# SAVED FOR A PURPOSE

*A Journey from Private Virtues to Public Values*

To MOC Staff,
Thanks for all the good
work you do.
James A. Joseph

## JAMES A. JOSEPH

DUKE UNIVERSITY PRESS   DURHAM AND LONDON   2015

Printed in the United States of America on acid-free paper ∞
Designed by Heather Hensley
Typeset in Minion Pro by Westchester Publishing Services

Library of Congress Cataloging-in-Publication Data
Joseph, James A. (James Alfred), 1935– author.
Saved for a purpose : a journey from private virtues to public values / James A. Joseph.
pages cm
Includes bibliographical references and index.
ISBN 978-0-8223-5896-1 (hardcover : alk. paper)
ISBN 978-0-8223-7554-8 (e-book)
1. Joseph, James A. (James Alfred), 1935–
2. Ambassadors—United States—Biography.
3. Executives—United States—Biography.
4. African Americans—Biography.
5. Ethics.
6. Leadership.  I. Title.
E748.J768A3 2015
327.2092—dc23
[B]
2015001927

Cover art: Photo by Barbara Banks, barbarabanks.com

# CONTENTS

*A gallery appears after page 92*

# PREFACE

William Lee Miller described his book on Abraham Lincoln, *Lincoln's Virtues*, as an ethical biography, "a book of a different sort from those whose authors write about moral ideals and moral choices from the perspective of a commune, a sanctuary or a library." Much the same can be said about this book. It is in many ways an ethical autobiography, a very personal account of a moral journey through a fascinating period of American history. It is a story of half a century of seeking to identify and apply values to all three sectors of American democracy: the private sector driven by markets, the public sector driven by ballots, and the third or so-called independent sector driven by voluntarism and the institutions of civil society. The manuscript was completed while I was in residence at the University of Cape Town, and in the best African tradition of storytelling uses seminal moments from my own experience to raise critical questions about the relationship between private virtue and public values.

I have been encouraged to write this book by my students and faculty colleagues at Duke and the University of Cape Town, by graduates of the leadership program I launched in South Africa more than a decade ago and in Louisiana after Hurricane Katrina, and by members of various audiences around the world who have invited me to lecture at their universities and to speak to civic groups in their communities. I write with both strong personal conviction and great passion. Yet this book was written with many audiences in mind: students in public policy, ethics, theology, business, and public management courses; those who are developing leadership programs and designing curricula for leadership studies; managers in business and the institutions of civil society in search of best practices; and all those in the general public who want their leaders to be more moral, their institutions more humane, and their communities more caring.

The narrative is set against the backdrop of a continuing public debate about the role of ethics in public life. The prologue recalls a defining moment in the South Pacific when my rescue from a plane crash in deep and distant Micronesian waters left not so much an emotional scar as a sense that I had been saved for a purpose. I took the trip to help sort out a moral dilemma in American foreign policy; but after hours on a life raft waiting and hoping to be rescued, I was led when I finally reached shore to ponder larger questions about the meaning of life and the genesis of the human capacity to engage adversity without being consumed by it.

Part I begins in the segregated South, growing up black in Louisiana's Cajun country. It was a time of brutal assault on both my dignity and my humanity; yet there was a refusal to hate and a development of the moral and spiritual intelligence that enabled me to rise above the hostility that could have so easily consumed me with rage. It was here in the 1950s that, greatly aided by the black church of my father, I learned to say no to the impulsive urge to respond in kind to those who used violence and intimidation to limit our reach, but could not stifle our dreams.

Part II chronicles the search for values to guide my engagement in the social movements of the 1960s. There is a firsthand account of the moral challenges in moments of great danger, trying to organize a movement and integrate a community in Alabama that served as the national headquarters of the Ku Klux Klan. There is also a report on painstaking but transforming experiences in California during the campus debate—often overshadowed by the Vietnam War—regarding the moral use of knowledge. The questions we raised about the civic responsibilities of a university, the public role of religion, and the emphasis on respect for the humanity of the adversary should have special relevance today for those who compete in the public square for positional leadership. Indeed, it was on the front line of activism in the turbulent 1960s that I learned that there is often no adversary more dangerous than the religious zealot or the self-described patriot who bars the door to social change because he is convinced that he is executing the will of God.

The chapters in part III share the insights of my efforts to apply ethics to the more traditional leadership roles of a democratic society. My constant concern with what was the right thing to do kept me in the domain of applied ethics, striving often to apply the ethical theories I had so studiously examined in my theological studies to real-life issues and dilemmas. It is a story of the professional challenge of a business executive seeking to make the case for capitalism with an ethic, including support in the 1970s for disinvestment from South Africa, a debate that led to the first of many trips to that country. It is the story of a government official seeking to distinguish private wants from public needs. It is also the story of a spokesperson for benevolent wealth raising moral questions and proposing ethical standards for the public use of private assets.

The chapters in part IV tell the story of four fascinating years at the end of the 1990s as the U.S. ambassador to South Africa, the period in which Nelson Mandela, Desmond Tutu, and others sought to reconcile both conflicting images of the past and the deep racial divisions caused by the apartheid policy of separate development. Looking through the special window of an additional fourteen years of part-time residency in that remarkable country, this section chronicles my efforts to distill lessons for the United States from the South African experience with forgiveness and reconciliation. It includes a look at what I learned from Nelson Mandela and concludes with a snapshot of the remarkable displays of presidential diplomacy by Bill Clinton when he delivered on a promise made to me earlier at the White House that he would come and visit.

Set in the early twenty-first century, the final section of the book is about leadership and public values. It tells the story of a partnership I launched and led between two world-class universities in South Africa and the United States to help build a culture of ethical leadership. It showcases the contributions of some of the young leaders in the program who have gone on to high-profile leadership roles in their communities and countries. The last chapter brings this narrative to a conclusion by identifying a lexicon of public values that have shaped and guided my engagement in public life, whether as a social activist, a business executive, a government official, or in the many other activities that have challenged me to integrate values into my work.

An epilogue offers a portrait of the resilience of the people of Louisiana as I joined them in rebuilding their lives and literally remaking their state after Hurricane Katrina. As chair of the board of directors of the Louisiana Disaster Recovery Foundation set up by Governor Kathleen Blanco, I was able to help empower groups that had long been denied access to the corridors of power where decisions about their future were made. The journey that began in Louisiana had finally come full circle. The passion that was once reflected in the strong drive to leave the state of my birth had been transformed into a passion to help change it.

## ACKNOWLEDGMENTS

I cannot name the many people who contributed to the writing of this book, both those whose insights are an important part of the story and those who helped put the manuscript into print. But to all those who recognize themselves in these pages, even when not mentioned directly, I express my heartfelt gratitude.

I owe special thanks to:

My wife, Mary; my son, Jeffrey; and my daughter, Denise, who all encouraged me to finally give birth to this mysterious manuscript that I seemed unwilling to let go.

J. Irwin Miller, the former chairman of Cummins Engine Company, who was a renaissance man and early mentor from whom I learned much about ethics and the bottom line of business.

Phil Sorensen, who brought me into organized philanthropy and encouraged me to think strategically about how social change takes place.

Pete Reckard, who was my predecessor as chaplain of the Claremont Colleges and who lured me to California when I needed some time away from the intensity of the 1960s movement I had helped organize in Tuscaloosa, Alabama.

Cecil Andrus, the former secretary of the interior, who persuaded me to join him in Washington as undersecretary of the Department of the Interior.

The fellows in the binational leadership program who encouraged me to share the lessons I learned from trying to apply ethics to leadership roles in business, government, and civil society.

My students at Duke, Claremont, the University of Cape Town, Yale, and Stillman, from whom I learned as much as I taught.

Arlie Schardt, a good friend who was willing to read this manuscript with the same thoroughness that led him to offer great editorial advice for my two previous books.

My staff in many settings for their valuable support throughout the process of this work.

# A Plane Crash in the South Pacific

It was August 1978. Jimmy Carter had been elected president almost two years earlier and I had been persuaded to leave a comfortable job in business to join his administration in Washington. But here I was on an overcrowded life raft, thousands of miles away from my new office a few blocks from the White House, waiting and hoping to be rescued. I had miraculously survived a plane crash in the South Pacific, had made it to a life raft, and was helping the wounded and hoping that my staff and other members of my delegation were all alive.

The experience of waiting on a life raft, wondering whether I would survive the Mariana Trench with ocean depths of more than 18,000 feet, is not one I wish to repeat or recommend. But I recall it here because it has caused me to reflect often on the meaning of that moment. Was I saved for a purpose?

For centuries, visitors to the mostly tiny islands of Micronesia have called them paradise, with some convinced that if we could re-create Eden, it would emerge as a Pacific island. Almost perfect in their beauty and intrigue, some are known for their sharp peaks, coral reefs, waterfalls, and beautiful lagoons. But others are remembered primarily for the bloody battles of 1944 when Allied troops sped across the Pacific to repel Japanese invaders. Names like Saipan, Eniwetok, and Truk still remind us of the nightmare of World War II.

My trip to the South Pacific started out primarily as a visit to Bikini and Kili to meet with Micronesians who had been displaced from the Bikini Atoll because of nuclear testing in the 1940s and 1950s by the U.S. military. The soil still produced radioactive coconuts and was obviously unsafe, but despite the danger to their health the Bikinians had voted overwhelmingly to resettle their ancestral home. My job was to decide whether the Carter administration should agree to their request, thus honoring the democratic process that had seen an almost unanimous vote of the elders, or act as guardian for the younger generation, who did not vote, but who by returning to Bikini would be sentenced to an early death.

The typical ethical decision involves a choice between right and wrong. The Bikini decision challenged policymakers in a different way. We were caught in a conflict between right and right. We were being challenged to choose between two courses of action in which each alternative was the right thing to do, but there was no way to do both. I had grown up in a black church and had often been moved by the "feel-good" inspirational ethics of my father, who was a Baptist minister. I had even gone to seminary to gain the tools for "objective" moral reasoning, but I had not really thought very much about what happens when there are multiple acceptable solutions—not the one right answer that I had been taught to find. Aristotle, John Stuart Mill, Immanuel Kant, Reinhold Niebuhr, and the holy host of ethicists whose teachings had fascinated me as a student at Yale Divinity School provided a good framework for reflection about right versus wrong, but here I was on my own in public life trying to decide between right and right.

I decided to go to the Marshall Islands to learn more about what had informed the decision of the elders. Had they fully understood the information provided, for example? The Marshallese language had no word for radiation and radioactivity or for strontium 90 or cobalt 60, terms very new to me as well. The translation in Marshallese was "sickness" or "poison," but the Bikinians could see lush growth everywhere. Some who had tasted the coconuts reported that they were larger and sweeter than those on the island before the people were removed.

In August 1968, President Lyndon Johnson had announced that Bikini was no longer needed as a nuclear test site, and that cleanup and rehabilitation would prepare the island for the return of its former inhabitants. The multimillion-dollar cleanup included burying test debris in fifty-foot pits, plowing up the entire island, and removing the topsoil. And in 1971, fifty thousand new coconuts were planted, and breadfruit and other foods indigenous to the Marshall Islands were brought in. One former resident reported that every house on Bikini was so close to a drinking coconut that it was like having a lemonade stand or free soft drink machine on the corner. To add to the magnetic pull of returning to their ancestral home, there was an experimental farm on neighboring Eneu Island where sweet watermelons, squash, and bananas were growing well.

The magnitude of the challenge I faced was obvious from the beginning of the planning for the trip, but while still pondering the dilemma involved, I decided to enlarge the trip to include the major district centers, and selected outer islands from the Micronesian group that included the Marshalls, Palau, Ponape, Truk, Yap, Guam, and other islands administered by the United States under a trustee agreement with the United Nations. We were negotiating the future status of the group of islands that had been taken from the Japanese during World War II, so as an advocate for some form of self-government it seemed important that I meet with as many representatives of the local people as I could reach in a two-week visit. Seeking to follow the standards of frugality that brought President Carter considerable attention, but in retrospect very little credit, I declined the use of the shiny new plane the navy originally offered for the trip and accepted the offer of the naval commander of the South Pacific region to use his plane instead. The budget savings were enormous.

Ruth Van Cleve, director of the Office of Territorial Affairs in the Department of the Interior, had persuaded me to make the trip. It was not difficult because oversight of territorial affairs was one of the many responsibilities I had been asked to assume when Cecil Andrus, the new secretary, and I discussed my role as the undersecretary. I would be the highest-ranking U.S. government official to visit the area, and the Micronesian leaders, who were part of a culture that was rather rank conscious, were very excited about my coming. I wanted them to know that the Carter administration took its responsibility for the group of islands very seriously. The people of Bikini wanted to know how soon they could return to their home. Others wanted to know where we stood on the completion of the status agreement.

A few months earlier, I had learned from Mrs. Van Cleve that Bikini was not yet safe for human habitation. This was very disturbing to the islanders who had been moved off Bikini in 1946. They had been relocated to Kili Island, five hundred miles to the south, but throughout the years they longed to return to the home of their ancestors. While Kili was safe from radioactivity, it was unsatisfactory for many other reasons, including the fact that the beleaguered Bikinians had been neglected for many years by their trustee, the U.S. government. I was especially eager to inspect the temporary facilities that were being constructed for the small group of returnees who had prematurely resettled on Bikini only to learn that it was still unsafe.

On my previous visits to the region, I had sworn in the governor of American Samoa and represented the United States in a ceremony celebrating the new status of the Northern Marianas as an American commonwealth. I had become friends with the governor of Guam and always enjoyed the hospitality of the people of Guam. This trip was not very different. I had spent a wonderful evening at the governor's residence and headed for the Naval Air Station early on the morning of August 15, arriving at about 9:00 AM for our scheduled 9:15 departure.

Our flight plan called first for a visit to Ulithi, an outer island in the Yap District where I was to dedicate a medical dispensary before moving to Yap itself to participate in a groundbreaking ceremony for a new dock. But as we prepared to leave Guam, I noticed oil leaking from the right engine of the plane. I pointed this out somewhat nervously to the navy admiral who had been my host and travel companion for the trip. He reassured me that this was not unusual and that the plane was one of the safest models ever built. I had no reason to doubt him, since we had been landing on coral reef strips and enjoying the aerial view of spectacular lagoons and small islands without incident for more than a week.

Occasionally during this trip, I read from a briefing book while flying between the beautiful and enchanting islands that give Micronesia its special allure. After leaving Guam and soaring comfortably high above the ocean that had once known the turbulence of a vicious war, I started fingering through pages that had been prepared to remind me of the politics of the region and the culture and economy of a community for which I had direct oversight. Suddenly there was an unusual sound from the right engine. To the astonishment of everyone on the plane, the engine slowly stopped. I started fingering through my briefing book again. I needed a diversion. The fact that I had read everything in the book several times didn't diminish the desire to go through the material again. As I contemplated the seriousness of our predicament, I wondered whether we would return to Guam where more sophisticated pieces of rescue equipment were likely to be available.

When it appeared that we were continuing straight ahead, I turned to Adrian Winkle, the high commissioner of Micronesia, to inquire whether we had reversed our course. I had appointed Adrian to his position despite some opposition from a powerful congressional committee chair, but all this was behind us now. Here we were settled together in the VIP seats of an old navy plane with Wallace Green, at that time my deputy, sitting directly across facing me, and Ruth Van Cleve, who, as my chief advisor on Micronesia, was sitting on my right. She said something about watching the horizon to see if the sun was in the right place. I had no idea which direction we were headed, so

I had no sense of where the sun should be, but I kept my thoughts to myself. Ruth as usual was elegantly dressed with high heels and expensive purse. She had once almost declined an invitation to accompany me to a ceremony at the White House because she did not have her white gloves.

Admiral Dave Cruden tried to reassure us that everything was under control by telling us that we were returning to Guam and the plane was capable of flying back on one engine. A member of the crew even gave us the expected arrival time in Guam, but we decided he was confused since his estimate of how long it would take and what time we would land didn't add up correctly. Ordinarily one would not bother to check out this sort of trivia, but I was not the only one who felt the need for diversion.

For the first time, I felt a little anger. Why had the navy allowed us to be placed in this predicament? Why had I turned down the more modern, but very expensive, plane originally recommended? After all, no one would give me credit for the budget-conscious decision to accept the admiral's offer instead. The anger soon gave way to a brief moment of anxiety and fear. There was tightness in my stomach, a shiver down my back, and a twitching on my face now tanned by the Pacific sun. Our plight was now obvious. We were informed that the plane was losing altitude and the crew would have to throw out our luggage. What an irony. Ricky Bordallo, the governor of Guam, had invited me to leave most of my luggage at Government House since we were coming back by way of Guam and intended to be in Yap and Palau for only a couple of days. I packed with this in mind, putting the things I needed in my tennis bag and attaché case, but I decided the next morning to take everything with me. After all, I needed the additional space to bring back the colorful storyboard art I had been encouraged to wait until Palau to buy.

I tried to step back from all negative emotions, to expel the emerging threats from consciousness. Suddenly, I no longer felt anxiety or fear. There was a surprising calm. My emotions were all positive. It was as if there was a limit beyond which fear could not go, and after it was reached, there was only calm. I remember very little of the fear, only the serenity with which I faced the succeeding moments. Having put on my life vest and assured myself that I knew the location of the flap that I needed to pull to inflate it, I focused on the exit door that I knew I must reach quickly when we crashed. We had determined in an earlier conversation that Adrian Winkle and I were the only two passengers who could not swim, but even this was behind me as I completely blocked out any negative thoughts. The back door was opened and members of the crew began to throw out both the luggage and the musical instruments of the thirteen navy bandsmen accompanying us to the gala ceremony in Ulithi.

I looked around for the envelope I had been instructed to use for my glasses, but finding nothing, I put them in my shirt pocket. Throughout all of this there was complete quiet, a silent discipline that reminded me of mock combat drills at Fort Devens in Massachusetts, where as a twenty-one-year-old company commander I had learned to repress my own emotions in order to set an example for the men under my command. My mind was suddenly fixed on the terror in the eyes of the crewman who had instructed us to put on our life jackets. I did not feel his fear, but I was moved by the tears visible in his eyes.

Very soon the instructions went out to close the back door. Shortly thereafter the plane touched down on the Pacific waters. I felt relief. It had been much smoother than I expected. I even felt gratitude to the pilot. But within three to five seconds, just as I started to unbuckle my seat belt, there was a second impact. This one was vastly more ferocious. The sound was deafening. The plane was breaking apart. Luggage or bodies (it must have been bodies as all of the luggage should have been thrown out) were everywhere. I was obsessed with one thought—get to the door quickly.

Once at the door, I stood for a moment and realized that even though I could not swim, I had no fear. How could that be? I was standing at ocean level and could see nothing but water in every direction. Suddenly, I discovered that to my left there was a member of the crew inflating a raft. He appeared to be the only other person ahead of me. I reminded myself to pull the string on my life jacket, but I had already decided that I could float to the raft even if my vest did not inflate. It was a strange time to think about it, but I remembered the hot afternoons spent in Sylvia Leeser's pool in Claremont, California. Having been denied access to the local swimming pool in Louisiana closed to blacks, I never did learn to swim, but I had learned in Sylvia's pool to float from one end to the other. The distance to the life raft seemed about the same.

I pulled the string, the jacket inflated, and I jumped into the water. Fortunately, I did not recall Ruth's observation during the life jacket demonstration that there had been no mention of shark repellent, which she thought was standard equipment for this kind of flight. While I had smiled at the time, thinking about it then would have totally immobilized me in the water. But I soon approached the raft, where a crewman already there helped me aboard. Then we helped others. They kept coming. I wasn't aware how many were alive, but I thought our raft was the only one afloat. I looked around for Ruth, Adrian, and Wallace Green, my deputy who had accompanied me on previous trips, usually by slow ships and fast boats, through the treacherous waters of Micronesia.

Our raft was soon full, and then overcrowded. We were piled on top of each other and there were still others clinging to the side. I helped pull Adrian into the raft. He was struggling to get over the side, muttering quietly that he could not swim. I grabbed a leg, and two crewmen also pulled. He made it into the raft, but I still saw no sign of Ruth and Wallace. I could see other people in the water, so I knew there was hope.

Off in the distance, I saw a bag that looked like mine. I wondered how long it would stay afloat. I could also see Wallace standing on top of the wing of the plane looking around; probably for me, since he had promised to stay close by when he learned I could not swim. After about ten minutes on the raft, right before our eyes, our plane sank. As it disappeared from view, I saw two welcome sights: a second raft off in the distance and Wallace in the water swimming to a third. It looked for the moment like all thirty passengers had survived.

A fixed-wing plane from the Guam Air Force base was now circling overhead. It could not provide any help directly, but it was comforting to know that we had been spotted. It was time to rearrange the raft. Two people were lying across my legs. One of them was in a state of shock. He kept saying that he couldn't breathe. Several of the people clinging to the side were bleeding badly. I looked around and realized for the first time that others in the raft were also bleeding. One of the young men who had been helping to pull others aboard actually had a deep cut across his hand. He had never complained but he was obviously in pain. I offered to tear off a piece of my T-shirt, but he had a blood-stained handkerchief and he only wanted help in tightening it. To my continuing astonishment, I suddenly realized that I had a long (although not very deep) cut on my right forearm and a shorter cut on my left hand.

One of the members of the crew had a radio that he could not get to operate, but he kept trying anyway. We all sat anxiously hoping that the plane we had seen above had notified someone who could arrange our rescue. We also wondered aloud why it was taking so long for rescue vessels to arrive. After all, we had been told that we were near Guam just before we touched down. Actually, we were farther out than we originally thought.

Finally a helicopter arrived. A couple of men—medics I hoped—jumped out and began to seek out the more seriously injured. They operated with a precision and competence that I found fascinating. As a young lieutenant in the Army Medical Service Corps, I had once taught medical evacuation classes to ROTC cadets in New England. But here I was sitting on a raft watching real craftsmen at work. They took those with the worst injuries and sent them up to the helicopter, going up with them as they were lifted by a cable.

When the badly injured had been secured on the helicopter, they offered to take me—as the ranking official—next. But I could still see others bleeding, and my cuts, including a third one I had just discovered on my forehead, were more superficial, so I declined and suggested that they take another one of the more seriously injured. A ship soon arrived, but it continued to another raft. Finally, a second ship also appeared. There was no ladder on board, so the crew threw out a rope, which I tied securely under my arms while three men on the deck pulled me up. Several hours after the crash, I was finally out of the water. But as I banged against the side of the boat, I even longed for the Jacob's ladder—a rope tied together to function like a ladder—which I had come to intensely dislike during other parts of my journey through Micronesian waters.

Once on board, I went below, stretched out across a bunk, and collapsed. Sometime later, I was awakened by someone wanting to know my name. I asked about survivors, but he had no information. He would check and let me know. I went back above to find that we were arriving in Guam. The other ship was already there and ambulances were parked on the dock.

I was met by Governor and Mrs. Bordallo and inquired immediately about Wallace and Ruth. They told me that they were checking. I was taken to the governor's limousine, where I waited to find out about survivors. He and Mrs. Bordallo soon returned and informed me that Ruth and Wallace were both safe but had injuries that would cause them to be hospitalized.

I felt both relief and dismay, wondering if my family had heard about the crash and how my wife, Doris, would explain to my two young kids, Jeffrey and Denise, where I was and how close they had come to losing their father. What I did not know was that Doris had already been called by relatives who had heard an announcement on the radio that a plane carrying a senior Carter administration official in the Interior Department had gone down in the Pacific, and it was not yet known whether there were any survivors. She had also been called by a friend with a diplomatic post abroad who, upon hearing the news flash on British radio, contacted the White House Situation Room. And just as she hung up and turned on the television for breaking news, she received a third call. It was from Cecil Andrus, the secretary of the interior, who had been monitoring the news from the Situation Room. He informed her that I was safe and would be able to travel in a few days. The dismay I had felt earlier soon turned to grief as I learned that two members of the crew had gone down with the plane.

Throughout my visits to small Micronesian islands and beautiful lagoons, I was reminded why no one at my level in government had ever visited most of these areas. The many risks I had taken partly explained why, but what I saw and learned made the risks worth taking. These islands were now the last American colony. They were poorly equipped to function in a modern world. We had used the islands and their people for our own national purposes and made ourselves responsible for them, but we had not acted responsibly. On my way to the hospital to visit survivors, I thought as much about the neglect of these islands by their American patron as I thought about the dangerous journey I had traveled in search of an answer for not only the people of Bikini, but the larger Micronesian dilemma.

After an evening at the governor's mansion, trying to sleep and watching Mrs. Bordallo stitch together the holes in my badly torn shirt—the only one I had left—I woke up to the local newspaper headline, "Saved for a Purpose." It seemed that after my rescue, while still struggling to find my bearing, I was lucid enough to interpret the day's event on a cosmic scale.

The sense of destiny I felt as a child was now reinforced, and while I could not imagine what lay before me, I knew in my heart that I had been saved for a purpose. As Carl Jung once said of himself, I felt as though my life was assigned to me by fate and had to be fulfilled. In the years since that fateful day in the Pacific, I have reflected often on my good fortune. While the incident has left no visible scars, it has certainly left its mark. When I look back, I think not so much about the moment of anticipation before the plane hit the water, the time on the life raft, or the rescue, as I do about the values that led me to Micronesia in the first place and how much my decision to go to the South Pacific was based on the same moral sentiments that now provide the integrating theme of this book.

# I

# The 1950s

THE GENESIS OF
MORAL CONSCIOUSNESS

# CHAPTER 1

# Growing Up Black in Cajun Country

I was born in 1935 in a small rural community in Louisiana called Plaisance. It was the year that our legendary governor Huey Long was assassinated. This chance connection seemed of no consequence at the time, but it took on a different meaning some years later when our portraits shared a wall in the Louisiana Political Hall of Fame. Set in St. Landry Parish, where large oak and pecan trees mixed with open grasslands, rabbits, and armadillos, Plaisance was a farming community that served as home to several generations of Josephs.

A few miles from where I was born, the Opelousas Indians once had a thriving settlement. There were very few traces of the earlier settlers who roamed the swamps and lagoons intermingling with the lush vegetation and diverse wildlife of the backwoods, but the community bore their name. The Cajuns and Creoles who followed them wasted no time in placing their stamp on the local culture. The two groups had very different origins and passed on distinct cultures, but their music had somewhat similar sounds and their cooking and folkways shared similar characteristics. The Cajuns were the white descendants of French-speaking Catholics who fled Canada in the late 1700s rather than pledge allegiance to the British crown. The Creoles were the light-skinned blacks with mixed blood who had a close French connection and a history of having been regarded as a distinct cultural group. But despite the present emphasis on the culture and cooking of the Cajuns and Creoles, both were heavily influenced by the Africans who settled in Louisiana as both slaves and freemen.

Few places in the world were more ethnically mixed than the area of southwestern Louisiana where I grew up. All of us, despite our differences in color, reflected in some way the fusion of Acadian and African culture with the equally varied cultures of the American Indians, Spaniards, French, Germans, Scots, Irish, English, Caribbean islanders, and other Latin Americans who intermixed at various junctures to form what the local people now call a "cultural gumbo."

My father looked like a Cajun and spoke fluent Creole, yet he did not identify with either group. His grandfather, Jules Joseph, was of German descent, but my father was self-consciously African American. My mother had Native American blood, but it was her African features that stood out. We were called "colored" then, but we were soon identified as Negroes and celebrated our African connection later when we became known as African Americans. My mother never let us forget that we were the descendants of kings and queens who flourished in very sophisticated African kingdoms when the ancestors of some of those who insulted and marginalized us roamed around Europe as barbarians. It was not unlike Disraeli's reaction to a taunt in which he responded, "Yes, I am a Jew, and when the ancestors of the right honorable gentlemen were brutal savages on an unknown island, mine were priests in the temple of Solomon."

My mother was a very proud woman. She had only completed the eighth grade when she was forced to drop out of school to help bring in the family crops. But her father, who was largely self-taught, was regarded as one of the most literate persons in the parish, and he taught his daughter the love of learning. It was my mother who constantly reminded my brother John and me that we had to be twice as good as any white person in order to have half a chance at success. My mother, like my father, saw education as the potential escape route from the boundaries and burden of race. While they prepared their children for a new era they believed to be on the horizon, they sought against poor odds to better prepare themselves as well. My father finished college one year before my older brother John, and my mother finished high school one year after I graduated from college. While we had limited assets and even more limited income, we never thought of ourselves as poor. Even among the most deprived in the local black community, there was a fierce sense of independence and self-reliance. Our worth and our identity were to be found in the quality of our minds, the mystical character of our souls, and the spiritual connection we shared with the universe. As long as we were prepared to outthink and out-work those who positioned themselves as our adversaries, our time would come. This was heady stuff for kids who read by a kerosene lamp and hated the darkness because it sometimes meant we had to stop reading. The little money we had was needed for food rather than light.

## Surrounded by Books

We grew up surrounded by books. Many had been used before and begged or borrowed, but we treasured them as if they were newly printed and bound in the best leather. My father's favorite book was the Bible, and he had a library before he had a car. It was while surrounded by his books that I used to sit for hours dreaming that I was a philosopher or a poet, a politician or a preacher, actually writing in my mind a future speech or sermon. And while I did not fully understand the contemporary politics from which I was legally excluded, I came to cherish Pericles's famous oration on the meaning of democracy as if it were my own. While still very young, I suffered with Socrates and studied Aristotle. I quoted Shakespeare and praised Longfellow. I was probably the only kid in elementary school to talk with my teachers about the writings of Bishop Fulton Sheen and the speeches of Douglas MacArthur while playing with toys my father made by hand because he could not afford to buy them.

When my brother John started school, I freaked out when told I was too young. He was about to be six and I was four, but while I could not legally enroll, the teachers allowed me to tag along from time to time. We were still living on my grandfather's farm, and we walked miles through rain and mud and sometimes waded in floodwaters, but we understood that our future depended on our being able to acquire as much education as we could. The state of public education for blacks in St. Landry Parish and throughout the South was deplorable, but this little schoolhouse in Plaisance was more precious than we knew at the time. As I was to learn later, it was one of over five thousand schools constructed for use by blacks as part of a program started by the philanthropist Julius Rosenwald at the suggestion of his friend Booker T. Washington. The Rosenwald Fund, which overhauled the structure of African American education, not just in Louisiana but throughout the South, required that blacks match its grants by contributing cash or labor to the construction of the schools. Black ministers, farmers, tenants, domestic workers, and small business owners joined together to buy and clear land, contribute lumber, and in some cases build the schools themselves. They also raised matching funds by holding festive rallies, planting and selling cotton, and raising and selling hogs. Fiercely independent and reticent to seek help from whites, the hard-pressed but resourceful Plaisance community became an active partner in providing a community school that, along with the local black churches, remained at the center of black life while serving as a symbol of black self-advancement and achievement.

It would have probably startled Julius Rosenwald no end if he had lived to see this little school set a career path for one of its former students to one day become a spokesperson for benevolent wealth as head of the Council on Foundations. It was only much later that I heard of Julius Rosenwald and still later that I learned that I had actually studied in one of his schools, but his largesse became a critical part of the examples I used to make the case for private philanthropy before congressional committees, opinion leaders, and wealthy families. It was a great example of both the value of collaboration and the multiplier effect of strategic philanthropy. During the period of the fund's work between 1913 and 1932, one in every five black schools constructed in rural areas was a Rosenwald School, serving one-third of the South's rural black schoolchildren.

One day, soon after enrolling in the Rosenwald School, my family moved to our own farm. It was not that we had accumulated large resources. It was simply the willingness of an aging farmer to bet on the hard work of my father, who walked clearly and even self-consciously in the footsteps of my grandfather. My mother and father got up early on the morning of the move. While my father readied the horses, my mother began to pack the wagon. John and I did not fully understand why we were moving, but our parents' enthusiasm was contagious. When the wagon was loaded (there really wasn't much to move), my brother and I happily took up positions in the back, watching the old house disappear in the distance as we moved slowly toward our new home.

It was fall, and the pastures were brown and the fields not yet plowed, but there was a tranquility that in its silence spoke to us of fond memories and happy dreams. Along the way, we talked about the happy days ahead. John and I would share a room to ourselves and we would one day be able to afford new bicycles and maybe even ride them to school.

We were not the most successful farmers. While my father's first love was the church and the pulpit, he worked hard in the fields only to find the market for his corn and cotton severely depressed. But I remember the joy and exhilaration of our rides into town to gin and sell cotton. The wagon was packed with as much as the raised sides could contain. The real fun was the return home with the meager, but welcome, money the sale of cotton brought. Always, there was the stop on the way home to pick up some cheese and sardines for my mother. This was the only real luxury she allowed herself. She loved her family and wanted every extra penny to be saved for our individual advancement.

It came as a surprise to learn that after two years we were moving again, this time into the city. The church my father founded was now beginning to generate some income and he had been called also to pastor a second church in Opelousas, the small town that served as the hub of St. Landry Parish, with local government offices, a cotton gin, small stores, a post office, and a church in almost every neighborhood. There must have been some irony in the fact that the house my father bought was across the street from a cotton gin. My brother and I still shared a room, but there was an indoor toilet and running water. We had to pinch ourselves to make certain we were not dreaming. We would be going to a city school and we could now watch the wagonloads of cotton as they arrived rather than packing them ourselves.

## The Boundaries of Race

Opelousas was to be the beginning of our contact with whites. Julius Rosenwald had always hoped that the black schools he had caused to be constructed would start the process of bringing whites and blacks together, but they remained segregated for many decades. While the Rosenwald schools focused on reading, writing, and arithmetic, and often did a fine job at that, many of them followed Booker T. Washington's emphasis on preparing black Americans for the jobs likely to be available to them, so they also taught agriculture, shop, gardening, and dressmaking. Yet it was this coming together to study and learn that opened new vistas for my generation and led to an emphasis on other disciplines that better prepared us for new economic and political roles. Out in Plaisance, we had worked our grandfather's land, gone to the black school and a black church, and saw whites only when we came into town. In Opelousas, our next-door neighbor was white. We were told that this was all right as long as we kept in our place. The conventional wisdom, we soon learned, was that in the South blacks (we were called colored then) could get as close to whites as they wanted as long as they did not get too uppity, while in the North they could get as uppity as they wanted as long as they did not get too close. It was many years before I understood this little bit of homespun wisdom, but it seems ironic now that those of us who were educated and self-affirming were first called uppity, later arrogant, and now elitist when we challenge or dare to compete with those with truly elite backgrounds.

It was the same irony that Frederick Douglass wrote about in his own life in *Life and Times of Frederick Douglass*. He was assigned by the Massachusetts Anti-Slavery Society to travel through part of the state with a white society member to sign up subscribers to the antislavery journal the *Liberator*. He wrote later that he was generally introduced to audiences as "chattel—a thing—a piece of Southern property with the chairman assuring the audience that *it* could speak." The abolitionist leaders wanted him to simply tell stories of his life as a slave, but he grew tired of this and wanted to engage his audiences more broadly on the philosophy of slavery. "It did not entirely satisfy me to narrate wrongs," he wrote. "I wanted to denounce them."[1] Because of his speech and demeanor, people said that he did not talk or act like a slave and would not be convincing if he got into philosophy. It would be better for him to act like chattel and use plantation speech rather than seeming as learned as his audience. There was a price to be paid for being uppity.

My brother and I were not dissuaded by this charge that blacks with our ambition and bearing were being uppity. We thrived at the St. Landry Parish Training School in Opelousas. Not only were we good students with good grades, but we got to travel to other schools around the state to compete in various forms of interscholastic competition. I was not very good in sports, as whites somehow assumed all blacks were, but it was a time in the black community in which great orators were analogous to great athletes. The spoken word well delivered was a powerful and honored skill. It was not just a way of telling a story or communicating a thought. The speaker who could mesmerize an audience with the poetry of his words provided not just useful information or empowering insights but often a form of entertainment for audiences with few outlets to expand their imagination or open their minds to new possibilities.

None of my classmates were surprised that while some of them went out for athletic teams, I chose to compete in original oratory and won the Louisiana state oratorical competition. I could not afford the expense of traveling to the national competition, but instead of feeling exhilarated about my victory at the state level, I felt disappointed that it was segregated and I did not have the opportunity to compete against whites. I longed to prove that I was just as good and likely better than most in the exercise of the mind as well as in the art of communication. The victory won me special attention. It helped me to become student body president, and while the annual homecoming showcased our best athletes, I was the one who got to escort the homecoming queen and to bask in a glory once reserved for athletes.

The decision to compete in oratory also led to the practice of putting my thoughts in writing, as I often take flight from the present moment to pen a few notes on a small pad or a notecard for use in a future speech or simply to inform a future conversation. Even in later years as I traveled or sat alone with my thoughts, writing became an important way of grounding my thinking in something more profound, often helping to clarify what I believe or to raise my consciousness of the values I should hold.

I developed a distrust of absolutes, questioning the notion of finality in the development of an idea or completeness in the evolution of time. I saw my life as a journey, and while I did not know where it would lead, I felt confident that it had a purposeful destination.

Our teachers at Opelousas's only black public high school were tough and uncompromising in their insistence that we study, work hard, and excel in whatever we did. They didn't stop with academics. They were determined to develop the whole person, placing as much emphasis on character formation as on academic excellence. Mrs. Emerson, my English teacher, worked on my self-confidence as well as my writing, spelling, and grammar. Mr. Douglas, my math teacher, also served as my speech coach, often keeping me late after school preparing for an oratorical contest. He made me repeat phrases and practice delivery sometimes until my throat was sore and my voice hoarse.

We may have had secondhand books, but our teachers were determined to see that we developed first-class minds. I was surrounded with heroes. The white kids across town may not have ever heard of Frederick Douglass, Sojourner Truth, and W. E. B. Du Bois, but I knew all about them, identified with them, and wanted to be like them. I could never get enough information about the black heroes who rebelled against the status quo and refused to let others define who they were and what they could become.

It was on our way to and from school that we were most often reminded of the burdens of race. Bands of roving young whites had taken to attacking black kids on their way home from school. They were transported home by school buses while we walked past the white school on our way home from the colored school. We learned early to ignore the harassment and insults, but occasionally the antagonism went from mischief to violence. Ray Gauthier, a young man in my brother's high school class, left school late one day and never made it home. The next day he was found dead, with scars and broken bones that told the story of a brutal beating.

We grew up knowing that we faced the daily threat of death for simply being black, but we disliked even more the ongoing disrespect for our humanity; having to go to the back of restaurants to get food handed out a small window while local whites sat inside enjoying the comforts of ceiling fans that blew away the heat and calmed the humidity; going to movie houses where we had to enter through the side door reserved for coloreds and sit in the buzzard roost, a balcony far up and far away from the screen. We disliked the knowledge and fear that one look at a white girl (even the return of a smile) resented by a white man could land you in a bayou with a rope around your neck or a bullet in your head. But we refused to be consumed by either fear or hate. Our primary passion was the drive to succeed, to transcend and someday transform the barriers around us.

As my brother and I began to look around for part-time jobs to supplement the family income, we found the doors of economic opportunity shut tight to black teenagers. During the summer months, we often got up before daylight and stood on the street corner waiting for the truck to come by to transport day workers to pick the cotton of white farmers. The ground still wet from the dewdrops of early summer and the moss hanging from large oak trees were almost eerie reminders that this was Cajun country. The white folks, mostly on the other side of the tracks, slept quietly and peacefully, totally oblivious to either our pain or our dreams, with no thought that these young black kids whose hands picked the cotton on the nearby farms would someday pick the leaders of this historic town. In truth, many of these youthful cotton pickers in time became the leaders who helped rescue a dying community from almost certain decay.

Those who gave us sacks in the daytime to bring in their cotton were often the same people who wore sheets over their faces in the evenings as they marched behind the burning cross of the Ku Klux Klan. We often knew who they were and even quietly whispered their names. Yet nothing forged a determined will to succeed as much as those days in the cotton field under the hot sun. During breaks for lunch, I would often lie under the wagons dreaming of a day when I would leave home and then return to the accolades of the sons and daughters of even those who now spent their days trying to devise ways to ensure that we were never a threat to white dominance.

### The Ethics of Civility

In *Civilities and Civil Rights*, William Chafe notes the presence of a "progressive mystique" among whites in North Carolina in the 1950s. Three underlying values enjoyed consensus: (1) conflict is inherently bad; (2) consensus offers the only way to preserve a genteel and civilized way of life; and (3) good manners are important in all social contacts.[2] Much the same could be said of small pockets of whites in Louisiana in the 1950s. In Opelousas, the Klansmen in sheets who engaged in many acts of terror and intimidation, including violence, made the headlines and dominated the political life of the community. But one could still find remnants of the progressive elite who had prevailed in the nineteenth century when Louisiana held back the tide of vitriolic racism sweeping across the South. In St. Landry Parish, there were free blacks who made a major contribution to the development of the area. They moved easily among the white upper class and enjoyed their respect. Their achievements were so notable that even after the Ku Klux

Klan had become an intimidating force and Jim Crow practices had become the norm, accounts of their work and wealth remained a part of the local folklore. They lived in some of the finest homes in the state and sent their children to France and other European countries for their education. Free blacks elsewhere amassed significant wealth and acclaim, but more came out of Louisiana than from all the other slaveholding colonies combined.

My father was not a descendant of any of these aristocrats of color, but even among the poor there was a strong sense of independence and pride as they told stories of a time when some blacks owned large cotton and sugar plantations; others were engineers, doctors, writers, artists, money lenders, and even humanitarians. The most legendary may have been Thomy Lafon, who was born in poverty but became one of the richest men in the state. The more money he made, the more he gave away, winning such wide recognition for his humanitarianism that the Louisiana legislature voted in 1893 to honor him by commissioning a bust in his likeness. This black man, from whom the city of New Orleans once borrowed money to meet its payroll, distributed his sizeable fortune indiscriminately to the needy of every creed and color.

It was the aristocratic blacks who had moved freely in the white community who were primarily responsible for the legacy that saw a few whites even as late as the 1940s and 1950s treating blacks with dignity and respect. But while these whites disagreed with local practices, their adherence to the culture of civility prevented them from doing anything that might cause conflict. Their rejection of black "agitators," therefore, was often not only racial but cultural. To create conflict by opposing the system was to violate the ethic by which upper-class whites lived. As a result of their silence, Opelousas became the state headquarters of the Ku Klux Klan almost by default. The fragile fabric of harmony among whites was no longer maintained by the mystique of civility, but by an intense fear of the Klan.

Blacks in St. Landry Parish had their own form of civility. It took several forms: (1) hospitality to the stranger; (2) generosity toward each other; and (3) deference and good manners toward whites. The etiquette of race relations practiced by the blacks of my father's generation reflected still another side of civility in which the ground rules were set by whites, and the blacks who followed them were deemed to be "good niggers." Those who operated outside of this ethic of accommodation were likely to be found hanging from a tree or floating down a bayou. But the deferential poses blacks had to strike in public in order to keep a job or physically survive sometimes masked an alternative culture of self-assertion that could be found in the black church, pool halls, barber shops, and street corners. It was at these gatherings that one was more likely to hear the incipient voices of protest articulated and encouraged. Those whites who thought their blacks were dumb and docile would have been shocked to hear the mocking humor of blacks making fun of the "dumb whites" who could not survive without the exploitation of blacks.

I graduated from high school in 1952 and was selected to give one of the two student speeches. I had won a wide variety of public speaking contests in Louisiana and throughout the southeastern United States, but on graduation day I was nervous. As I started to speak, my legs began shaking uncontrollably, but I was armed with my usual insights from philosophers, poets, and prophets. Before long I was in full control of both my body and the audience. It was one of the many times during those melancholy years of youth that I realized the power of words. As I returned to my seat, I looked at my mother and wondered what she was thinking. She told me later that she was proud of the way I was beginning to sound like my father, and that she was sure I would someday be a preacher too.

She failed to mention that I might have been walking in her steps. My father was the preacher in the family, but my mother had her own oratorical flair. She was president of the Women's Auxiliary in the Baptist Association and her annual address was as much a highlight as my father's speech to the Southwest Missionary Baptist Association, which he also served as president. Without doubt, our family collected more than our fair share of leadership positions, but it was the emphasis on serving others that stood out. We set out first to serve. Leadership is what followed.

# CHAPTER 2

# Sunday Mornings in Louisiana

The one consistent moral force in the early years of my growing up was black religion. Sunday morning in Louisiana was more than simply a time of worship. It was a time of shaping one's values and learning how to use them, a time of developing a deeper understanding of who we were and what we could become. Yet being a minister's son set special boundaries around what I could say, do, or enjoy. A friend of mine even lamented that if an activity was fun—playing cards, dancing, going to movies on Sunday, and such—it was very likely to be off limits for me.

I was baptized in a pond on the side of a gravel road near my father's church in the rural community of Plaisance. While still too young to fully understand either the ritual of baptism or the theological affirmations it reflected, I knew that Sunday morning in Louisiana was something special. Everywhere I looked, I saw people dressed in their best clothing, headed off to sing, pray, and "cheer the preacher on." The church lit up with a very special glow of excitement and anticipation when my father approached the pulpit to present the Sunday sermon.

Baptism was a very special event in the life of the black church, so when my time came to be led into the muddy waters, I was excited. I had come to know baptism as a rite of passage and always felt something special when the congregation burst out in unison with a chorus of the old spiritual "Down by the Riverside." I had heard the song and participated in the ritual many times, but instead of my usual role as a spectator, this time was different. It was awesome to realize, as I followed my father into the water, that this moving melody was now being sung for me. I was still in elementary school, young and innocent, but people were already beginning to say that I would be a preacher like my father. In my own admiration of his skills as an orator and after watching Sunday after Sunday how people were moved by the power of his words, I saw him as a tough act to follow; but on that day when he gently plunged me into the water, I felt like I had been singled out to someday carry the torch.

I am sure that because of its worship style, preaching and singing, Star Light Baptist Church would now be described as evangelical; but it bore little resemblance to either the moral imperatives of the new evangelicals who have captured the public imagination or the prosperity gospel preached in high-profile megachurches. Very few whites knew much about the black churches that proliferated across the landscape in both the rural and urban areas of St. Landry Parish. They were susceptible, therefore, to negative images like those created by the television sound bites of a very narrow slice of black religious life during the 2008 presidential campaign of Senator Barack Obama. These sound-bite depictions, out of context and representing a small part of a vastly larger story, did not nearly reflect the full reality of the black church that helped shape my own moral consciousness or, for that matter, the wider ministry of the Chicago church so badly maligned.

It is easy to overlook the pluralism of black churches. I came from a long line of Baptists who built churches and prescribed moral behavior in Plaisance, but two blocks from where I grew up in Opelousas was a black Catholic church that read its Mass in Latin and boasted of a unique heritage in which interracial worship with integrated seating arrangements was permitted long after a rigid segregation had become the norm for Protestant churches in Louisiana. These black Catholic churches had a different history, different worship styles, and a different theological culture and often appealed to a different subculture of blacks; but they too shaped community values and provided therapeutic relief from the racial pathology that afflicted not only the South, but the entire nation.

While blacks left the white Protestant churches in large numbers during Reconstruction to form their own congregations, most of the black Catholics in Louisiana continued to attend integrated churches throughout the Reconstruction period. These churches fought consistently against the idea of requiring blacks to sit in separate pews. A Methodist minister once described the history of integration in the Catholic Church of the period in astonishment: "In her most aristocratic churches, lips of every shade, by hundreds press with devout kisses the same crucifixes, and fingers of as great variety in color are dipped in holy water." Another observer praised the conduct of priests and parishioners, noting that "the prince and peasant, the slave and master, kneel before the same altar in temporary oblivion of all worldly distinctions. They come in but one character, that of sinners."[1]

It is no wonder that so many blacks in Louisiana remained Catholic. Their influence was everywhere. Black Catholics, now with separate churches and their own alternative culture, had their own network of black schools, religious orders, and social clubs. The churches tended to serve a different clientele, many of whom were descendants of the mixed-race "free people of color" of the antebellum period, when they were regarded as a separate class from slaves and free blacks. They accepted Roman Catholic rituals, accommodated Anglo-Saxon music, and mixed easily in Louisiana society—some even changed their identity and disappeared into the white community. Yet, in the period following the Civil War, when free people of color were no longer distinguished from other blacks, many became the backbone of black leadership in the Republican Party of that time and remained active leaders in parish politics until the 1890s, when those privileges were taken away.

While my world as a child was essentially that of a black Baptist, I heard occasionally about another form of black religion that was known as Voodoo. It originated from the ancestral religions of the African diaspora, but the variations that continued to thrive in Louisiana were often reinforced and influenced by Haitian immigrants. During the days of slavery, the Africans were forbidden from practicing Voodoo under the penalty of death. In Louisiana, they were often forced to convert to Catholicism, but many used Catholicism as a cover, syncretizing some of the names and aspects of Voodoo into those of the Catholic saints. Voodoo found its way into the Protestant churches as well. In the early twentieth century, a Christian sect was founded in New Orleans that incorporated Catholic iconography, the ecstatic worship of the black Protestant Pentecostal churches, and a large dose of spiritualism. Voodoo was in many ways an alternative religion viewed with suspicion by many black Christians, but while it took root in and around New Orleans, it attracted followers from other parts of the state as well.

Algiers, the part of New Orleans that is across the river to the west, was the center of a folk belief and practice known as Hoodoo. It had no organic religious connections or connotations, but it was often confused with Voodoo. It was fused instead into the beliefs and "magical" practices of individuals rather than institutionalized into religious rituals and ceremonies. My father made occasional, but rather mysterious, trips to Algiers to meet with Hoodoo practitioners known as root doctors. The purpose of the trip was never made explicit, but one heard talk of the power of "hot foot powder" sprinkled around doors, "mojo," and the gypsy women referenced in the blues and other songs of the time.

In other parts of the state, one could find great diversity among Protestant churches that appealed more to the rising black middle class and the old black elite. Episcopal and Presbyterian churches, for example, practiced the same status and social division that Richard Niebuhr described in his classic *The Social Sources of Denominationalism.* Yet most black churches have long been multiclass, cultivating the spiritual life, shaping the moral consciousness and bringing help, healing, and hope to congregants of all social and economic levels.

The pluralism of the black church was expressed in many additional ways. Some were black institutional members of predominantly white denominations and others were members of predominantly black denominations. Some black Protestant churches emphasized the independence of the congregation and the priesthood of every believer, while others practiced a more structured, even hierarchical, polity and sought more conformity in theological beliefs and worship styles. What all these black churches shared in common, however, and what has caused many interpreters of black religion to speak of a single black church rather than black churches, was the need and capacity to provide healing and wholeness to congregants facing a daily diet of racism and marginalization.

Most black churches, not just in Louisiana but wherever blacks gathered to preach and pray, were safe spaces and supportive places where people who may have differed widely in status and standing came together to seek spiritual guidance, support each other's aspirations, celebrate a common history, and debate fervently how best to make their faith real in the larger society.

Maya Angelou, the black poet and literary icon, was expressing this supportive role when she said in an interview, "If you are black and still the last hired, still the first fired, still the butt of even white liberal jokes, find yourself a black church . . . because when these things hit you—and be sure they will hit you—you need to be able to join with people who understand what is happening to you; people who can embrace you and say I feel your pain; people who will know how to pray for you; elders, deacons and ushers who will say, Oh no, we cannot have that happening to you, honey."[2]

Maya is reminding us that people who wake up daily to attacks on their humanity simply because they differ in color or culture will seek out on Sunday morning people and places where they feel grounded and reaffirmed. They are not as much concerned about the fact that 11:00 on Sunday morning is the most segregated hour in America as they are about what the church does during the rest of the week. Blacks in Opelousas understood that what kept us apart on the weekend was what kept us apart during the week. Even if the doors had opened to those of us seeking to rid ourselves of the impediments of segregation, many would have refused to enter. It is only when people find reassurance, fulfillment, and an active social ministry in predominantly white churches, when they are able to find respect for their differences as well as their commonalities, that they are likely to play a more aggressive role in helping to change the demographics of Sunday morning worship.

### The Prophetic Tradition

The emphasis in the black churches, in St. Landry Parish where I grew up and in Baton Rouge where I went to college, could be seen most clearly in the independence of the pulpit and the freedom of the minister to both comfort and disturb. It may seem strange to some today to learn that the priestly ministry that provided theological meaning, spiritual comfort, and social relief came interspersed with a strong, sometimes radical, condemnation of society and the denunciation of its leaders. Yet even in the 1950s, a decade before the foot soldiers of the civil rights movement marched into many living rooms courtesy of television, black ministers were reminding blacks and whites of the Hebrew prophets who consistently denounced the social order in language so extreme that they were often seen not simply as angry voices but as representatives of an angry God.

The more educated whom I met regularly at Sunday vespers and weekly chapel at Southern University also reminded us of the Greek philosophers who, while providing keen insight into both the human condition and the imperatives of civic life, so disturbed the status quo that their lives were often in danger.

The ministers I met in the many gatherings of black Baptists to which I tagged along with my father, often to meet other preacher kids with my ambition, were effective because they were able to fill a prophetic, priestly, and ecclesiastical role simultaneously. I came to understand later that even when parishioners disagreed with the rhetoric used in services that seem to outsiders more like a public pep rally than the worship of a religious community, they remained loyal members of the congregation because of the role the church played in the community and in their own personal and spiritual lives. Many people, for example, who disagreed strongly with Martin Luther King Jr. on the Vietnam War, and especially the rhetoric he used to denounce it, remained loyal supporters of his ministry and larger mission. As someone once observed, the thought of disowning him would have been as unlikely as Jesus disowning John the Baptist. Moreover, the members of a black church do not have to concur with everything the minister believes, says, or does to remain deeply committed, and deeply indebted, to a local parish as a nurturing and caring community.

Historians have not given sufficient attention to the many ways in which black Southern activists like those with whom I worked in the 1960s got their strength from prophetic religion. It was often the source of their solidarity and self-sacrifice. In *A Stone of Hope*, David Chappell argues, quite correctly, that the story of black Southern activism is not a story of the ultimate triumph of liberal ideas, as sometimes assumed. It is the story of the ultimate triumph of prophetic religious tradition.

It was no accident that the three men who founded the Tuscaloosa Citizens for Action Committee with me in 1963—a local civil rights organization discussed more fully in a later chapter—were all ministers. I did not bring the same sense of a religious revival to our mass meetings, but I soon learned that the exclusive appeal to reason did not inspire the same passion or release the same power as the prophetic tradition of the Old Testament. The leaders with whom I worked saw themselves as in the tradition of the Old Testament prophets. They understood that in order to stand apart from society, often apart from the traditional leaders of their community, the dramatic change we sought could only be instigated through an appeal to the prophetic tradition of the black church. I heard social critiques in language that I could never use, but I saw sacrifices that I could never make and compassion I could only try to emulate.

Some of the Northern allies who had fought on our behalf before we gained our own voice were often as committed as we were, but many had settled for an appeal to human reason rather than direct action rooted in the prophetic tradition. Indeed, some of them urged us to go slowly, fearing that pushing too hard and speaking too passionately would provoke a violent reaction. Yet in the end, some took a prophetic stance as readily and as faithfully as those of us who spoke the language of Jewish and Christian faith. The alliance between those driven by the moral theology of the black church and those driven by a liberal faith in human progress enabled us to join hands against the cattle prods, billy clubs, and fire hoses of the time, but the unraveling of that once-strong alliance after the 1960s may not be as baffling as it first seemed. We were both motivated by a common commitment to change, but the alliance was not based on a deep ideological or theological affinity. Chappell reminds us that there were two very different kinds of optimism and confidence: one came from a strong sense that one was morally right, while the other came from a sense that one had been called to set things right. The idea that one is morally right is easy and common;

to believe that one is going to defeat one's enemies requires rather extraordinary faith.[3]

## What Constitutes Moral Conduct

My own experience of both the appeal and tensions of black moral theology had to do not only with the application of the prophetic imperative, but with some of the theological affirmations as well. My father was a theological conservative who believed in the literal truth of the Bible. While some of our views began to diverge when I was quite young, I never allowed our differences to get in the way because they paled in comparison to the many things we shared in common. Religion for my father was as much a set of rules as it was a source of meaning and moral authority. But while my own sense of personal ethics was less absolute and more broad in scope, I must credit my father for developing within me a sense that I was not here alone, that I did not exist for myself alone, that I was an integral part of something bigger and more mysterious than myself.

There developed at an early age a spiritual hunger that no orthodoxy seemed to satisfy, a yearning for something deeper and more profound than the spirituality I often saw around me. Religion for me was a matter of both the heart and the head. Pascal said the mind builds walls and the heart jumps over them. While it was only in later years that I came to understand what he meant, I refused from the beginning to see the heart and the head as antagonists.

My early struggle with the microethics of the black church saw me develop a keen interest in ethical questions and what constitutes moral conduct. But while others were interested primarily in determining what is right or wrong, good or evil, I was always asking how we arrive at ethical judgments or decisions. Why do people who claim the same moral grounding, appeal to the same moral authority, and use the same moral language arrive at altogether different conclusions about what is right and good? I respected those who saw ethics as having to do primarily with individual actions like smoking, drinking, or sexual behavior, but I came to regard this as far too limited. How could members of a community relegated to second-class citizenship not include the interaction between the individual and society in their discernment of the domain of ethics? It was not simply whites as individuals who denied our dignity and limited our dreams, but the laws of the state and the legacy of institutions as well. I accepted the definition of ethics as the science of behavior having to do with what ought to be, but I felt a moral requirement to help bridge the gap between what was and what should be.

Time and experience caused me to focus more on the macroethics of public institutions than the microethics of individual behavior, but I never lost sight of the connection between the two. The imprint of Star Light Baptist

Church, founded by my father, who served as its senior minister for more than fifty years, can be found in everything I have done, every profession I have pursued, and every job I have held. It was partly because of Star Light Baptist Church that I grew up knowing who I was, where I wanted to go, and what I needed to do to get there. It was in Sunday school that I improved my reading skills. It was in the youth programs and special pageants that I developed public speaking skills. It was in the worship service, with its emphasis on the power of the spirit and the common human condition, that I first became fascinated with the possibility of a different future. It also helped to be surrounded by a caring congregation of people who believed in me and refused to let me fail.

In the early years of my growing up, my father seemed to be consumed with a very narrow slice of the moral imperatives of his faith, but I found on my first visit home after I was established elsewhere that he had become very active in seeking justice and promoting equal opportunity for those blacks I had remembered as preoccupied with private virtue. It was then that I came to realize that, like many of his generation, he refused to do anything that might jeopardize opportunities for his children; but as soon as we left home, he pulled off the mask of civility and docile manners that had once made him seem oblivious to a much larger understanding of the moral imperatives of religion in public life.

The white churches in Opelousas were not only unwilling to affirm this marriage of private virtue and public values as a central tenet of Christianity, but they either remained silent or strongly supported the racial theories and theologies of the white supremacists who dominated local politics. We were all claiming to be moral persons. We simply had different ideas about what constitutes moral conduct. The meetings of the Ku Klux Klan opened with a prayer, and its members frequently sang religious songs as they lynched black men who also hummed the songs of their faith as they went to their death. It was not unique to find two very different views of the moral life.

The moral theology of that little black church on the side of the road that launched my hunger for answers to difficult moral questions was both universal and particular. The rural location and the rural people who populated it may have suggested to the outsider an isolation from the world of ideas and progressive social thought, but long before the rise of black liberation theology, some of us were asking questions that seem now to have been far ahead of our time. I can remember wondering why none of the people depicted in the Sunday school literature looked like me. There were hints in the Bible that some came from cultures and places that were not Anglo-Saxon, but I did not fully engage that issue until I was much older.

Yet even at an early age, I was asking in my own mind many of the questions now associated with black or liberation theology. I saw it as a logical manifestation of my faith rather than something special or different. Growing up black in a white community where Jesus was visually portrayed as white, we had to take charge of our own faith and think of it in ways that were relevant to the circumstances of black people. We did not claim any exclusive identification with the historical Jesus because we believed that all people in their goodness and in their humanity had something of Christ within them. The centrality of Jesus to our faith revolved not around race, therefore, but around his identification with the suffering and struggle of the oppressed.

While my father and his generation never spoke of a black messiah, they did their best to free theology from the racial, cultural, and political myopia that limited the depiction of his humanity to strictly European features. Like the later black theology movement, their theology was formed and expressed by the faith and life of black people. It was only in this way, by doing theology in context, that they could worship the same God as those who sought to deny their humanity and destroy their dignity.

### African Roots

As I grew a little older, I began to think more deeply about the myriad questions surfacing in my young mind. I was rather unsophisticated about what I came later to know as theology, but in retrospect, the roots of the little black church that nurtured my theological and moral growth were grounded in cultural heritage as well as religious imperatives. While the preeminent beliefs were those of Western Christianity, there were traces of an African humanism as well.

The ancestry of the first blacks in southwestern Louisiana can be traced almost directly to the west coast of Africa and Angola. Others came from the French islands, such as Martinique and especially Haiti. All brought with them the theology and practices of African religion with its unique cosmology and metaphysics.

When the French, the Spanish, and other Europeans came to Louisiana, they brought with them a worldview that defined the individual in two basic ways. The first emphasized the individual as thinker in the tradition of René Descartes—"I think, therefore I am"—and Thomas Aquinas, who sought to marry faith and reason. The second emphasized the individual as worker in the tradition of Martin Luther and Karl Marx.

The belief systems brought to Louisiana by the first Africans placed emphasis on three other dimensions of humanity that found a home in the new world of black religion. The first was the idea that individual identity is communal. The emphasis was on the group and the individual's obligation to its members. Along the bayous and the nearby cotton fields, black children were brought up by the whole community, and the elderly were cared for as if they were members of the immediate family. Slavery had caused a terrible rending of the fabric of black family and community life, but there was a kinship created by common adversity and shared dreams. Despite a concentrated effort to break up the old ties that once bound them together, there was still a spirit of community, of shared joy and shared grief, of shared resources and shared responsibility. There was not much room for individualism in the Western sense, for while a high value was placed on individual human worth, it was an individualism that found its highest expression in a communal context. The individual was regarded as part of a network of kin that functioned as an economic, political, and religious unit with its own customs, traditions, and rituals. As the core communal unit, the extended family was able to make demands that normally overrode all other duties and obligations.

The second idea that fostered identity and shaped moral behavior was the notion that each individual has both the capacity and the need to celebrate life even in the midst of tragedy. This understanding of human nature could be seen both in the personality of individuals who appeared to be happy when all around them were reasons to be sad, and in the vitality of the African funeral ritual, which was preserved and practiced in the black churches not only in Louisiana but wherever members of the African diaspora settled. The celebration of life did not mean the acceptance of the conditions of life, but rather the ability to look beyond the worse moments of life to see the possibility of something different and deeper.

The third idea was the belief that human beings are visionary mythmakers who are able not only to imagine different life alternatives but also to create them. Long before Martin Luther King Jr. held the world spellbound with his "I Have a Dream" speech at the Lincoln Memorial, the notion of the individual as dreamer had become central to the moral theology of the black church. The parishioners at my father's churches in St. Landry Parish were admonished regularly not to settle for life as it was, but to think of life as it ought to be. They were repeatedly reminded, "Keep your eyes on the prize." While the prize sometimes appeared to be simply an otherworldly escapism, the emphasis was on perseverance rather than resignation. And that is why so many whites in St. Landry Parish, where the Ku Klux Klan flourished, were surprised to find one day that those whom they thought were focused on an afterlife were demanding justice in this life. The idea of men and women as dreamers, of the possibility of a widely different future, was also an important way of contextualizing the biblical adage, "Where there is no vision, the people perish."

Just how aware the first Africans to settle in Louisiana were of these weighty metaphysical ideas is a matter of conjecture. Certainly, most were not intellectuals, but they had so internalized the worldview of their tribes and regions that these were not so much concepts to be debated or learned in some form of cognitive development as they were the unconscious realities of everyday life.

These realities predated the birth of the black church, but the religious institutions developed by the freed slaves managed to put their fingerprint on almost every aspect of African American life. Like all expressions of religious faith, it was in many ways unique to the people who fashioned it, but its theology and moral claims were consistent with those of early Christianity.

### The Impact of a New Pluralism

In the years since my childhood experience in Louisiana, there has been considerably more tolerance of the new pluralism that has seen the United States become the most religiously diverse nation in the world. While Louisiana remains primarily Protestant and Catholic, it is nevertheless increasingly difficult for many to accept the view of my father's generation of Christians that it is only the Christian tradition that provides the foundation for authentic moral reasoning. They seem to be in good company in that regard. Scholars like Marcus Borg, author of the best-selling *Meeting Jesus for the First Time*, argue that when Christianity claims to be the only true religion, it loses some of its attraction and credibility. I agree, yet, as for them, the Christian tradition is home for me. I was born into it and grew up in it. Its stories, language, music, and ethos are familiar to me. It nurtured me, even as, along the way, I have had to unlearn some of what I was taught. I also know that under different circumstances other religions could have been home to me—had I been born in India, Japan, or Indonesia, for example. Krister Stendahl, a former dean at the Harvard Divinity School, spoke of this openness to other religions as a kind of "holy envy," the ability to see beauty in other religions.[4] This describes me fully, but the truth remains that my moral consciousness was shaped by the cultural, religious, and even political context in which I grew up. The passion I feel for justice, and my identification with the oppressed and marginalized, as well as my hunger for reconciliation and community, all had their genesis in what I came to understand about the life and work of Jesus.

As I look back on the theological journey I traveled, I must admit that there were moments when I believed and other moments when I doubted; but there is no question that the moral consciousness I carry within me had its genesis in the teachings of that little black church in rural Louisiana. Yet, as I confess and describe in a later chapter, I continued to struggle with the question whether morality needs religion.

...................

# CHAPTER 3

# On the Banks of the Mississippi

I was ready and confident when I arrived in 1952 as a freshman at Southern University in Baton Rouge, Louisiana. The fragrance of magnolia on campus, located on Scott's Bluff overlooking the Mississippi River, mixed with the smell of oil refineries down shore. The history of Southern paralleled the history of the state of Louisiana. Chartered in April 1880 by the Louisiana General Assembly, the college opened its doors a year later "for the education of persons of color." The concept of an institution for black Americans was put forth by Pinckney Benton Stewart Pinchback, the first person of African American descent to become governor of a U.S. state. Born free in Georgia, he moved later to Louisiana, and, after serving as lieutenant governor, in December 1872 he was sworn in as the thirty-fourth governor.

I arrived on campus at a time when Southern served as the black alternative to Louisiana State University, which only admitted whites. Many of us had excelled in high school and were eager to demonstrate that we were as capable as any white student, but we knew our time would come, so we saw Southern as a necessary first step. It had grown from a student body of twelve in 1880 to more than ten thousand. These were the days before integration in the South, but many of the black faculty members had graduated from prestigious schools in New England and the Midwest. Black students from the best high schools in the United States also found their way to Southern.

My father and my brother had gone to Leland College, a small private school operated by black Baptists, but Southern offered me a partial scholarship with the promise of a job washing dishes in the kitchen of the student cafeteria to help pay for tuition. I had first visited the campus as a high school junior to participate in Bayou Boys State and returned later as a counselor and deputy to the director. Thus it was with fond memories of the campus and the professors I had met at Boys State that I arrived on campus on a hot and humid summer day, registered for classes, and was assigned to live in Barracks B. I did not realize at the time that it was somewhat unusual for college students to live in discarded military barracks with as many as fifty jammed together in one long open room. But this was just the beginning of my experience of segregation in higher education. It was not very different from high school—old run-down buildings, very little equipment, but great teachers.

My experience at Southern was not unlike high school in other important ways, especially the opportunity to serve in leadership roles. While I served as president of my class and other social and fraternal organizations, it was as president of the Baptist Club that I found myself reexamining some of the beliefs and practices that had been such a central part of my early life. As I started to meet faculty and students who were not Baptist but who claimed to share my faith, I began to realize that I was part of a larger and far more diverse faith community than I had been taught in Sunday school. Like Opelousas, the rest of Louisiana had a very large population of Catholics, so I soon learned that the religious life for them meant knowing and believing in formal creeds and doctrines, participating in rituals, and honoring saints. It was also the first time that I began to see my faith as one among many. I even became friends with students who were raising questions about some of those biblical stories that I had heard repeatedly in Sunday school. I remembered especially those about Joshua stopping the sun, Moses parting the sea, and Jesus turning water into wine without adding grapes, and while I could not understand how, I kept the faith because I had started to feel that faith was deeper than belief.

I had many role models at Southern who exposed me to the career options available to young blacks with ambition. One of the first and foremost was Felton G. Clark, the president of Southern, who was a scholar and nationally respected leader. Under his leadership, the university had grown from a small college in Baton Rouge to become the largest black university in the United States. Yet its impact came from more than its size. Felton Clark had successfully recruited some of the best teachers and scholars in black America. He had persuaded many companies to hire Southern graduates and many professional and graduate schools to recruit them. It was not surprising that within a few years after I arrived, the Southern faculty was raided by newly integrating white institutions encouraged by court decisions to expand their reach. My sociology professor became a college president, and the head of the political science department became an Ivy League dean, while two of his colleagues soon occupied similar positions in the Midwest and on the West Coast.

Clark managed to meet this new challenge by keeping Southern alive and professionally relevant, but the times were changing, and while he was focused on sustaining the institution, a new generation of students were more interested in changing society. It was the early years of civil rights activity, and students at Southern joined the movement. On March 20, 1960, seven students participated in a sit-in at the lunch counter of the S. H. Kress store in Baton Rouge and were arrested. The next day, Southern students organized more sit-ins that were followed by more arrests, and thousands of students marched through the streets of Baton Rouge. Louisiana Governor Earl K. Long demanded (some say ordered) that Clark take decisive action to stem the tide of "disruption" that was placing Southern's future in danger. Faced with the moral dilemma of many black leaders of his time who sought to keep black institutions open, he bowed to the pressure and expelled eighteen students. Feeling betrayed, hundreds of students withdrew from the university, and two years later Clark was forced to close the school for a brief period.

Later in the decade, the rift between the students and the Clark administration began to heal, and some years later I was invited to serve as the commencement speaker at a ceremony conferring honorary degrees on the students who had been expelled. But the image and accomplishments of the once highly revered Felton Clark had been tarnished. He was the victim of two very different visions of how social change takes place: keep black educational institutions open and available at all costs, or risk closing them in order to build a better future. When my opportunity came a few years later, I chose the latter, but I could still feel Felton Clark's pain as he agonized over a moral dilemma faced by many of our elders. Subservience was the price they paid to make our assertiveness possible.

A few years before the civil rights protest, some of us had dared to confront Felton Clark about the quality of life on campus. As one of the organizers of the campus protests, I was seated onstage for a rally in which we asked him to meet with us to discuss our demands. As students gathered in the auditorium, the mood turned ugly, and when President Clark was introduced there was a loud burst of boos that made it impossible for him to speak. When it became clear that some form of intervention was necessary, I stepped to the podium and began to recite the New Testament prayer that was so often a part of our assemblies. About a third of the way through the prayer, the booing subsided enough for me to complete the prayer and make an appeal to the students to give Dr. Clark a hearing. He shared with us the impediments posed by limited resources, but he surprised us by identifying with our discontent and promising to do his best to make the changes we sought. We left the meeting with a greater sense of empathy for his predicament in trying to stretch the institution's limited budget to provide for our general well-being as best as he could.

During my years at Southern, I took in everything I could and sat at the feet of some of the great men and women in black America. While many were on the faculty, even more came as visitors, from an aging Mary McLeod Bethune to a young Martin Luther King Jr. I had lunch with Benjamin Mays, the famed president of Morehouse College, and served as student host for the visit of Samuel Dewitt Proctor, who was president of Virginia Union University at thirty-three. I especially remembered Proctor because he shared stories with me of how he had first met Martin Luther King and the lively conversations they had about how to reconcile their Christian faith as Baptists with the brand of liberal theology taught at Crozer Theological Seminary, where they had both been students. It was as the student speaker for the Founders Day Convocation that I met Mrs. Bethune, and I was often on other programs in the auditorium that served as the assembly hall for distinguished visitors. Dean Martin Harvey, who was a spellbinding liturgist for Vespers and a friend of many of our visitors, made certain that I was able to spend some time with each of them. Like many of his colleagues, he did everything he could to expose Southern students to some of the most inspiring leaders in the nation. This too was part of the uniqueness of Southern. As early as 1901, President William McKinley spoke at the university, and in 1943 Eleanor Roosevelt visited, making Southern one of the first historically black colleges to receive a First Lady.

What made Southern special was not simply its role in exposing its students to the ideas and movements of the time, or even facilitating cognitive development—enhancing the ability to think and to learn—but its role in affective development as well, enhancing the capacity to feel the pain and share the burden of others. It was at the feet of my father that I learned the importance of the microethics that build character, but it was at Southern that I learned to appreciate and value the macroethics that build community. No one used the language of a third sector or civil society, but we were being urged to find the balance between our calling as students and our calling as citizens, between the need to build a career for ourselves and the need to help build a better life for our communities. We heard often that our generation would be called upon not simply to help establish justice, but to help remake our democracy. While the rigidity of segregation made these claims seem unrealistic to some, I had written in my high school yearbook that I wanted to be the first black senator from Louisiana, so I did not need much persuasion.

Southern was also unique in ways that are often overlooked when we debate the role of black colleges in present-day America. It not only attracted the best and the brightest, but it also took underprepared students from underprepared high schools and transformed them into very competitive adults. That in the end may be the most important legacy of black colleges like Southern. The best students would have succeeded anywhere, but many who might have been rejected elsewhere because of inadequate appraisal of their potential ended up with careers of distinction.

## Competing with Whites

I made a decision as early as my freshman year to join the ROTC (Reserve Officers' Training Corps), partly for the small monthly subsidy and partly because the army was beginning to provide opportunities for young black men with ambition. It was in ROTC summer camp at Fort Hood, Texas, that I got my first opportunity to compete against whites. The army had been formally integrated some years before, but with colleges and universities in the South still segregated, this meant that our ROTC units were also segregated.

It was not an easy summer. We were only a handful of blacks facing the wrath of angry and resistant whites from universities still segregated. While we were training to be officers and actually carried the rank of officers in our respective units, summer camp was very much like boot camp with rotating assignments. Those of us who were black were disproportionately assigned the menial tasks of washing dishes and cleaning out the latrines. But there were also taunts, name-calling, and provocations that we were determined to resist. Yet while some of my classmates from Southern felt the sting of discrimination in the final ratings, I discovered something that summer that was to remain with me for the rest of my life. One of the training officers was a white captain from West Point. He took an interest in me and gave me every opportunity to compete, ensuring that I had leadership as well as subordinate roles. And because he and a few others like him were fair, some of us from Southern ended the summer camp with excellent ratings. It was the first time I had encountered a white person who was willing to give me an equal opportunity to compete, and it helped me to recognize that the whites I had known in Opelousas did not represent the full spectrum of white attitudes.

The graduates of the Southern University ROTC now read like a Who's Who in the U.S. military. The most notable may be Lieutenant General Russel L. Honoré, who brought order to New Orleans during the chaos of Hurricane Katrina, but it also included Brigadier General Sherian Grace Cadoria, who was the first African American female to reach the rank of general in the U.S. Army, and Lieutenant General Joe Ballard, who was the first African American to serve as commander of the U.S. Army Corps of Engineers.

During my last year at Southern, I continued to excel in intercollegiate debate and original oratory while serving again as class president and in many other leadership capacities. I was selected to carry the university colors and to march at the head of my class for the commencement ceremony, but I was also honored as a distinguished military graduate and commissioned a second lieutenant in the Medical Service Corps. Two of my classmates rose to the rank of general: Robert Dinkins, a superb football player who in other times might have played professionally, and Donald Delandro, who after retirement from the army became a very successful businessman.

I left Southern in 1956 with an academic degree in my hand and ambitious dreams in my head. It was May, and while I had been commissioned as a second lieutenant, my duty assignment did not begin until the end of the year, so I headed to Houston, Texas, in search of a job. I was quickly reminded that in the eyes of many whites an "educated Negro" (some used the other "N" word) was still regarded as inferior to any white man, even if that man was illiterate.

I had heard that one of the largest and most prestigious department stores in Houston was hiring, so I headed to the employment desk and was sent to the room marked "colored." It was next door to the waiting room marked "white," separated only by a low partition that allowed applicants to see what was going on in the next room. As I started to fill out the application form I had been given, a white man on the other side of the partition asked me if I could read. Upon hearing that I could, he asked if I would help him fill out his form. Feeling good about my obviously superior education, I agreed. After meeting with an interviewer, we both exited about the same time, so I asked him if he had any luck. It turned out that I had been offered a job in the basement baling used cardboard boxes that came down a chute from many floors above, and he had been given a job on one of the upper floors that paid twice as much.

Life changed considerably in December when I finally arrived at Fort Sam Houston in San Antonio, Texas, for my initial orientation to the Medical

Service Corps. Upon completion of my medical service training, I was sent to Fort Devens, Massachusetts. As a twenty-one-year-old college graduate fresh out of the Army ROTC, I was assigned to a special infantry brigade where I served as commander of a medical detachment. The men in my unit were all white and much older. They were very experienced in the affairs of military life, but my authority to lead came from the power of my position and the capacity to coerce. My leadership assignment was called a command, and I was described in the organization chart as commanding officer. It was a paradigm of leadership where authority was maintained as much by disincentives as by incentives. The leader received an order and passed it on. The order was followed because of the threat of court-martial or other forms of punishment.

Yet there was another element in my experience, in which I had to learn about leadership from those I led without losing my influence or authority. As a young lieutenant with little actual field experience, I had to learn as much as I could from my senior noncommissioned officers while still maintaining control and retaining their respect. Learning from those you lead is a principle of leadership that remained with me throughout my professional career.

There was one additional aspect of the principles and practices of leadership in the U.S. Army that influenced my understanding of the role of the leader in other settings. The leader is not so much a leader of followers as a leader of leaders. I did not simply lead subordinates. I led other leaders. There was a chain of command, but each soldier had to be prepared not just for a military specialty in which he was the expert, but had to be prepared to step in at any minute and assume the leadership role of a fallen comrade. Each soldier was taught that leadership has to be everyone's job.

Leadership training in the U.S. Army now places more emphasis on "being" (what it means to be a leader) than in my years as a first lieutenant, when the emphasis was almost exclusively on knowing and doing, on giving orders and ensuring that they were followed; but I learned even then that effective leadership was essentially a way of being grounded in something deeper than the power of position. It was preferable for the men in my unit, and it was only men then, to follow me because they wanted to rather than simply because they had to. I learned that even in leadership roles where authority is vested in a position, it was still important to show respect for others, care for their well-being as persons, help them find meaning and value in their work, value diversity, promote tolerance, practice kindness, and treat people fairly without regard to position or context.

I was promoted to first lieutenant and urged by the post commander to make the military a career, but when my two years of required service ended,

I returned briefly to Louisiana and applied to teach in the public school system while waiting to begin graduate study at Yale. The school board official who made assignments greeted me by asking, "What can I do for you, boy?" To which I replied, "I have just completed serving my country in a capacity where everyone in my unit called me 'sir,' and I am not about to allow you to demean your country and yourself in this way." He uttered something unintelligible but got his revenge by assigning me to teach third grade in a distant rural school rather than the premier high school I had been led to believe would be my assignment. Teaching at that level for half a year may have been my most difficult teaching assignment, although I taught later at the undergraduate, graduate, and continuing education levels.

Something else happened at this elementary school, in Grand Coteau, that helped me to better understand southwestern Louisiana. The school had been private and Catholic and was in the early phase of integration into the black public school system. I was the first and only Protestant on the staff and one of only two men, but the nuns, who were much better at working with young third graders, practically adopted me as they tutored me on both teaching and black Catholic culture. In return, I taught them what I knew about public speaking and how to play basketball. I still remember the sight of nuns in habits and long dresses shooting free throws. They were some very tough and competitive sisters, but it was their compassion for the rural students that stood out. I kept in touch with them for many years and saw the elementary school become a high school, with many of my former students going on to college.

I left home after a year for graduate school, but my brother remained and eventually became the mayor of Opelousas. My mother did not live to see him become the first black mayor or to see me elected to the Louisiana Political Hall of Fame and honored at a large gala in Baton Rouge as a "Louisiana Legend," with former president Clinton describing me as "not only a Louisiana Legend but a national treasure." But in every step of our journey, we could still see her smiling presence on the front row, where she sat so often through the years of our growing up. She would surely have appreciated the irony of the complimentary articles by the once-racist press announcing my appointment to senior executive or advisory positions by four U.S. presidents, including undersecretary of the interior and U.S. ambassador to the Republic of South Africa.

The years at Southern were a time of immense personal growth. They instilled within me an intellectual curiosity and a love of learning that have served me well for more than half a century. Some of my memories are romantic—vivid images of moss-covered oak trees, the almost mystic influences of

Cajun and Creole cultures, and the vitality of an educational institution that was rigidly segregated, but whose students refused to be rigidly subservient. My other memories are less romantic and less mystical. It was in quiet moments on the banks of the Mississippi that I also pondered the burden of being black in America and what I had to do to overcome the structural barriers waiting for me once I graduated.

# II

# The 1960s

APPLYING VALUES TO
SOCIAL MOVEMENTS

CHAPTER 4

························

# A Spiritual Journey at Yale

In my junior year at Southern, I was sent as a delegate to a YMCA conference in Kansas. It was a cold winter and the first time I had seen snow, but that was not the most important memory I took back to Louisiana. The experience that lingered for many years was the opportunity to hear a student from Yale Divinity School talk about his faith, and somehow feeling instinctively a kinship with this stranger who was neither Baptist nor black. I made it a point to meet him and to talk not just about what he had said, but about the place where he was studying. I peppered him with questions. How did his professors explain the existence of God? Did his institution respect those who had moments of doubt? Was he encouraged to ask critical questions? I liked his answers and came to realize that he was in seminary not just to learn more about Christian doctrine and church history, but to engage in critical analysis and to put biblical theology in perspective. He made quite an impression on me, but I went back to Southern and got so engaged in other pursuits that I kept a growing disquiet about what my faith asked me to believe under wraps, realizing that it would be very disappointing and disturbing to my family and devout friends to acknowledge that one moment I believed and the very next moment I had grave doubts.

It was not until 1958, when I was nearing the completion of my military assignment, that I thought again about the student I had met earlier from Yale Divinity School and how much his moral and intellectual concerns reflected my own. I had taken quickly to military life and was a model junior officer with various awards for performance, but despite the greater opportunities in the military at that time for young black men like me, this was not the future I imagined for myself. I wanted to get involved in changing the society rather than simply defending it. I was beginning to ask deeply moral questions about the public obligations of the nation-state to its citizens. I was starting to feel a calling not just to change public institutions and practices, but to change the hearts and minds of the traditionalists who believed that their faith had called them to protect and preserve the status quo.

I was stationed in Massachusetts and often drove through Connecticut on my way south, but the next time I passed through New Haven I decided to tour Yale's historic campus and visit the divinity school. Shortly thereafter, I got in touch with school officials, investigated the requirements for enrollment, and, on a beautiful day in late August 1959, arrived in New Haven as a seminary student in pursuit of a divinity degree. The professors I met—Richard Niebuhr, the younger brother of Reinhold; Roland Bainton, the British-born church historian; Robert Calhoun, the systematic theologian; David Napier, the Old Testament scholar; and many others—were well known to most of my classmates, but to a young Baptist from Louisiana they were strangers whose works I quickly read for the first time.

I had married the year before, and my new wife, Doris, had no indication that the young lieutenant she had first met on a double date while I was working with Hungarian refugees at Camp Kilmer in New Brunswick, New Jersey, was interested in seminary. She not only adjusted well to the frugal life of a graduate student who arrived on campus with no savings and only a promise of a small scholarship and part-time work, but she was a great asset, both in the upper-class white church in Stamford, Connecticut, where I did my field work—a sort of internship—and in my summer work for the Connecticut Council of Churches with migrants in the tobacco fields. With a degree in social work, she quickly found a job and added economic support to her many other contributions that greatly improved the quality of life we enjoyed. When she became pregnant during my last year and was no longer working, I took on three part-time jobs while still studying full time. Fortunately, one was as a security guard with the Yale police that simply required me to sit at the divinity school's entrance on one of New Haven's quieter streets; and since my hours were late into the night when my fellow students were in their rooms studying and visitors were rare, I was able to read books and write papers while on duty.

This served me well at the end of the year when Doris went into labor just as I began final exams. Studying in a hospital waiting room was a challenge in itself, but my excitement about the birth of our first child was tempered by the anxiety about final examinations that would help determine whether I would be remembered and recognized as much for my academic achievements as for my curious and questioning mind. My parents were already making plans for the commencement and the long drive from Louisiana to Connecticut, one that Doris and I had made many times for holiday visits, often with Grady Poulard, an old friend from Louisiana also studying at Yale. Jeffrey was born in the Yale–New Haven hospital on May 18, 1963. I graduated a few weeks later with very good grades on my exams and two gifts from my very pleased parents: their presence at the ceremony and a clerical robe I still cherish. I had not yet fully worked out the tension between the private virtues that I had been told in my early years were absolutes and the public values that I was now better equipped to affirm and practice, but I had been liberated—at least in my own mind—from the stigma once associated with playing cards, drinking alcohol, and dancing, although I never fully recovered from not having started early enough to develop any real skill in the latter. More importantly, I still felt a call to ministry, but now I saw the world as my parish and the call of the Old Testament prophets for social justice as my primary message and mission.

## An Age of Belief

The theologian Harvey Cox could have been describing my own personal journey when he described a three-stage way of envisioning Christian history. He wrote about an age of faith, an age of belief, and an age of the spirit. While the time line of the stages was far from precise, the period in my early life in Louisiana was for me an age of faith. I pushed aside the questions about what I should believe and whether I should walk in my father's shoes, as many suggested, and began to consider my faith as a way of being grounded in what I could learn about the faith *of* Jesus, rather than simply what had been fashioned by those who years later sought to codify what it means to have faith *in* Jesus.

The professional shift from military life to the graduate study of religion launched a parallel shift in my way of thinking about the relationship between religion and public morality. Yale Divinity School was concerned as much with the intellect as with faith. This was great for my inquiring mind, but not the same for some theologically conservative critics who saw those two ways of knowing as in irreconcilable conflict. They were the ones I met along the way, even at Yale, who questioned whether I was too ecumenical in my approach to holiness and too focused on public values to include a proper consideration of the private virtues they wanted me to affirm as absolutes for the nation.

An issue that had troubled me from an early age emerged anew as I began to think more seriously about whether morality needs religion. I discussed it in the classroom with my professors and in the lobby on long cold nights with my fellow students. I was reminded that for most of modern history, religion and ethics have been closely intertwined. I learned that the folklore of almost every civilization contains an account of how the laws and rules that guide private and public behavior had their genesis in some form of divine revelation. While I had not explored the assumption that morality needs religion with my devout family and friends, I felt free to raise it at Yale, but first as a provocateur rather than as the expressions of one who was regrounding his faith.

The period at Yale was for me an age of belief. I was trying to anchor my faith in something that answered, rather than simply raised, critical questions about the Sunday school stories I had once accepted as a matter of faith. The increasingly intense intellectual inquiry was directed at the writings of early scribes and interpreters of the Bible, as well as later reformers who brought into fuller light what they believed to be the central tenets of Christian faith. I was also greatly influenced by Reinhold Niebuhr, especially his book *Moral Man and Immoral Society*, where he argued that while we know a lot about what is right and what is to be revered in individual behavior, we have made relatively little progress in applying morality to the problems of our aggregate existence, whether as nations, institutions, or communities. I knew from experience that there were many confessed believers who focused primarily on what is right and what is wrong in individual behavior, but I was intrigued by Niebuhr's distinction between individual and group morality and what he had to say about bringing them into balance.

The years at Yale were also the beginning of my life as a social activist. Faculty and students at Yale Divinity School were deeply involved in the civil rights movement. I had come to know the activist chaplain Bill Coffin through a course on religion and higher education. He invited me to assist him for a semester as a volunteer in his work with international students and became a mentor and icon. I had never met anyone whose words could create such electricity. He was clearly the most erudite minister I had ever met, and his sermons were spellbinding. I knew in my heart that I had finally found the model of ministry I wanted to pursue. Coffin became a lifelong friend whom I called on occasionally for help when I became a university chaplain and a civil rights and anti–Vietnam War activist.

It was at Yale that I also met two white Southerners who would remain a part of my life far beyond graduate school. Both Joseph Hough and John Maguire were as committed to social justice as I was. While their accents reminded me of people I had come to dislike in my early experience of segregation, they defied all the stereotypes I had developed of white Southerners.

One day, I walked into the lobby of the divinity school where a large crowd was gathering and found John Maguire at the front of the group saying, "We go forth to war." He was organizing a street protest on the New Haven Green in support of James Lawson, a Vanderbilt divinity student who had been expelled for his civil rights activities. I joined the march and regularly repeated it as we expanded the protest to include a denouncement of Woolworth's stores in the South, where blacks were being denied service at their lunch counters. I got to know the manager of the New Haven Woolworth's, who made it clear that he did not support the practices in the South and invited me to visit his lunch counter. When he found out that I would not leave the protest march even while very thirsty, he went back in and brought me a drink of water.

Many of my classmates and colleagues at Yale left for public life rather than the parish ministry. We had all been touched by the times as well as the theology we studied. John Danforth became a U.S. senator. Gary Hart became not only a senator from Colorado but a candidate for president of the United States. Lynn Jondahl had a long career in the Michigan legislature, where he chaired the budget committee. John Maguire became a university president and Joe Hough a seminary president and lifelong friend. Grady Poulard, seemingly the least likely to go into the parish, went into the parish ministry until he left to become a foundation executive and to pursue other areas of public life.

While in New Haven, I changed my denominational affiliation from Baptist to Congregationalist (now the United Church of Christ). It was not just the more liberal theology of the Congregationalists that I found attractive, but the social activism of a church that had opposed slavery, fought long for the elimination of segregation in all its forms, and put justice at the center of its moral mission. Having left Europe to seek spiritual freedom, the Congregational churches founded by the Pilgrims set out to create a model for a just society in their ecclesiastical practices as well as in their engagement with the larger society. They were at the center of the first act of civil disobedience in U.S. history—the Boston Tea Party. They were among the first Americans to take a stand against slavery. When enslaved Africans broke their chains, seized control of the schooner *Amistad*, and were later arrested, Congregationalists organized a successful campaign to free the captives. In

1798, they were the first white Protestant denomination to ordain an African American.

The work of the Congregational Church had first come to my attention in 1957 when they united with the Evangelical and Reformed (E&R) Church to form the United Church of Christ. The new community brought together the traditions and practices in which the Evangelical and Reformed theologian Reinhold Niebuhr had preached a sermon that introduced the now-famous Serenity Prayer: "God, give us grace to accept with serenity those things that cannot be changed, the courage to change those things that should be changed, and the wisdom to distinguish the one from the other." The E&R theologian Paul Tillich, who wrote *The Courage to Be*, proclaimed as one of the books of the century, was also a part of the tradition I was now choosing to join.

The new Congregational community embraced a wide variety of spiritual traditions, including those of African, Asian Pacific, and Native American origin. But it was not just the rich history that appealed to me. It was the leadership in the civil rights movement of the 1950s and 1960s that attracted my attention as well. When in 1959 Southern television stations imposed a news blackout on the growing civil rights movement, it was to the United Church of Christ that Martin Luther King Jr. appealed for help. Under the leadership of the church's Office of Communications, an appeal was made to the federal courts that culminated in the ruling that the airwaves were public, not private, property. The decision led to a proliferation of people of color in television studios and newsrooms. Of course, within a decade of my graduation, the United Church of Christ ordained the first gay person as a minister in a mainline Protestant denomination. It was not surprising that my three Baptist friends from the South—Grady Poulard, Joe Hough, and John Maguire—also joined the United Church of Christ.

It was while at Yale that I began to think about the relationship of the United States to the rest of the world. Kofi Opoku, a fellow student whom I first knew as Nathan, added greatly to my expanding worldview. He was from Ghana, and I was eager to learn about his country and culture, but as we became close friends, we debated larger issues having to do with the role of the United States in the world. I drove him to Washington, DC, for a weekend to align his distant view of the city with an actual experience of its population and policymaking. He became so interested in American politics that, much to Doris's dismay, we sat up all night in our tiny apartment waiting for the returns and listening to the commentary on the election of John F. Kennedy.

It was largely because of my conversations with Kofi that my own moral consciousness expanded to include the teachings of world religions, especially the traditional religions of West Africa. I came to realize that placing moral authority within a religious context served three purposes: (1) it provided authority for prescriptive moral behavior by relating ethics to the transcendent claims of divinity; (2) it provided a communal context that kept morality from becoming a matter of individual preference; and (3) it provided a universal context that kept morality from becoming simply the choice of individual communities.

Understanding the utility of religion as a moral authority did not fully satisfy my curiosity about whether society needs religion in order to be moral. I came to understand that my problem was with the grounding of morality in elaborate theological systems. If, as Søren Kierkegaard suggested, religion is not so much a doctrine as an existence, my quarrel was with those who used religion not to enhance consciousness of the good but to judge or prescribe behavior that was often culturally rooted.

While the theological debate about religion and morality was a factor in my choosing to study at Yale Divinity School, I left feeling that while the moral teachings of religion must be a part of the public discourse about values, no faith should assume that its parochial claims about private virtue should be transformed de facto into the public values of the nation-state. What became most important to me was that there was abundant evidence to suggest that the best interest of society is served when the authentic voice of religion is heard.

### An Age of the Spirit

The conversations with Kofi about world religions helped launch what became for me an age of the spirit. The awe and wonder that consumed me in the encounter with mystery, the difficulty with doctrine, and the rejection of ritual led me to look more deeply at what was happening at the core of my true self, not just where one locates insight and imagination but in the ability to see the sacred in everyday life. While my father was a Baptist minister and I grew up in an Afrocentric black church, I was discovering something that could be informed, but not contained, by what is normally described as organized religion.

Religion was for many of my classmates at Yale a set of coherent answers to the existential problems of humankind. For others, it was the lockbox that enabled them to find meaning in mystery, while still others used it to affirm moral absolutes. But when I reflected on what had kept me centered in times of great challenge and resilient in times of great adversity, I was persuaded that it was a special form of spiritual intelligence. Religion can both open and close minds. It can lead to remarkable demonstrations of love, and it can also lead to hatred of the other. What I was coming to call spiritual intelligence cultivated openness to the unknown, the unexpected, and the unexplored. While I had once tied religion exclusively to doctrines and traditions, a new consciousness was emerging that found me leaning toward the kind of God Spinoza described as one who reveals himself in the harmony of nature. It was what Einstein called religiousness, the sense that behind everything that can be experienced there is something that our minds cannot grasp.

It was surprising to learn that the word "religion" is not mentioned in the Bible or any of the early texts of other faith groups. It is in fact the product of an early Latin term that in its earliest usage had no doctrinal or theological content. It was used instead to simply refer to obligatory practices and duties. With the spread of Christianity across the Roman Empire, it came to be used primarily to refer to belief.

I learned much during those years of personal reflection about being in touch with my inner self and at ease with my own strengths and weaknesses. I found that I was happiest and most in harmony with myself and others when I practiced compassion, forgiveness, tolerance, and patience. I also found inspiration from others with whom I felt a deepened sense of presence. I have not always had to retreat from the noisy sounds of either the streets or the workplace, because stillness does not always mean silence. For some, it re- quires detachment from secondary attractions. Yet it has continued to be my experience that it can also come from a short break-away moment, from the magical sound of the ocean, the mystical seduction of a Nat King Cole song, the singing of a bird on the limb of a tree, or simply the rustling of the wind.

I have found increasing numbers of people who might once have de- scribed themselves as religious eager to explain how being religious for them differs from some of the doctrines or institutional practices of conventional religion. They are the ones who are most likely to describe themselves as spiritual. Many clerical leaders take exception to this claim that one can be a spiritual person but not religious. This is in some ways understandable. Some who claim to be spiritual engage in what Harvey Cox has called "mere navel- gazing, a retreat from responsibility in a needy world."[1] Others pay huge fees to travel to luxurious spas that promise a weekend of spiritual renewal by providing a sauna, a pedicure, and even a guru who will help them cope with the stress of a demanding job. This may provide an opportunity for personal renewal and even self-reflection, but the experience is often void of content or connection.

It is in the need for theological grounding and communal support that one comes to value the role that belonging to a religious community provides. I came to feel most at home in a community centered in the life and legacy of the Christ I met in the New Testament, where what we now call religion was described not as a doctrine but as "the Way." As with the followers of many other religions, the experience of the divine is more important to me than creedal formulations about divinity. I can thus feel comfortable about my Christian identity while still remaining a rebel on some of the doctrinal claims that others find a necessary part of their faith.

There was no way I could have anticipated in the 1960s that I would be invited back to Yale Divinity School in 2013 to receive the Lux et Veritas alumni award for "excellence and distinction in applying compassion to the diverse needs of the human condition through the wider world of government, business, academia, philanthropy and not-for-profit organizations." I had chosen the world as my parish, where everything I did, I saw as a form of ministry—seeking to infuse values into all sectors of society, promoting justice and compassion, preaching sermons in secular places, and the like—and I was now being honored for it. All because of those years at Yale when my faith was strengthened and in many ways regrounded.

# CHAPTER 5

# Alabama

*The Search for an Ethic of Protest*

On a bitter cold day in January 1963, George Wallace, the newly elected governor of Alabama, delivered an inaugural address that was a defining moment for race relations in the old South. Standing where Jefferson Davis once stood, he warmed up the shivering crowd with a rhetorical flurry of defiance that was to become his trademark: "I draw the line in the dust and toss the gauntlet before the feet of tyranny, and I say: segregation now, segregation tomorrow, segregation forever."

Five months later, armed with a freshly signed graduate theological degree from Yale, I found myself on the way to Alabama to take up the challenge. Yale Divinity School had been a great place for the study of theology, and I had job offers from a variety of Northern institutions that would provide an opportunity to compete in the integrated arena I had long sought, but I felt a call to return to the South. Ostensibly, I was joining the faculty and administration of Stillman College, a private Presbyterian school with a black student body and a predominantly white faculty. But it was George Wallace and the plight of blacks in the South that was on my mind.

New Haven had been a comfortable and convenient place for protest at the village green when events in the South touched the national conscience. The Northern cities had their own problems, but the time had come for me to shed the security blanket of the sanitized protests on the streets of New Haven and join those on the front lines of the struggle in the region where I felt a special affinity.

Shortly after my family and I arrived in Alabama, we found ourselves on a hot Sunday afternoon part of a small group of blacks enjoying Southern barbecue and the fragrance of magnolia in a white colleague's backyard in Tuscaloosa. As the blaze of the charcoal started to fade and the conversation warmed up to the danger posed by an integrated gathering, word came from one of the guests, a young man named Jimmy Hood, that he was withdrawing from the University of Alabama "to avoid a complete mental and physical breakdown." Hood and Vivian Malone had only a few days earlier taken the bold step of enrolling at one of the South's premier bastions of segregation. George Wallace, in predictable demagogic showmanship, stood in the doorway blocking their entrance, but he finally yielded to the federal marshals and permitted them to enter. It was a moment that has remained etched in civil rights lore.

Hood acknowledged that while he had tried to merge into campus life after his enrollment, he faced vicious reminders of opposition to his presence. He received not just threats to his life, but harassing phone calls at all hours of the day, and a dead black cat had even been mailed to him. While he did not specifically mention it, he was also a little shaken by the assassination of Medgar Evers the day after he enrolled. As the field secretary of the NAACP, Evers had helped overturn segregation at the University of Mississippi.

Tuscaloosa was the national headquarters of the Ku Klux Klan. Except for the infamous confrontation between George Wallace and the federal marshals, Tuscaloosa had not been in the news. Birmingham had its water hoses, cattle prods, and Martin Luther King Jr.'s "Letter from a Birmingham Jail." Montgomery gave birth to the bus boycott that catapulted Rosa Parks to international acclaim. But Tuscaloosa was the home of Robert Shelton and his hooded Klansmen, who spread fear throughout both black and white neighborhoods. Outsiders who came to town in search of a movement were invited by local black leaders to take their songs of protest elsewhere. They feared a confrontation with the Klan even more than they resented economic and political marginalization.

When my plane landed in Tuscaloosa at the beginning of the summer of 1963, I felt for the first time a little anxiety and even doubt about the wisdom of my decision. The brave talk in New Haven was tempered by the reality of having actually arrived in alien territory. The accents at the airport and the shimmering heat of the Southern summer reminded me that I had returned to what I had once struggled so hard to escape. The romance of the village green protest in New Haven was gone. Here I was in George Wallace country, the epicenter of Klan intimidation and violence. Off in the distance, I could hear the sound of the country music that I had come to dislike in Louisiana because it had often provided the background when the Klan gathered to wreak havoc on the black population. Louisiana had been bad enough, but we had several generations of populist members of the Long family who gave our politics lots of flair, yet often spoke with reason and restraint about race. In Alabama, the political mood seemed more threatening, the prejudice stronger, and the Klan meaner.

I gathered my thoughts, and the mood of defiance that had brought me to Tuscaloosa slowly returned. I was on a mission, and nothing was going to distract me from having taken the first step on a journey that I simply had to travel. I wish I could say that Doris and our three-week-old son, Jeffrey, shared my passion. Far too young to understand, Jeffrey had no idea what was in store for him. Doris had reluctantly consented to try life in the South, but it was a region of the country where she had assumed she would never live. On the day of our arrival, a sweltering Sunday afternoon, life seemed suspended. We kept our thoughts to ourselves, collected our bags, and silently headed to the Stillman College campus.

The president of Stillman was a white Southern Presbyterian minister who was committed to the education of blacks, but who in his Southern gentility wanted to avoid racial conflict at any cost. Yet to avoid conflict was to accept the status quo. He could hardly have known when he greeted me and my family so warmly that while I shared his views about the importance of education, we differed in very significant ways about how best to bring about social change. We settled into a modest—very modest—home near the campus, but far enough away to be a part of the Southern housing pattern where whites and blacks often lived next door to each other. My compensation was so meager that I built my own desk, my living room sofa, and even a guest bed from discarded wooden crates and old doors; but I was determined to be a part of the effort to build a new South and to demonstrate that we were part of a movement that demagogues like George Wallace could resist but not stop.

## Organizing around Principles

My job was both administrative and academic. I was to teach a course on ethics and to help identify and recruit outstanding black faculty and students, but I soon became chairman of a college self-study project and took on responsibilities that placed me at the center of decision making about the present and future mission of the college. This additional role was welcomed by the president and the predominantly white faculty, even though many were uneasy about the fiery speeches I was making in the community about the need for change.

The uneasiness reached a crescendo shortly after the opening of the school year. We had a chaplain and regular chapel that scrupulously avoided reference to the movement sweeping across the campuses of colleges around the country. On my second visit to the chapel, I asked for time to make an important announcement. I stood before the altar and made an impassioned plea for students to return to their rooms and get their toothbrushes and whatever else they needed for a night in jail. I urged them to join me on a march to the county courthouse to protest the signs designating black and white restrooms in this newly constructed building. To my surprise, many of the students walked out with me. This may have seemed bold, but it was nothing compared to the letter three local ministers and I had addressed to the city fathers demanding that the signs come down.

The letter created a lively controversy. The Klan and the city leaders could not believe that there were blacks in Tuscaloosa willing to challenge the status quo. Some black leaders, including a black dean at Stillman College, went downtown to assure the white officials that we were outsiders who did not speak for the local black community. Meanwhile, the press played up our audacity as if we represented a growing protest movement that had finally come to Tuscaloosa. We had made no contact with any civil rights organization, and the four of us had actually acted on an impulse with no consideration of what additional action might be appropriate. But the publicity persuaded us that we had to do something. So we called ourselves the Tuscaloosa Citizens for Action Committee and decided to call a mass meeting at the African Baptist Church, a stately building pastored by the Reverend T. Y. Rogers, one of the three other black ministers who had signed our statement. We simply announced the date and place for a public meeting and hoped that at least some of the members of the churches my colleagues represented would show up. None of us was prepared for what happened next.

On the evening of the meeting, a huge crowd showed up, packing the building and filling the parking lot as African Americans of all ages waited eagerly to find out who we were and what we were up to. There had never been so many blacks in one place in Tuscaloosa, not even for a basketball game at Stillman. Of the three ministers, none was widely known. Will Herzfeld was a black Missouri Synod Lutheran pastor whose name and church both seemed out of place in a black community. N. W. Stevens served a small African Methodist Episcopal congregation, and T. Y. Rogers was the newly arrived pastor of the premier black Baptist church in the city.

We took turns telling the audience that the time had come to stand up and be counted. After some inspirational singing by a local choir and some impassioned appeals in the best rhetorical tradition of African American churches, we found that we were connecting with our audience. It was my first exposure to the power of the mass meetings that became a staple of our new movement, but I found that my skill at debate and my experience in original oratory served me well in this new role. It was not exactly what I had learned about the art of preaching at Yale Divinity School, but my father would have been proud of the crowd's response. (He had once overheard one of his parishioners tell me after my first sermon that I had given a good talk, but she was looking forward to my learning to preach.)

This was the background that led to my call for support at the Stillman chapel. Many students had come to the mass meeting, and there were reasons to believe that they were ready to join us, but I had no idea that so many would march out with me to participate in our first demonstration, scheduled to begin at the African Baptist Church and to end at city hall. The faculty was far more reticent. Many feared the loss of their jobs if they were arrested.

Marching quietly and with great dignity, we made our way to city hall, where we found Klansmen with baseball bats waiting on one side of the street and state troopers with billy clubs and cattle prods blocking the entrance to the courthouse. Up to now, this had all been rather simple and nonthreatening. We had received disturbing telephone calls, and I had been followed regularly by the local police, who claimed to be protecting me, but this now seemed much more dangerous. Our plan was to walk up to the steps now occupied by the police and to read a prepared statement announcing the birth of our movement and our intention to place Tuscaloosa on the right side of history. True to our plans, the four leaders left the group just before we reached our destination, walked up boldly toward the state troopers, and turned around to read our statement. Suddenly, I felt for the first time the powerful electric sting of a cattle prod and the brute force of a billy club. Without even taking a step (as best I can remember), I ended up across the street where the Klansmen were swinging their baseball bats. With blood flowing in the streets, we regrouped and headed back to the church. Only one arrest was made. A white visiting professor who was part of a faculty exchange was pulled from the line and badly beaten before he was placed under arrest and taken away. He was the only white person in the demonstration, and they intended to make an example of him. As we were reminded later by a local member of the faculty at the University of Alabama who supported us but did not join in the demonstration, the only thing that the local whites hated more than "niggers" were "nigger-lovers."

We did not know where to turn. We were not a part of any organized national movement and we knew that no one in the local black elite would help us, so we set up alternating teams of members of our group to keep a close, but sufficiently distant, all-night vigil around the jail. We had heard too many stories of people disappearing from jail to feel confident that our colleague was safe. The four leaders of the movement spent the night together while the members of our families slept close by under the protection of the volunteer security we had hastily put together.

We had survived the first confrontation and we were now preoccupied with changing Tuscaloosa. Our white colleague was let out on bail the next day. We now knew that we needed the watchful eye of the national press and the support of national organizations more experienced in local demonstrations. Word of our movement had spread across the country. The first to seek us out was James Bevel, an official with the Southern Christian Leadership Conference, where he, along with Andrew Young, was one of Martin Luther King's chief lieutenants. Bevel was a fearless mystic who wore a skullcap and relished a fight as much as anyone I ever met. He was totally committed to nonviolence, but he could move a crowd to action with the best of them. He came to Tuscaloosa looking for me. We met as I was about to leave for a luncheon meeting scheduled with the local black ministers association to tell them about our movement and to solicit their support. After being introduced, I introduced my new friend, James Bevel. When Bevel finished much later, the meeting was adjourned, and I was never invited back. The ministers did not take too kindly to his description of their role in the community as sellouts who were letting black people down. I often wished he had been more diplomatic, but time proved him right in his assessment of the state of their courage. Bevel and I became friends, and we were to meet many times later.

### Martin Luther King Jr. Comes to Town

Thanks to Bevel, we were able to get a commitment from Martin Luther King Jr. to address a future meeting of our group. It was a dramatic moment for all of us when he showed up at our next gathering. The whole city was in a state of alert. Blacks were excited and whites were uneasy. The pews of the church were crowded with a wide spectrum of the city's blacks, young and old, some doing reasonably well and many less well off. They were packed in the aisles, peering through the windows, and straining to hear in the parking lot. The church was at that moment what churches are supposed to be at all moments, a place where the rivers of diversity empty into a common stream.

In *God's Trombones*, James Weldon Johnson penned a prayer that is popular with many black preachers. "Take him Lord," Johnson wrote. "Fill him full of the dynamite of thy power. Anoint him all over with the oil of thy salvation and set his tongue on fire."[1] This prayer was unnecessary for Dr. King, whose oratorical skills consistently moved audiences and energized communities. He began by praising us for having the courage to stand up to George Wallace, Al Lingo (the head of Alabama's notorious state troopers), and Bobby Shelton (the national head of the Ku Klux Klan, who resided in Tuscaloosa). In typical introductory fashion, he spoke in a deep voice with slow cadence. He was good and the audience was with him, but we were eager for him to take his message to the next level, to tell blacks in Tuscaloosa what he had told the skeptics in Montgomery after Rosa Parks was arrested for refusing to sit at the back of the bus. He had said then in his very first political address, "My friends, there comes a time when people get tired of being trampled by the iron feet of oppression. There comes a time when people get tired of being thrown across the abyss of humiliation, where they experience the bleakness of nagging despair. There comes a time, my friends, when people get tired of being pushed out of the glittering sunlight of life's July, and left standing amidst the piercing chill of an alpine November."[2] This was the Martin Luther King Jr. that my colleagues on the organizing committee wanted to hear, the wordsmith with the inspiring and motivating rhetoric that transformed solemn assemblies into cadres of troops eager to wage nonviolent war.

We were not disappointed. Dr. King soon shifted gears as only he could. His cadence became more rapid, his voice more penetrating, and his audience more responsive. He had arrived in town to a screaming headline in the local newspaper accusing us of seeking to provoke another Birmingham, arguing that we were wrong to push so hard for change in a city that had been free of racial disturbances. Dr. King wanted to make it clear that we were not wrong, that even in the heartland of the Klan blacks were refusing to trade the demeaning and debilitating practices of segregation for tranquility. His tongue was now on fire. "These young ministers are not wrong," he thundered. "If they are wrong, the Supreme Court is wrong. If they are wrong, God Almighty is wrong."

We could now feel the power. The audience was excited, and they were responding as we had hoped. Dr. King did not stop there. "If they are wrong," he said, "Jesus of Nazareth was merely a utopian dreamer. If they are wrong, justice is a lie." A few of us had heard these words almost verbatim before, but they had a freshness as if they had been written for Tuscaloosa. The city was never the same again. The rally ended with a commitment to nonviolence, an explosion of new energy, and ironclad determination to see the struggle through to victory.

There were some humorous moments in our efforts to bring down the signs saying "white" and "colored" that seemed to be everywhere. A white colleague on the faculty at Stillman had recently arrived from Germany. His wife went to a laundromat to do the family laundry. Totally confused when she saw the signs, she took her white laundry to one side and her colored clothing to the other.

My own sphere of activity began to expand as I received invitations to speak to groups in nearby communities that had not yet been touched by the wave of civil rights activity flooding the South. Asked to address the annual meeting of the black teachers association in the adjacent county, I accepted with enthusiasm. Upon arriving, I found myself onstage with the local white superintendent and members of the all-white board of education. The superintendent commended the teachers for not engaging in the kind of subversive activities that were now part of the daily diet in Tuscaloosa. When he finished, I was introduced for my speech. I had been so busy, I had not had time to talk to the organizers about what they wanted to hear from me, but it did not matter. I had only one message. It was the reverse of George Wallace's "segregation now, segregation forever." We were out to prove him wrong and to tear down the old walls that not only set boundaries around black ambition but robbed the region of the human and intellectual capital it needed for social and economic development.

I proceeded to explain as carefully and thoughtfully as I could why many of us had concluded that segregated education was doing more harm than good, why the time had come for teachers to move to the front lines with us. I moved next to a flurry of passionate arguments about why their time had come. When I finished the speech, the audience seemed to retreat in silence, sitting quietly as I headed to my seat next to the superintendent. I wondered whether I had misjudged them or whether they had simply been intimidated by the presence of local white officials, including the police. But just as I began to feel a tinge of disappointment, I could hear the faint sound of a few hands coming together in applause. By the time I took my third step and was about to sit down—within the space of a few seconds—a deafening roar encircled the building. The whole audience rose to their feet in unison. It was obvious that the teachers in Greene County, Alabama, were ready to join the movement.

Meanwhile, the Tuscaloosa Citizens for Action Committee had become a full-service movement with a wide variety of strategies. We cast our nets more widely and found a few whites who were willing to work with us. My friend William Sloane Coffin, the Yale chaplain who was an early freedom rider, came to provide moral support. He was a man with a reputation for spellbinding oratory, and we hoped that he could bring more whites into the movement. But to our surprise, Coffin could also speak with the same magnetic appeal when addressing blacks. We had a great time together in college halls with academics, in living rooms with local teachers and black professionals, and even in kitchens with cooks and other domestic help. Yet his boldest move was to call on Paul "Bear" Bryant, the legendary football coach at the University of Alabama. Coffin sought, unsuccessfully, to convince Coach Bryant that he was the only man in Alabama strong enough to take on George Wallace. I was undaunted by Coffin's failure and arranged a meeting at the home of one of the campus chaplains to explain the objectives of our movement. A few students and faculty members were brave enough to meet with me, but the meeting was broken up when a large crowd started to gather outside looking for that "nigger Joseph." My host sneaked me out the back door, and that was my last attempt to penetrate George Wallace's stronghold at the university.

But it was only one of many close encounters with the threat of violence. Vivian Malone had become a friend of Doris's, with whom she shared an occasional meal and other forms of escape from the strains and stresses of life in Alabama in the 1960s. Vivian and Doris were members of the same sorority and had developed a special bond. One evening, as they were about to attend a social function, they received word that the location had been changed. The next morning we learned that there had been a mysterious explosion at the building where the social event had been originally scheduled. Needless to say, this did not go over too well with Doris, who was already questioning whether the public contribution I was making was worth the personal risk. We not only received constant threats, but they were increasingly focused on what would happen to my son Jeffrey, not yet one year old, if I continued as a leader of the Tuscaloosa Citizens for Action Committee.

## A New Way of Thinking: A New Way of Acting

The movement soon shifted gears and turned to economic strategies. The Alabama legislature had recently passed a law making it illegal to advocate an economic boycott, so we were careful to call this leg of our strategy a selective buying campaign. However, after a public meeting in which I punctuated my call to action with numerous references to the new selective buying campaign, the local newspaper came out the next day with the bold headline, "Joseph Now Advocating Boycott." After a few anxious days, I decided that my indiscretion (actually the newspaper's almost costly misrepresentation) had gone unnoticed or at least unchallenged, so we stepped up our campaign. We were amazed at its success. The downtown merchants were soon hurting and wanted to talk to us. This was our first such campaign, and we were mystified at how it could work so well with very little publicity. As fate would have it, I went downtown one day with one of the ministers in our leadership group and discovered two young black men tearing up the bags of someone who had decided to ignore the boycott. We scolded them for taking matters into their own hands, but questioned later whether it was their action, as much as our own, that made the boycott successful.

This incident caused us to think more deeply about the moral and theological implications of what we were doing and to ask ourselves whether it was ever appropriate to permit nonviolent action to benefit from the use of force. I also had to come to grips with the reality that while I was out emphasizing the importance of nonviolence, I took great pleasure on returning home one evening to find my neighbor sitting on his front porch with a shotgun, guarding the entrance to my home.

Over the following months, we talked more about the values and vision of our movement. We developed workshops on nonviolence, selective buying, and voter registration. What had started out as a protest movement was transformed into an all-out effort to introduce both a new way of acting and a new way of thinking. We were no longer focusing simply on what we were against. We now had to articulate a vision of what we were for. We often quoted Albert Camus's definition of a rebel as one who knows altogether as much what he is for as he does about what he is against.

But the quieter, gentler behind-the-scenes reflection and strategic maneuvering did not exempt us from the cold realities of life in Alabama. In 1963, four little black girls were killed by an explosion at the Sixteenth Street Baptist Church in Birmingham, only fifty-eight miles from Tuscaloosa. It was a year in which George Wallace's message started to reverberate not only in Alabama and the South, but also in the outer reaches of the country. It was also the year that President John F. Kennedy was assassinated in Dallas. The bombs in Birmingham, the ugly face of racism on national television, and the shots in Dallas all seemed connected. A new meanness was tearing the nation apart. Yet we retained our commitment to nonviolence and urged our members to meet hatred not with hostility but with love. Those who saw love as an emotional feeling were confused. The black community, they argued, wanted justice, not love. We were thus confronted with the perennial question in theological ethics—what is the relationship between love and justice? The difference, however, was that this was not an abstract debate in the common room of a theological seminary where the moral teachings of Reinhold Niebuhr, Paul Tillich, Dietrich Bonhoeffer, and Aristotle could provide both answers and authority.

The practice of viewing love and justice as two different imperatives has deep and enduring roots. Joseph Fletcher, the author of the book *Moral Responsibility* and a proponent of what is often described as situation ethics, liked to quote the popular black entertainer Sammy Davis Jr. to illustrate this point. When Davis decided to repudiate his Christian identity and become a Jew, he said, "As I see it, the difference is that the Christian religion preaches love thy neighbor and the Jewish religion preaches justice, and I think justice is the big thing we need."[3]

Justice was what we needed in Alabama in 1963, but we refused to accept this inferred contradiction between justice and the concept of love that we spoke about so often and so passionately. In *The Theology of Culture*, Paul Tillich argued that love is the ground, the power, and the aim of justice. He even went on to say that love without justice was like a body without a backbone.

### Loving the Enemy

While justice was at the heart of our movement, the admonition to love the enemy was equally revolutionary. It was left to a community that had known so much suffering and pain to take the lead in emphasizing the common humanity of both the oppressed and the oppressor. It was often with loud chants of "Jesus" in the background that I had heard my father regale his audiences with the words taken from the lips of Jesus: "Love your enemies, bless them that curse you, do good to them that hate you, and pray for them that despitefully use you, and persecute you" (Matthew 5:44). But this only came to make sense to me when I first heard him introduce the notion that *loving* the enemy and *liking* the enemy were fundamentally different moral concepts. I learned later from the powerful meditations of Howard Thurman, the black mystic, poet, and theologian who was a mentor to Martin Luther King Jr., to soften the notion of enemy by using the word "adversary" and defining it in three varied categories, with each requiring a different moral response.

The first is the personal adversary, one who is in some sense a part of one's primary group, one who at some time may have been a rather intimate part of one's world, but who has now caused conflict or become alienated from the present circle of community. Loving the enemy in this regard requires reconciliation, the will to reestablish a relationship. It involves the restoration of a former relationship with one who has a former claim on one's sense of duty, obligation, and community.

The second form of loving the enemy is a little more complex and difficult. It involves those with whom there has been no prior relationship. On every street corner in Opelousas and Tuscaloosa, I met someone who fell into this category: the shopkeeper who would not even consider me for a job because I was black; the white kid next door whose parents forbade him from playing with me because I was black; the white minister who preached about the same God as my father but would not let me attend his Sunday school or worship in his church because I was black.

I was taught that to love such people is to look beyond the circumstances of their rejection of you and to see how their world is limited, and their humanity damaged, by the denial of the humanity of another person. They are more to be pitied than hated, for they are trapped by their own cultural myopia.

The third type of enemy is pathological. Members of this group are usually obsessed with the superiority of their own kind and feel a special calling to use whatever means are necessary to keep members of less favored groups in their ordained place. They join the Ku Klux Klan, the White Citizens Council, the Aryan Nation, the skinheads, and assorted militias who take up arms to prevent the "unnatural" mixing of blacks, Jews, and gays with members of their community.

It is here that the distinction between liking and loving becomes most relevant. Some of these people are despicable and violent. They form "we" groups and reject certain "they" groups as outside the pale of their humanity, making it easier to exploit them, mistreat them, and even kill their leaders without feeling the constraints of conscience or the restrictions of religion.

When the Klan surrounded my car in Tuscaloosa, Alabama, and threatened to kill me for leading a boycott and mobilizing the black community against local segregation—an incident described more fully later in this chapter—it was hard for me to remember my father's admonition that no evil deed represents the full intent of the doer. It was even more difficult to remember the moral notion that not only do I share with the enemy a common humanity, but we are both part of a universal spirit and, in my father's language, we are children of the same God.

In the wide sweep of the moral requirement to love the enemy, one is challenged to do that which appears to contradict what we know about human nature. The only way to free oneself from the natural temptation to return hatred for hatred and hostility for hostility is to develop a painstaking inner discipline that is grounded in something deeper and more mysterious than the human will. And that is the role the black church played, introducing a concept of divine will that, from its origin in plantation meeting camps and Protestant missions to its role in the civil rights movement, enabled black Americans not simply to survive but to transcend. I was taught very early in life that in not succumbing to the temptation to meet violence with violence, I was demonstrating a moral power that could someday subvert the system of segregation and convert even those who were our sworn enemies. In my mother's words, I was a bigger person than them and would ultimately benefit if I could continue to occupy the moral high ground.

The admonition to love the enemy caused as much confusion and concern in Tuscaloosa as talk of forgiving the perpetrators of human rights violations in South Africa. Both Martin Luther King Jr. and Nelson Mandela called for respect for the humanity of the evildoer while despising and seeking to change his evil deeds. It was for both of them recognition that hating the enemy corrodes the personality of the hater and impedes the prospect for genuine community.

Dr. King was a social reformer who brought a new civility to confrontation. He insisted that while we were engaged in activities that could of necessity cause alienation, a demonstration of respect for the humanity of the adversary could leave a crack in the door for reconciliation. Like Nelson Mandela, he believed in a form of restorative justice where both the perpetrator and the victim of civil and human rights violations could be restored to full standing in the community. This was as difficult a standard for those of us who led the movement as it was for those who followed us into potentially violent confrontations. I remember the hours of debate and just plain listening that preceded the decision on strategies or a specific course of action.

Dr. King also urged us to listen to those whose beliefs and practices we opposed. He put it very succinctly in a prayer at the beginning of our movement in Tuscaloosa: "Help us to see the opposition's point of view, to hear their questions, to know their assessment of us. From their view we may indeed see the basic weakness of our condition, and if we are at all mature, we may learn and grow and profit from the wisdom of our brothers whom we call the enemy."

Loving the enemy also involved persuading our allies that this elevated form of human potential was actually possible. And that is one of the reasons why the mass meeting was so critical to our movement. Before every major street march or public demonstration, we assembled in a church or an auditorium, usually a church, to inspire and persuade each other not simply to face the hostile bystanders, the police dogs, and those who stood behind them with clubs and electric prods; we had to keep those who stood with us focused on the potential of the human spirit as well.

Leadership required as much inspiration as organization. Some of our colleagues instinctively understood the importance of process and were good at organizing neighborhoods and communities, but in the end the power to persuade was just as critical. The black preachers in our communities had demonstrated for generations how to make use of stories, metaphors, imagery, and alliteration to appeal to the hopes and aspirations of those who might otherwise lack confidence or give in to fear. The meaning and messages of our mass meetings were reinforced by songs and slogans. When we finished telling the collective story of African Americans in the language and myths of "the children of Israel," the group was ready to take on the worst that anyone could throw at us.

It was that same narrative that enabled us to keep hope alive in what appeared to others to be almost hopeless situations. As Martin Luther King once put it, "We must accept finite disappointment, but we must never lose infinite hope." "Basic to our philosophy," he would say, "is a deep faith in the future. Ours is a movement based on hope because when you lose hope the movement dies." That is why the movement song stated, "We shall overcome / Deep in my heart I do believe / We shall overcome someday." When we faced hostile mobs, when we were thrown in jail, and when we faced physical death, there was something special about being able to sing, "We are not afraid. We shall overcome someday."

Once inspired and ready to tackle the Klan and those who joined them in opposing change, it was difficult to keep the movement realistic and practical about what was doable. The compromises that often followed our carefully considered demands were possible only because they were part of the plan. We learned early that we could stand on absolutes and please our conscience but accomplish nothing for our constituents. While compromises are never popular, we had to persuade our colleagues that victory often means that both sides in a dispute must receive some benefit. The moral requirement is to set the ethical parameters beyond which the group is not prepared to go and to negotiate within those parameters. Both King and Mandela are best known as moral leaders who called others to a higher and nobler purpose, but they were also practical men who knew how and when to compromise. They were successful because they were always searching for common ground where both sides in a dispute received some measure of benefit. Stephen Covey in *The Seven Habits of Highly Effective People* called this win/win, a frame of mind and heart that consistently seeks mutual benefit in all human interactions.

In everyday usage, the word "love" continued to have a romantic connotation in Tuscaloosa, so the best solution we found was to talk primarily about justice when we were discussing the ideals and aims of the group. Justice, at least, did not suffer from being oversentimentalized or romanticized.

After an intellectually exhilarating discussion of the underlying principles and ultimate purpose of our movement, we often went home to face another evening of telephone threats and racial insults, making it easier to think about retributive justice than distributive love. But we refused to be intimidated or to give up on our commitment to nonviolence or our affirmation of the love-justice relationship.

## The Politics of God

The public role of religion and faith leaders in the public square is now a matter of great debate. But when I joined with the three other young ministers in Alabama in 1963 to establish the Tuscaloosa Citizens for Action Committee, we had no doubt that God and the Constitution could share a place at the lunch counter, the workplace, and the county courthouse. We were demanding initially that the signs for colored and white be removed from the water fountains, restrooms, and public seating arrangements, but we soon expanded our demands to include equality in education, employment, and public accommodation. We were motivated and driven by the moral teachings of religion, but we differed in very important ways from many who now argue that they speak for God, that their politics reflect God's will.

First, and probably most importantly, we did not seek to transpose the private virtues affirmed by our faith into the public values practiced by the nation. We avoided the politics of virtue and the parochialism of dogma by appealing directly to the public values given legitimacy and moral authority by the framers of the American Constitution. When they thought about the public values that should guide this new experiment in democracy, the architects of our political system wrote that if we were to form a more perfect union, we would have to establish justice, and if we were to ensure domestic tranquility, we would have to promote the general welfare. They included security in this lexicon of public values by calling on succeeding generations to promote the common defense. While it might have been expected that our nonviolent movement would be silent on this latter civic imperative, we accepted and affirmed it with the assertion that the best way to demonstrate the efficacy of our democracy to critics abroad is to demonstrate that it can work equitably for all of our citizens at home.

A second important difference between our moral claims in the 1960s and those religious leaders who now get the most press is that while our movement was led primarily by ministers, our strategy was one of moral persuasion rather than religious pronouncements. We did not claim that God was on our side. Like Abraham Lincoln, we prayed that we were on God's side. We were strong and uncompromising on those values the framers of the Constitution considered paramount, but our political opinions on other matters did not rise to the level of God's will.

This brings us to the third difference, and one that might seem strange to some religionists. We did not claim that God's truth is fully knowable. We were more likely to use the language of the Apostle Paul, reminding others as well as ourselves that "we see through a glass darkly." We certainly did not hold that God spoke to one group more than others or that any one of our differing views on personal morality uniquely represented his will. We were as one on the larger issues of peace, justice, and opportunity, but we were all over the map on the personal issues that now rise to articles of faith.

In retrospect, we were in agreement with former senator John Danforth, whom I first met at Yale Divinity School, that to infuse our personal opinions with the moral language of religion would be to make religion serve political ends and to distort the role of reason and analysis in a faith that calls upon the faithful to use their minds. Christians too easily forget that in Paul's letter to the Romans he said, "Do not be conformed to this world, but be transformed by the renewing of your minds, so that you may discern what is the will of God—what is good and acceptable and perfect" (Romans 12:2). Danforth likes to refer to Paul's letter to make the point that God gave us brains and we are supposed to use them.[4]

To do the work of God in the world, according to Danforth, takes more than a good heart or even strong convictions about moral imperatives we come to regard as absolutes. We can become very emotional about our politics, but Paul tells us that Christianity is more than emotions. It engages and renews the mind. Christianity is not anti-intellectual. It is not a matter of feeling overcoming thinking.[5] Paul tells us also that through renewing our minds, we "may discern what is the will of God." At times, as Danforth reminds us, the will of God comes in a flash, as it is reported to have come to Paul on the road to Damascus. But Paul seems to be saying that such revelations are the exception. More often, discerning God's will takes hard work. It requires us to think, to use our reason, to use judgment. Normally, we do not passively receive the will of God. We have to discern it.[6] No human being has a corner on the market of truth. It is, thus, a mistake to assume that God's will is being provided for us by some external emissary with a special capacity to discern his will. There are, of course, moral leaders like Martin Luther King Jr. who appeal to our nobler instincts and even fire our spiritual imagination, but this is no substitute for thinking and reasoning. Moreover, King appealed to the public values around which there has always been a moral consensus. He did not try to lift up the private virtues of his faith to the level of law or legislation.

It is true that the leadership ranks of our movement were filled throughout with high-profile ministers, but it was not that they claimed to be more moral than others in the community or simply that they exerted enormous social authority. Of critical importance was the fact that they were part of a leadership class that was independent economically and often politically. They were part of a long tradition of maintaining independent institutions without the need for white approval or support. They could take independent action and speak truth to those in power without fear of economic reprisal. They were independent voices with independent resources.

The local ministers with whom I worked in Alabama were also men of considerable ability. From the beginning of the formation of separately organized black churches in the eighteenth and nineteenth centuries until the end of legal segregation, Protestant denominations had regularly recruited some of the most gifted in the black community for ministry. With so many other professional fields closed to bright young black men, they went into the church, where they occupied positions at the center of black life. Black religious institutions not only provided moral leadership and committed activists; they also groomed and provided political leadership. When blacks began winning elective office, it was not surprising that the most visible among them were ministers, including, first, Adam Clayton Powell and, later, Walter Fauntroy, Andrew Young, and William Gray. It was not surprising that even in my own life I went to seminary before I took to the streets to promote civil and human rights and to protest ill-advised wars.

The legacy of the civil rights struggle is a legacy of public values that have great implication for the larger society as it seeks to reform or transform itself. Those who seek to forge a link between personal and social ethics might well turn to the black religious institutions of the 1960s as a model. They were strong on issues of community values, sexual integrity, and personal responsibility, but they were equally strong on issues like poverty, peace, and social justice. When Martin Luther King Jr. decided to link the civil rights struggle with the Vietnam War, some supporters broke ranks, urging him not to marry international peace with social justice at home. But he resisted any effort to narrow the boundaries of the moral claims of his faith to include some but not all of his values. He was living, after all, in perhaps the bloodiest and most violent century in history. It was a century in which between 167 million and 188 million people died because of organized violence.[7] According to Harvard history professor Niall Ferguson, World War I killed between 9 million and 10 million people. Another 59 million died in World War II, and it is estimated that sixteen other conflicts in the last century took more than one million lives, a further six claimed between 500,000 and a million, and fourteen killed between 250,000 and 500,000.[8]

Like Dr. King, the ministers with whom I worked in Tuscaloosa were both pro-poor and pro-peace, pro–government initiatives to increase access to health care and economic opportunity, and pro–personal responsibility. We never saw these as ideological or theological polarities as some now do. For most of us in the 1960s, both personal and social responsibility had a religious grounding. We maintained that it would be a mistake to opt for one and overlook the other as moral imperatives. But we saw one as the domain of private religion and the other as the duty of public values.

While we were fearless in the presence of each other or after a mass meeting, where we were often psyched up for days, there were times out on our own when we were terrified. One such time for me was a visit to a shop at a local hotel with a friend to pick up an airline ticket. Grady Poulard had just returned from work in India with the Student Christian Movement and was a volunteer participant in the National Council of Churches Freedom Summer in Mississippi. He had come to Alabama for a few days' break from the violence and intimidation in Mississippi.

While I was waiting for Grady outside the Stafford Hotel, where George Wallace had stayed the night before his infamous confrontation at the University of Alabama, a Klan meeting was breaking up inside. The rumor spread that I was about to try to integrate the hotel. Very soon, a crowd started to gather. I could feel and almost smell danger, but Grady was still inside and I could not leave him, so I sat in the car anxiously waiting for his return. When he finally appeared, the crowd let him through and he made it into the car. But once the door was closed, the crowd completely encircled the car and started to rock it back and forth.

Faced with a crowd that was getting noisier and angrier, I decided to start the engine and see what would happen next. To my surprise, the crowd opened up a path just wide enough to permit us to drive off. It was several days before I returned to normalcy and came to realize the psychological toll that my family and I were forced to pay for our efforts to improve the quality of life in Tuscaloosa. With the insults and threats of the Klan still ringing in my ears, I wondered almost aloud whether I had now been on the front lines too long. Had the time come for me to move on and to make my contribution in another arena? I had seen too many cases of shell-shocked activists who maintained the intensity of the struggle too long for their own good or the good of the movement in which they were engaged.

After consultation with my wife and the three ministers with whom I had embarked on this high-risk venture, I made the decision to accept an offer from the Claremont Colleges and relocate to California. George Wallace was not on the run, but Tuscaloosa was beginning to change, and many in the black community had gained a new sense of pride, dignity, and determination. The local movement was now very strong and had caught the attention of city officials, who had already removed the signs from the water fountains and the bathrooms in the courthouse building. The boycott had successfully led to commitments from local merchants with promises to hire and promote blacks. Several restaurants and the local hotel had opened their doors. The local black community was now fully integrated into the leadership of our movement, and I had no doubt that the momentum of the struggle could not be contained. In many ways, I felt the call to a new adventure, but I was also beginning to feel burned out and in need of a quieter and less dangerous period of personal and spiritual renewal.

Thus, it was with a mixture of joy and sadness that I bade farewell to my colleagues with whom I had shared a year of extraordinary leadership and learning. I had successfully recruited some of the best high school graduates in the South to attend Stillman College, and the student leaders were determined to keep the pressure on the administration to comply with the new mission statement and the other recommendations of the self-study. It had been an incredible year of strategic interventions, moral reasoning, and living dangerously on behalf of those who had finally been awakened after decades of deep silence—and while I still felt some anger every time I heard George Wallace on television, I had learned to control the rage within and to channel it into constructive action. Even more importantly, I had developed skills and insights and made a commitment to a set of public values that would be the cornerstone of my professional life wherever the future took me.

Alabama was changing, but not George Wallace. His national influence was just beginning. He was flamboyant in his politics and dead wrong on race, but he went on to mobilize a national constituency of angry, alienated, and resentful whites. His attacks on liberals, government bureaucrats, and intellectuals helped usher in a new brand of right-wing populism that fundamentally changed the political landscape. Yet, thirty years after the march from Selma to Montgomery, George Wallace was one of the few whites to attend the commemoration of that momentous event in Selma. He sat on the stage with Joseph Lowery of the Southern Christian Leadership Conference and greeted many of the aging veterans of the movement as though they were old friends. If there were any doubts about his change of heart, he issued a statement in which he apologized for segregation. Sounding almost like those of us whom he had once so strongly opposed, he expressed his concern that so many people were turning away from trying to overcome our differences and retreating to resegregation. As he put it, "If it was wrong when I was supporting it, it's no less wrong now." The notion of George Wallace one day redeemed and repentant is something we could not have imagined when we started the movement in Tuscaloosa, but there he was linking arms with a band of battle-weary blacks on Alabama soil and singing "We Shall Overcome."

# CHAPTER 6

# California

*The Other War on Campus*

In the summer of 1964, I left Alabama for a new life in Southern California, where I could finally work in the integrated arena I had long sought. I was returning to a place I knew well, the home of the Claremont Colleges, where I had once spent a year on the chaplain's staff as a graduate intern from Yale Divinity School. The city of Claremont was an idyllic community set against the backdrop of Mount Baldy, with its snowcapped peak in the winter and beautiful wildflowers and vineyards in the summer. It was a place where one could go swimming in the valley on a warm December day and skiing on the mountain after only a few minutes' drive.

The founders of Pomona College, the oldest of the Claremont group, had set out in 1887 to establish "a college of the New England type" with small classes, close relationships between students, and a green jewel of a campus in a desert landscape. From that audacious beginning, the Pomona College I came to know while serving as a Danforth Foundation intern in 1961 had become one of the nation's premier liberal arts colleges on a campus where ivy and palm trees coexisted under habitually sunny skies. Over the years since its founding, the trustees had added additional colleges on adjacent land rather than expanding Pomona, making Claremont a unique consortium of seven independent institutions collaborating in a manner similar to Oxford University in England.

I arrived in the summer of 1964 after a cross-country drive from Tusca-loosa to find that the idealism and activism sweeping across the country had not yet visibly touched the Claremont campuses. The civil rights movement was on the minds of a few, but the vast majority went about their academic pursuits with little notice of the problems and pathos only thirty-five miles away in Los Angeles. Some even took pride in their isolation. The racial revolution had almost totally escaped Claremont. I could find very few blacks in any of its institutions or the larger community.

Coming directly from Alabama, where I had fought against segregation and prided myself on organizing protests and tackling long-standing injustices, I saw Claremont not as an escape but as a challenge. The moral outrage I had felt in Tuscaloosa quickly returned. I had no illusion that the old Claremont would somehow wither away, but I saw instantly the need to help focus the colleges on the moral and social responsibilities of a university. As if to make certain that I never forgot the miseries and mind-set of the South, Myrlie Evers, the widow of the recently slain Medgar Evers in Mississippi, decided to relocate to Claremont to study at Pomona College. She was seeking a quiet place far away from the nightmare that had befallen her family. I was committed, on the other hand, to generating a new social and political activism. I had returned to Claremont for a period of personal renewal and recess from the dangers and daily threats of life as a civil rights leader, but social reform was too much a part of who I had become to sit on the sidelines. Myrlie and I became good friends, and both of us found a great measure of what we were seeking. A few years later, I performed her wedding ceremony when she decided to remarry. She in turn became the godmother of my daughter, Denise.

It was altogether fitting that I should end up in Claremont after the racial turmoil in Alabama. Claremont had first come to my attention while participating in a civil rights demonstration on the village green in New Haven. Marching next to Harry Adams, a Yale Divinity School professor, I learned about an internship program conducted by the Danforth Foundation to attract graduates of American seminaries to careers in the campus ministry. I later applied and was accepted, only to find out that I was about to be assigned to a black university very much like the one at which I had done my undergraduate studies. I suggested that since I had grown up in a segregated black community and gone to a segregated black university, it might be useful for me to spend the internship year in an integrated environment. I wanted the opportunity to demonstrate that I could be successful in any institution, regardless of its racial composition.

Bob Rankin, the director of the internship program, had once been the chaplain at Claremont. His boss, Merrimon Cunningham, the president of the foundation, was also a former chaplain at Claremont. Pete Reckard, an advisor to the program, was the present chaplain at Claremont. I was not surprised when informed that I had been assigned to the Claremont Colleges.

I was well received at Claremont, where I developed a large student following and a good circle of faculty friends. So when Pete Reckard visited me in Tuscaloosa several years later and discovered the intensity of my daily clashes with the Klan, he and my wife, Doris, hatched a plan to extricate me from the front lines of struggle in Alabama. The plan worked, but my return to Claremont was very different from my earlier years as an intern serving as an assistant to the chaplain. As an intern, I spent considerable time observing and learning how to be a chaplain. I was now a seasoned activist concerned not just with private virtue and the role of the Christian community as a worshipping community, but with changing society. I had not been in Claremont very long before the threatening calls from the Klan in Alabama were replaced by calls from members of the John Birch Society and other right-wing groups making threats very similar to those that had become an almost daily occurrence in Alabama.

### A Mississippi Summer

Determined to continue contributing to the movement in the South, I decided after my first year at Claremont to take key members of the faculty and student leaders for a summer in Mississippi. The college church had become a socially engaged community. We were supporting Cesar Chavez and the National Farm Workers Association, tutoring blacks in the city of Pomona and the Watts community in Los Angeles, demonstrating at the Los Angeles federal building, and constructing a coalition against the Vietnam War. While it was ecumenical in its worship and Christian in its theological orientation, the college church soon attracted a following that represented a wide diversity of religious beliefs. What participants shared in common was a sense of moral outrage and the quest for a center of meaning and spiritual fulfillment.

The purpose of the Mississippi project was to help register voters in rural areas of the state. We were invited by the Delta Ministry of the National Council of Churches to spend the summer in Edwards, Mississippi, a small community near the epicenter of Klan activity. So we set out to raise money and recruit volunteers. We ate grits in symbolic fasting, collected clothing and books for schoolchildren, and even managed to secure several Volkswagen minibuses to transport the kids to and from school.

It was a motley crew of about fifteen volunteers who arrived in Edwards in the summer of 1965 to deliver the supplies we had collected and to do voter registration. We wanted a local partnership and broad local ownership of our project, so we went to leaders of the local black community and told them that we had come to help. To our astonishment, voter registration was not even on their list. What they wanted was a public swimming pool.

Bob Meyners, a professor of religion at Claremont Men's College, volunteered immediately to lead our group in building a swimming pool. Recreational facilities were still segregated, and the amenities available to blacks were minimal. After recovering from the shock of both the request and Bob's response, we were able to determine that Bob was, indeed, serious. He had built his own swimming pool in Claremont, done most of the repair work on the vehicles we had donated, and was capable of leading us through an effort no one else in our group had ever undertaken.

We managed to build a swimming pool, develop a black history curriculum for preschoolers, help renovate the facilities we were occupying, tutor community kids, and even survive several close encounters with the Ku Klux Klan before the summer was over. But even more important, the local people with whom we worked took the leadership, with our encouragement and support, in doing voter registration. Our decision to go to Mississippi also brought home to the college presidents, faculty, and other students the importance of civic engagement, the long-term value of getting involved in the needs of others. It also built a core constituency in Claremont that would later be mobilized in opposition to the Vietnam War.

The earliest signs of change in student attitudes at Claremont occurred among black students in the mid-1960s, about the time of the emergence of the Black Panther Party for Self-Defense. In Alabama, I had been part of a movement in which young people hoping to gain basic civil rights and access to public accommodations marched in the streets, boycotted white business establishments, and sat in at lunch counters. But in California, I found a different tone and temperament, a far more defiant brand of young students. Some picked up guns and demanded to be heard while others simply engaged in intimidating rhetoric and dress. At Claremont, the tranquil campus where black students had only recently become a visible presence, there were also stirrings of a new militancy. The students did not join the Panthers, but a few supported them, raising many eyebrows (and causing some indignant calls to me) when several solicited support for them after an offering at College Church. While the Panthers were known by the larger public primarily for their excesses, the students also noted that the Panthers organized voter education drives, engaged in sickle-cell testing, and established a free breakfast program for children in impoverished neighborhoods.

### An African Summer

It was while serving as chaplain of the Claremont Colleges that I made my first trip to the African continent, a visit that I was to repeat many times in later years. The Reverend James Robinson, director of Operation Crossroads Africa, invited me to lead a group of college students from the United States and Canada to West Africa to build a community center in Jamasi, a small village in Ghana just north of Kumasi, the ancient capital of the Ashanti Kingdom. We were joined by students from colleges and universities in Ghana.

The region surrounding Jamasi was the epicenter of Ashanti culture. Kumasi still housed the Manhyia Palace, the seat of the traditional king of the Ashanti, and in nearby villages artisans specialized in crafts such as goldsmithing, wood carving, cloth painting, and the weaving of kente cloth. The zeal of traditional African religion was so evident and engaging that I returned in the 1970s to study at the University of Ghana in Accra, examining how the former animistic rituals and beliefs were being integrated into Christianity.

Jamasi was a rural area with no electricity, water, or paved roads. Yet we adjusted quickly and spent our days working with the local chief and villagers to build a community center for village use. Our evenings were punctuated with intriguing discussions of Ashanti culture and the insights of traditional democracy. The only signs of some of the comforts we had known in the United States, Canada, and even Accra were to be found at the local Catholic church, where the priest welcomed us to the rectory and even the use of his kitchen on special occasions. It seemed strange to find a vibrant congregation of Catholics in the heart of the Ashanti region not too distant from the palace of the Ashanti king. No one in Jamasi seemed to be aware at the time of our visit of the deep roots of Catholicism on the African continent that had once produced three popes. Moreover, the church had long supported a network of schools like the one in Jamasi where the children lined the dirt road on each side to welcome us to their village.

While the Catholic Church did not authorize the use of local vernacular in the Mass until the Second Vatican Council of 1962–1965, the church's indigenization was already in full steam even in the rural areas that were home to us for three months in 1966. African songs and dance were incorporated into services, although it was not until later years that young African priests took charge from European missionaries. In the Ashanti region and throughout Ghana, the Catholic influence was eventually joined by evangelicals, especially among the young. They now have twice as many members as the Catholic Church, and their influence is inescapably present on billboards and leaflets showcasing dapper pastors, often called prophets.

Our interest in traditional Ashanti culture led us to visit the much-discussed Manhyia Palace for an audience with the king and conversations with members of his court. The palace had a courtyard and a courtroom where matters of customs and the constitution were still deliberated upon by a traditional council. We had become so fascinated by the legend of the Golden Stool and the role it played in Ashanti religion and political history that we were eager to see the fake one that had once been used to mislead the British colonizers who demanded that the stool be turned over to them. The real stool was still kept at the palace, but it was now considered so sacred that it was not allowed to touch the ground and not even the king was allowed to sit upon it.

The nearby village of Ahwiaa, known for its woodcarving, became a favorite place to take breaks from our work in Jamasi. It was here that I commissioned a local wood carver to carve out a replica of the Golden Stool that according to legend was the strength of the Ashanti Empire. Local people curious about the foreigners in their midst came from far and wide to watch us working with our hands to chip stones and carry them in basins—sometimes on our heads—to the location of our work. They were especially concerned about my allowing the young American women in the group to sit on top of the rafters with hammers and nails while helping build the roof. They quickly learned what I had already learned. These young women were not about to be restricted to less demanding or less dangerous work.

My interest in local history and culture caught the attention of the local chief, who made me an honorary chief and offered me a local wife. I accepted the first, but declined the latter. My being robed in kente cloth was a humorous gesture to my students, but it reflected the highest respect and honor the chief could bestow on a visitor. It was, however, the only time I dared to wear the local symbol of my new stature. On one ceremonial occasion, however, I was presented with a drink of palm wine with an audience watching as I brought the ceremonial cup to my mouth. To my shock, there were flies floating on top of the wine, which had obviously been sitting in the sun as it fermented. It was the first time I had to pretend to be enjoying local cultural practices and fake a drink of the wine. It worked so well that not even the students noticed that my lips were tightly shut as I appeared to be consuming the wine.

My students and I returned home transformed by the experience of an extraordinary summer. We had arrived a few months after the overthrow of

Kwame Nkrumah as president. The shelves in the stores were almost empty. Food was in short supply even in local markets, and there were rumors of CIA involvement in the overthrow of Nkrumah. While we were welcomed everywhere with open arms, the American ambassador, who occasionally visited us in Jamasi and welcomed us to the embassy in Accra, was under a cloud of suspicion. This had no impact on our visit except for the shortages that were so obviously affecting the quality of life of people in both the cities and rural areas. The funds committed by the government of Ghana to support Ghanaian student participation in our project were no longer available when we arrived, so the American and Canadian students agreed with my suggestion that we stretch our already limited budget to cover our Ghanaian counterparts as well. Fruits and vegetables grown locally were plentiful, and we survived the summer with healthy ease, except for discovering at the festive celebration on our last day that the barbecued meat provided was from the goat presented on our arrival, who had become everyone's favorite pet.

Thus it was with a tinge of sadness that we packed our bags and as our final act placed a plaque on the center wall acknowledging our work in Jamasi as representatives of Operation Crossroads Africa. We quickly recovered the joy that had been pervasive throughout our stay as we passed the schoolchildren once again lined on the side of the dirt road singing, throwing flowers, and waving good-bye as we left for a few days in Accra before returning home. Africa was now on our radar screen in a very special way, and we all became strong supporters of the idea of immersing oneself in a foreign culture in order to better understand ourselves and our world.

I had first heard of Operation Crossroads Africa in a speech by President John F. Kennedy about the origin of the U.S. Peace Corps. At the White House on June 22, 1962, the president had praised Jim Robinson for pioneering a model of public service that led to the development of one of the crowning achievements of his administration. He described the group and Robinson's efforts as the "progenitors of the Peace Corps." Like those of us who spent the summer of 1966 in the small village of Jamasi, the president understood the importance of the Crossroads motto, "Make a difference for others. See the difference in yourself."

### The Politics and Principles of War

It was later in the decade that Claremont became a hotbed of moral outrage. A few days after the students arrived for the 1969 school year, I was invited to a Southern California rally against the Vietnam War. It was held in Claremont, but no one at the colleges expected it to have any real impact on the students since, as I had been told often, most of the local opponents of the war were over sixty-five. It turned out that Claremont was also home to a large retirement center for ministers and missionaries from the progressive Congregational Church (now reorganized as the United Church of Christ). They were the major activists in town, trying unsuccessfully to attract support from their young neighbors.

With good marketing and the promise of good entertainment, the organizers of the rally attracted a very large but unenthusiastic gathering. I was invited to be one of the speakers. I had thought as early as my days at Stillman that I should speak out against the war, but I was preoccupied then with George Wallace and our efforts to dismantle the structures of racism in the old Confederacy. Like Martin Luther King Jr. and some of my former colleagues in the South, I had now come to the conclusion that these could no longer be separate battles. Young black men were dying bravely as they had done in previous wars, but the black community was reaping little of the benefits of their heroism. I saw this as an opportunity to appeal to the young students to take responsibility for something beyond their studies, to supplement academic life with a contribution to the world they would soon inherit.

My speech was not long. It began with a recital of the evils I had experienced growing up in Louisiana and witnessed again in both distant Alabama and nearby Watts. I moved quickly to a recitation of the evils of the Vietnam War—the massacre of civilians in the village of My Lai the year before, for example. The crowd was sitting on the grass in an empty lot where they had been enjoying the music, drinking beer, and listening to some boring speeches. To my surprise, my speech struck a chord. Within a few minutes, members of the crowd were on their feet and cheering loudly. I put away my notes and spoke from the heart as the cheers got louder and louder. It was the beginning of what became a two-tiered ministry: to the retirees over sixty-five and the young students mostly under twenty-one. Most Southern Californians in the 1960s seemed more concerned with what they regarded as an erosion of American values and civility than with the cause of the Watts uprising or the student revolt against the Vietnam War. They worried about sexual mores, dress codes, and traditional standards of civility. But at least one American principle was actually strengthened during the period. It was the principle of conscientious objection to war. If an opponent of the war expressed opposition to killing, either as a religious belief or as an individual ideology, that person was legally entitled to seek an exemption from wartime combat. We had some heated debates about the moral imperatives of patriotism and the meaning of pacifism, but the idea of conscientious objection that had been primarily associated with the historic peace churches (especially Quakers and Mennonites) became a mainstream value. The courts, mainstream Jewish, Catholic, and Protestant organizations, and many individual Americans reaffirmed it.

Throughout most of the twentieth century, pacifism had been a marginal and controversial idea, but in the 1960s the country moved from requiring a religious creed for conscientious objection to requiring no religion at all. It was during World War II that conscientious objector status was first granted based on individual belief, but it was not until the Seeger decision in 1965 that the Selective Service System made it clear to local draft boards that identification with the teachings of a religious group was no longer required.[1]

Confusion about who qualified for exemption from the draft led me to establish a Draft Counseling Center at the McAlister Center for Religious Activities for Claremont area students. I had long since been drawn into the center of Vietnam protest and the debate about both selective opposition to war and conscientious objection on the basis of individual belief. The students decided, therefore, that McAlister Center should be the nerve center of their movement. Some camped out on the adjacent lawns as they spent their days holding teach-ins and their evenings debating strategy. On one such evening, I joined in an all-night vigil trying to persuade the more radical students not to pursue a course of action that might discredit our movement and set back the gains we were making. Surrounded by the almost invisible brilliance of bright stars struggling to break through the California smog, I experienced for the first time the signature scent of incense mixed with marijuana drifting in my direction.

I now found myself closely associated with a movement in which a few of the most radical students were nearly out of control. The sleepy, conservative Claremont that Myrlie Evers had chosen as a new home because of its tranquility had now become a noisy clutter of disparate voices. It was time to talk about the larger moral issues at stake, the relationship of means to ends, and what we needed to do to be effective rather than simply to please our individual consciences. A discussion was initiated with the college presidents about using the influence of their institutions to make our case directly to influential lawmakers in Washington rather than confining our activities to Southern California. I had become a popular speaker on the anti–Vietnam War circuit, often accompanied by a folk singer named Clabe Hangan and even appearing with the legendary Muhammad Ali on one occasion. Clabe and I made a great team, but there seemed to be more of a feel-good quality to our rallies than an effective attempt to influence the policy we were protesting. Marching, demonstrating, and letter writing had their place, but we decided we had to find a way to do more.

So we went to Washington. Joe Platt, the president of Harvey Mudd College, went with us. He opened many doors as we spread out across Washington to tell policymakers and opinion leaders that the time had come to bring this sad chapter in American history to a close. This was in many ways a turning point for the Claremont movement. We continued to demonstrate on campus and in the streets, but we expanded our strategy to include influencing our elected officials and persuading a badly divided public that this was not a liberal versus conservative issue. Some fundamental American values were at stake.

The cost of the Vietnam War went far beyond the 57,685 Americans killed and some 153,000 wounded. Less measurable, but leaving a terrible scar on the national psyche, was the increased distrust of American leaders, the questioning of institutions, and the sense of self-doubt engendered by the war. But the real legacy may have been the heightening of moral sensitivity. What started out as small sparks of idealism soon came to burn so brightly that students decided to take their reform crusade to other sectors of American life. They turned their attention internally to the social responsibilities of the university, raising questions about the impact on communities, access to knowledge by the disadvantaged, and apparent complicity with national policies and programs that were difficult to justify morally.

### The Politics of Knowledge

Meanwhile, back in Claremont we were growing frustrated with the backlash against the University of California from those who resented the role the institution had played in firmly guarding academic freedom and the right of students and faculty to dissent from national policy. The Claremont students joined their colleagues on state campuses in protest against efforts by Ronald Reagan, the newly elected governor of California, to cut the higher education budget and reinvent the state university system.

There were anti–Ronald Reagan demonstrations with effigy hangings on many campuses, so when a group of students at Pomona College decided to hold a local rally, it was not big news. I agreed to speak at the gathering with one condition; there would be no symbolic acts of violence. As the campus chaplain and a strong advocate of nonviolence, I could not be seen to be associated with the effigy hangings that had become a popular staple on public campuses. The students were true to their word, but after the demonstration was over one student burned a large photograph of Governor Reagan.

The next day the headline in the local newspaper read, "Chaplain Speaks at Effigy Burning." As expected, the demonstration caught the attention of many supporters of the Claremont Colleges who did not share our outrage at what was happening to the nation's premier state university. Some threatened to stop contributing, but the presidents held their ground. They may have been uncomfortable with our activities, but they supported our right to peaceful dissent.

The focus on the politics of education in public higher education led the Claremont students to raise deeper questions about the nature of the academic enterprise. The student bodies of the Claremont Colleges were becoming more diverse, but they still fell far short of what seemed like an appropriate response to the social needs of the time. We set out to convince those with responsibility for admissions and academic policies that access to knowledge in an information society was a fundamental issue of social justice. If access to capital was a major determinant of economic well-being in the industrial age, access to knowledge is just as clearly a key social justice issue in an information age. To be without it is to be severely handicapped.

We joined the national debate about admissions procedures and standards, but we soon went beyond the debate to develop Project Open Future, a program to prepare and provide support for students from academically disadvantaged backgrounds to matriculate at the Claremont Colleges. Pete Reckard, my predecessor as chaplain, was now serving as provost. He took the lead in designing the program and raising funds for this new initiative. We set up an advisory board, developed a partnership with elite prep schools in California, and hired Bert Hammond, a prominent black educator, to head the project.

The program turned out to be very successful both in the number of students recruited and in the academic success of those admitted. In light of subsequent national policy debates about affirmative action, it is important to note that after a summer enrichment program and special support during the freshman year, Project Open Future students were able to stand on their own.

Many are now very accomplished professionals who bear neither the scars nor the stigma some critics claim to be the by-product of affirmative action. This was a method of addressing a social problem that fell clearly within the academic function of the colleges and received broad support from the college presidents, the faculty, and the community.

A special linkage developed between the Claremont Colleges and the Los Angeles black community as students and local black leaders in Watts beat a steady path back and forth between the two communities. Ron Karenga, the leader of a black nationalist group called us and later the founder of the

African American holiday Kwanzaa, became a friend and frequent visitor. The College Church, already infused with the music of the Beatles, now reverberated with the words of black street poets and the voices of black musicians.

With this new connection also came controversy, but there was no thought of retreat. The colleges were now more diverse and their reputation for academic excellence not only intact but enhanced. Nothing was sacrificed and much was gained.

The conflicts on campus soon took another turn. Colleges and universities were under pressure from corporate supporters and other special-interest stakeholders to provide practical education, to make certain that what students learned was useful. The quality and integrity of the academic programs at Claremont made it an appropriate place to offer a careful distinction between useful knowledge and useless information, between what is permanent or profound and what is temporary or trivial. When previous generations used the term "knowledge," they usually had in mind the discovery of permanent facts. But knowledge was losing its sense of permanence. In far too many places, "to know" had come to mean "to be informed."

Early societies believed that knowledge belonged originally to the gods. When they wanted to know what was right, good, and useful, they asked, "What have the gods revealed?" In early religious thought, knowledge was believed to come to humankind through the revelation of the deity. It was assumed that humanity came to know only what the gods chose to disclose. But there is a parallel tradition in both Judeo-Christian and Greek thought, the idea of revelation through rebellion. The story of Adam and Eve eating from the forbidden tree underscores the discovery of new knowledge as a potentially dangerous act of rebellion. In his *Protagoras*, Plato portrayed the discovery of fire as a similar leap in consciousness. Both of these stories are attempts to answer questions about how things work and what are the sources of knowledge.

Later societies moved from a focus on knowledge through divine revelation and rebellion to the idea of knowledge as process. Knowledge was seen as always evolving. No idea, therefore, should be considered absolute, no ideology final, no institution closed, and no individual infallible. Unfortunately, this altogether valid emphasis on the search for new knowledge and new ways of knowing has led to a vision of social order as a state of being that is achieved primarily through the use of higher levels of technology. The computer has become so integral to every facet of our lives that we are all too often giving priority primarily to those things that are part of a computable domain.

### Literacy in Moral Reasoning

When the students at Claremont sought to shift the focus of public discourse in Southern California from what we can know to what we should know, they were concerned with three basic issues. The first was economic: What should we know in order to provide for the general welfare? The second was political: What should we know in order to exercise power humanely? The third was social: What should we know in order to live as neighbors in an interdependent world? All three issues had an ethical dimension that fell legitimately within the students' concern about the moral use of knowledge.

The paramount challenge to the university was how to prepare a new generation for literacy in moral reasoning. The students were seeking an education that enabled them to develop principles by which to live and govern, to make judgments about good and evil; standards by which to develop priorities; the power to think clearly; and the knowledge to live in a highly technological civilization without confusing means and ends.

When one realizes that the questions the students were raising went to the heart of what it means to be a university, it is not surprising that they were perceived as tearing universities apart. The fundamental question was whether education should seek to be value free, aiming at absolute objectivity; whether it is sufficient to help students understand their world, gaining the power to think clearly, without giving them some concept of the life they might lead, the values they might need. This was a discourse I found easy to join. These themes became the subject of my sermons at the college church and my speeches at social clubs and rallies for various causes. Along with some of my colleagues on the faculty, I made the point wherever I could that while the forces that move the world need to be informed and disciplined by the intellect, they are rarely in themselves intellectual.

Our critics replied that while this might in some ways be true, the concern of the colleges should be with the minds and not the hearts and feelings of students. We wanted the colleges to help strengthen the nobler instincts, to prepare students for citizenship and a lifetime of moral reasoning. They preferred to focus on scholarship and the pursuit of truth. We argued that these were not contradictory objectives. They insisted that the primary values of the college are academic and that it should be neutral on all others.

When I reflected on what made my own undergraduate education at Southern University, a segregated black school in Louisiana, so useful to me, I was reminded that it was there that I learned to integrate the cognitive with the affective. I learned not only how to think clearly, but how to feel another person's pain and the need to share another person's burden.

Of course I also learned that a society must provide for its material existence, for the running of its machines; that a society needs its skilled workers to feed it and clothe it, its doctors, economists, teachers, and preachers. But I was persuaded that the quality of civilization also depended on something neither of these approaches really defines. It depends on its standards, its sense of values, and its idea of what is good and what is not.

### How Should Moral Education Take Place?

While many university presidents, faculties, trustees, and alumni agreed with us, they were left with the pedagogic question of how moral education is to take place. In the earliest approaches to moral education, both presidents and professors were often called upon to present a compulsory series of lectures on moral philosophy, usually to the senior class. This was aimed at pulling together and giving meaning and purpose to the student's entire college experience and course of study.

The student activists with whom I worked wanted something different. Intellectually, many understood the genesis of this mid-nineteenth-century practice, when moral philosophers still thought in terms of a common moral code that could simply be passed on from one generation to another. The students in the 1960s were more likely to look to role models, living examples of people engaged in principled behavior, rather than simply the study of moral philosophy. They were in this sense more likely to agree with Aristotle, whose basic admonition was, "If you would know virtue, behold the virtuous man." In his *Nicomachean Ethics*, he suggested that morality cannot be learned simply by reading a treatise on virtue. The spirit of morality, said Aristotle, is awakened in the individual only through the witness and conduct of a moral person.[2]

Survey courses on moral philosophy had their place, but they tended to offer a survey of various ethical theories rather than focusing on the moral dilemmas students faced in deciding how to deal with the draft, whether to take time off to try to set the world right, or how to respond to the sexual permissiveness that seemed to accompany the activism of the flower children in their midst. It was not simply the private virtues essential to good character that concerned them. They were struggling with the big issues of how government decided public policy, how multinational corporations dealt with foreign governments, whether large stockholding groups should be persuaded to divest from South Africa, and how university admission policies might be changed to address issues of quality and equality simultaneously.

The 1960s also saw the emergence in California of a plethora of sometimes bizarre and frequently unorthodox expressions of religious feeling. As director of the religious activity center, I heard chants, witnessed rituals, and fought for the religious freedoms of groups that were very different from those I had experienced in either Louisiana or Alabama. But while they appealed to the sense of adventure of some and the genuine quest for a spiritual center by others, many did not provide the moral grounding or theological guidance needed to cope with a world beset with complex issues of moral ambiguity.

Many of the students who had been attracted to role models of moral behavior now wanted to make educational institutions paragons of integrity and virtue as well. They craved some sign that the leaders of the institutions also cared about the great moral issues of the day like peace, poverty, and injustice. While the first wave of their protests sought to persuade universities to address social issues through their nonacademic functions—issuing political statements, divesting stocks, and boycotting suppliers—they were now demanding that they address social needs through their normal academic functions. Here the claims of neutrality were of doubtful value. The students were now asking educators to take account of the values and concerns of society in deciding on which academic programs to establish, which courses to prescribe, and which students to admit.

The 1960s were a time of moral ferment throughout American society. Churches, universities, and corporations felt the urgency with which people were asking moral questions and seeking moral answers. But when thoughtful activists sought to understand what their questioning had spawned, they were often disappointed to find that many people were seeking not a moral perspective out of which to search for answers, but moral absolutes that provide answers. While we wanted the teaching of ethics to go beyond the relativism some of our colleagues were finding attractive, we argued that ethics must be less concerned with presenting solutions than with engaging students in active discussion to encourage them to perceive ethical issues, listen to contending views, and ultimately arrive at thoughtful, reasoned conclusions.

It seemed ironic to some that it was the college church which proclaimed that no religion offered absolute clarity or self-evident truth. True to our own sense of orthodox moral teaching and to the academic milieu in which we operated, we argued that moral reasoning should lead to a perspective out of which to search for truth, that in matters of faith and morals the right question is usually more important than the right answer to the wrong question.

While there are many people who would now like to forget the 1960s, focusing primarily on its excesses, many of the demands of that decade have now been accepted and inculcated into the ongoing life of our colleges and our communities. Many academic institutions have dismantled the psychological walls around their campuses. They now make a special effort to be good citizens in their communities with concern for both their students and their neighbors, recognizing the relationship between a healthy community and a good university. Others are careful about how they vote their stocks and make a conscientious effort to recruit minority students. There is also increased concern about the ends that colleges and universities choose to serve, the social responsibilities of research, the potential threats to objectivity that come out of linkages with industry and government, and the social role of credentialing in controlling access to the professions.

## Life at Home and in the Office

My experience in the 1960s in Alabama and California may have seemed to observers to be only about changing society, that of the activist consumed with ending the Vietnam War, fighting poverty, and eliminating segregation. But there were also the great joys of private moments with the family and the personal interaction with faculty and students. Living on campus in Claremont, I saw the flower children of the period leaving roses, wildflowers, and even notes on my front porch and dropping by, often without notice. They loved to come by and play with Jeffrey or take him for a walk. One of the students even brought her friend Mike Garret, the Heisman trophy winner at the University of California, to meet Jeffrey. The word spread that he was at our home, and our modest residence at the center of the campus was quickly surrounded by faculty kids eager to get an autograph or just a glimpse of this celebrated icon.

The mood of the 1960s also penetrated my office in personal ways. One day I received a call from a student very anxious about rumors of an impending raid in search of drugs in her dormitory. She was someone who was active in College Church and a model of personal morality and self-discipline, but on this occasion she seemed unduly anxious as she blurted out that she had some pot in her room and was terrified that it might be discovered. After getting over my own surprise, I told her to flush it down the toilet and to come immediately to my office so we could discuss it. She quickly arrived, and when I asked her about the drugs she had flushed down the toilet, she pulled a little package out of her purse, put it on my desk, and asked me to dispose of it. I sent her to the bathroom to flush it herself. It was probably the first time the religious activity center had been used in this way, but it was an opportunity to do some deep and very satisfying counseling for a student who was about to get in serious trouble.

While Jeffrey remained the darling of the campus and a popular student at the Scripps College nursery school, my premarriage counseling with students had come to include a session on the personal joy and social benefit of adoption. As Doris and I explored the process together, we concluded that Jeffrey needed a little sister and this might be a wonderful way for us to expand our own family. We adopted a beautiful baby girl in 1969, and all three of us, Jeffrey included, began the process of caring for her. We named her Denise, and she joined Jeffrey as one of the new stars on the block. While only three months old at the time, she never ceased to amaze us when she heard music. I could feel her little body shaking to the beat while she was in my arms. We marveled at her love of music at such a young age and celebrated her disciplined behavior until we took her to her first restaurant, where she enjoyed throwing baby food against the window. As Jeffrey sought to take control and let her know that this was not a good idea, Doris whispered to me that it probably was not wise for me to have assured him that the three of us would take care of Denise together. But he loved his little sister and remained a proud big brother, protective and full of advice even though he was only five years older.

Doris was heavily engaged with faculty wives and working part time in the Department of Religion at Pomona College while also very involved in the College Church and the programs of the religious activities center. Claremont was a special joy to her, not just because we were no longer in Alabama, but because it was such an ideal place for young families and close friendships. Sylvia Leeser, a local elderly woman of some means, practically adopted all of us and became a part of the extended family and a supporter of every good cause in which I was involved. Her major project was to make sure I overcame my fear of water, a hangover from days growing up near bayous where snakes were always close by. Much to her dismay, while I enjoyed floating in her backyard pool, I never did learn to swim; but she and Doris made certain that Jeffrey and Denise learned the skill as early as possible. Jeffrey had an embarrassing moment as a four-year-old when Father Larry Rouillard, the Episcopal chaplain and his godfather, picked him out of the water and threw him into the air. Larry liked the hearty laugh that usually came from Jeffrey on such occasions, but this time Jeffrey went up and his swimming trunks went down. He may have been only four at the time, but he knew that this was not the picture he wanted his mother to take.

## The Responsible University

My experience of trying to transform Claremont in the 1960s led me to conclude that there are at least three traits that should stand out whenever an academic institution is morally responsible. First, it should provide for the development of the moral instincts of its students, producing graduates who are not only informed and articulate but also thoughtful and responsible. Just as it is not possible to teach students all they need for a career—they must be prepared for a lifetime of learning—so they must be prepared for a lifetime of moral reasoning.

Second, it should provide and encourage opportunities for community service, helping students gain a more lasting appreciation for the values and concerns of the different communities in which they will someday live and work. It should also help develop an appreciation for the linkage between the future well-being of the most fortunate and that of the less well off.

Third, it should make a special effort to demonstrate that scholarship and the more traditional modes of higher education are not antithetical to being an engaged and responsible institution; that civic engagement is not simply a good thing to do. It is—in an interdependent world—a necessary part of cognitive development. The university should use its capacity for creativity to find appropriate and imaginative ways to respond as an institution to some of the problems that plague the society in which it is set.

When we think of the 1960s, we think primarily about the civil rights and antiwar movements, but the principles and practices of that period also include the legacy of vigorous debate about why and how universities and colleges should use both their academic and nonacademic resources to serve the public good. The decade that began with Clark Kerr publishing *The Uses of the University*, celebrating the triumphs of the modern "multiversity," came to a close with students protesting the ends that universities chose to serve. "The Columbia Statement," issued in the 1960s by students at Columbia University in New York, went further than most in arguing that some universities had actually become a clear and present danger to large sectors of the society. The students wrote, "We lived in an institution that channeled us, marked us, ranked us, failed us, used us, and treated masses of humanity with contempt." They went on to argue in the fiery rhetoric of the 1960s that "for years, Columbia trustees had evicted tenants from their homes, taken land through city deals, and fired workers for trying to form a union. For years they had trained officers for Vietnam who, as ROTC literature indicates, killed Vietnamese peasants in their own country."[3] The language was harsh, but the students were raising some fundamental questions about the moral basis of the university and its social responsibilities. It was these concerns about the ends universities chose to serve that preoccupied me for much of the second half of the 1960s.

Graduating from middle school in Opelousas, 1948.
AUTHOR'S PERSONAL COLLECTION.

As a freshman at Southern University, Baton Rouge, 1952. AUTHOR'S PERSONAL COLLECTION.

As a young officer in the Medical Service Corps of the U.S. Army, 1957.
AUTHOR'S PERSONAL COLLECTION.

Reverend Adam Joseph, the author's father, circa 1960.

With mother, Julia Joseph, and brother, John Joseph (at left), the first
African American mayor of Opelousas, 1962. AUTHOR'S PERSONAL COLLECTION.

Welcome by village chief and wife at greeting ceremony in Jamasi, Ghana, as leader of
Operation Crossroads Africa summer project, 1966. AUTHOR'S PERSONAL COLLECTION.

As chaplain of Claremont Colleges with wife, Doris Joseph, and son, Jeffrey, 1968.
AUTHOR'S PERSONAL COLLECTION.

As vice president of Cummins Engine Company with J. Irwin Miller, board chair and
early mentor, 1977. AUTHOR'S PERSONAL COLLECTION.

In Guam with Admiral Cruden, Ruth Van Cleve, and Wallace Green before plane crash and rescue in Pacific Ocean, 1978. U.S. STATE DEPARTMENT PRESS PHOTOGRAPH.

As undersecretary of the interior in meeting with President Jimmy Carter and his cabinet, 1978. WHITE HOUSE PRESS PHOTOGRAPH.

With Doris Joseph at the Executive Yuan with Prime Minister Sun Yun-suan of Taiwan, 1980. U.S. STATE DEPARTMENT PRESS PHOTOGRAPH.

Son Jeffrey after graduation from Princeton, 1985. AUTHOR'S PERSONAL COLLECTION.

With President George H. W. Bush after appointment as an incorporating director of the Points of Light Foundation, 1990. WHITE HOUSE PRESS PHOTOGRAPH.

With Ruth Shack and Sandy Cloud after working with the mayor of Miami Beach to pass resolution honoring Nelson Mandela and reversing earlier snub, 1992.
AUTHOR'S PERSONAL COLLECTION.

In Johannesburg presenting resolution honoring Nelson Mandela from city of Miami Beach, reversing earlier snub by southwestern Florida mayors, 1992.

With daughter, Denise, at presidential ball after inauguration of President Clinton, 1993.
WHITE HOUSE PRESS PHOTOGRAPH.

As chair of the board of directors of the Corporation for National and Community Service with First Lady Hillary Clinton welcoming AmeriCorps volunteers to the White House, 1994.
WHITE HOUSE PRESS PHOTOGRAPH.

With wife Mary Braxton Joseph at swearing-in as U.S. ambassador by Supreme Court Justice Sandra Day O'Connor, 1996. U.S. STATE DEPARTMENT PRESS PHOTOGRAPH.

With President Nelson Mandela in Cape Town after presenting credentials as U.S. ambassador, 1996. U.S. STATE DEPARTMENT PRESS PHOTOGRAPH.

With Mary Braxton Joseph toasting UN ambassador and Mrs. Andrew Young after serving as best man in Young's Cape Town wedding, 1996. AUTHOR'S PERSONAL COLLECTION.

With Secretary of State Warren Christopher, Archbishop Desmond Tutu, and Minister Dullah Omar at ambassador's Cape Town residence, 1996. U.S. STATE DEPARTMENT PRESS PHOTOGRAPH.

With family on boat en route to Robben Island, where Nelson Mandela was imprisoned, 1997. AUTHOR'S PERSONAL COLLECTION.

With Kofi Annan and Mary Braxton Joseph on Robben Island, 1997.
U.S. STATE DEPARTMENT PRESS PHOTOGRAPH.

With President William Clinton and First Lady Hillary Clinton at ambassador's residence in Cape Town, 1998. WHITE HOUSE PRESS PHOTOGRAPH.

President Thabo Mbeki presenting the Order of Good Hope, the highest honor South Africa bestows on a citizen of another country, 1999. U.S. STATE DEPARTMENT PRESS PHOTOGRAPH.

With Governor Kathleen Blanco after selection as chair of Louisiana Disaster Recovery Foundation in aftermath of Hurricane Katrina, 2005.

With Mary Braxton Joseph, 2010. AUTHOR'S PERSONAL COLLECTION.

# III

# The 1970s and 1980s

THE APPLICATION OF

MORAL REASONING

# Cummins Engine Company

*Capitalism with an Ethic*

We have all had moments when things come together in an unexpected way, when events that could never have been predicted seem to guide us in a new direction. Carl Jung called this "synchronicity." In 1970, after a decade on the cutting edge of two great social movements, I accepted an invitation to help develop the philanthropy of Cummins Engine Company and the Irwin-Sweeney-Miller Foundation. The two foundations were not well known outside of Indiana, but they were beginning to play a larger role in support of equity and inclusion in both the communities in which the company operated and the work of the foundations nationally.

Many of my colleagues and friends were surprised that I would leave Claremont for life in a small Indiana town. What they did not know was that I was being offered a national platform and resources to resume the work I had started in Tuscaloosa and continued in Claremont.

J. Irwin Miller, the chair and CEO at Cummins and patriarch of the Miller family, had played a major role in the passage of the Civil Rights Act of 1964, which, among other things, forbade places of public accommodation—including restaurants, hotels, theaters, and even barbershops—from discriminating on the basis of race. Miller was the first lay president of the National Council of Churches and played such a key role in galvanizing churches in support of the bill that Georgia senator Richard Russell, the leader of the filibuster against the bill in the U.S. Senate, wrote to a friend after the bill passed, "We had been able to hold the line until the churches joined the civil rights lobby in 1964."[1]

Martin Luther King Jr. called Miller the most progressive businessman in the United States. Clay Risen, the author of *The Bill of the Century*, called the epic battle for the Civil Rights Act far more than the work of Lyndon Johnson and those usually given credit for its passage. He specifically cites the work of J. Irwin Miller as critical to the success of the bill in making its way through Congress.

Miller was one of the remarkable figures in twentieth-century business. He developed a small family business into the world's leading manufacturer of heavy-duty diesel engines. In 1968, *Esquire* magazine featured him on the front cover as "the man who should be the next president of the United States." Not very well known by the larger public, Irwin Miller had no interest in running for office and probably would not have been a good politician, although he would likely have been a great president. He was both a renaissance man who read widely and thought deeply, and a business executive who produced a quality product and cared about his workers and their communities. He did much of his civic work privately and quietly, but he was an advisor to presidents and enjoyed the adulation of social reformers across a wide spectrum of activities.

I met Miller for the first time in 1967, shortly after Phillip Sorensen visited me in Claremont, California, and invited me to join him in an effort to further develop the private giving of Cummins Engine Company and the Miller family. Sorensen, a close friend of the Kennedys of Massachusetts (his brother Ted was a speechwriter and trusted advisor to President Kennedy) had just lost a close race for governor of Nebraska and had decided to take his career in a different direction. I was very impressed with Phil, but I had never heard of J. Irwin Miller or Cummins Engine Company. Yet I accepted the invitation to visit Columbus to meet Miller, his family, and executives of Cummins and his other family enterprise, Irwin Management Company.

Arriving at night in the town that because of its support for quality architecture would soon be known as the Athens of the Prairie, Doris and I woke up the next morning to see cornfields framing the picture of the landscape behind the local motel. At that moment, Southern California never looked better to her; but the people we met, the buildings we saw, and the commitment of the Miller enterprises to building a more just America were so unusual that the whole place seemed unreal. Here was a small Midwestern town full of big ideas and, of course, cornfields, but beginning to acquire international acclaim for its collection of some of the finest architecture in the world. The American Institute of Architects later rated Columbus sixth on the list of the top ten American cities for architectural quality and innovation, right up there with Chicago, New York, and San Francisco. More than sixty public buildings, from schools to firehouses, were built by a veritable who's who of architects—I. M. Pei, Eero and Eliel Saarinen, Harry Weese, Cesar Pelli, and Robert Venturi, to name a few.

But it was the commitment of Miller, his family, and his business associates to improving the quality of life for all Americans, especially those long excluded from the privileges and benefits of democracy, that led to our decision to leave Southern California for Indiana. We could already imagine Jeffrey studying in an I. M. Pei school and the family worshipping in a Saarinen church while still making a national contribution to resolving the issues that concerned us in Tuscaloosa and Claremont.

It was Irwin Miller whose values and vision shaped and defined both Cummins and Columbus. He was the Miller family patriarch, a successful business executive, a great manager, and a pace-setting philanthropist. Like the Old Testament prophets and the Greek philosophers whose work he read in Greek and admired, he was always teaching. Every board meeting, every lunch, and every appointment in his office was a teaching moment, not just for me but for all those who served on his management team.

Miller was respected and admired—in business schools and among many of his colleagues—as the prototype of the responsible corporate statesman. Cummins was widely known for both the superior quality of its diesel engines and the corporate values by which it operated. It was, from its beginning as a tiny machine shop in 1919, a values-driven company, and it became the subject of case studies for students in business schools eager to learn how it was managed and why it had a strong commitment to ethics. The rise from a small family business in a small town to the world's leading producer of heavy-duty diesel engines is a story that still resonates with important lessons about how to be both profitable and responsible.

The early years of Cummins were a time best characterized as a period of informally cultivating the values of the founding family. Considerable attention was given to private virtues: good managers are good people, for example. But there was also an emphasis on corporate values, the idea that those who seek to behave responsibly in their personal lives have every right to expect, even demand, that their institutions do the same. Miller was one of the first business leaders to introduce the idea of an obligation to other stakeholders as well as shareholders.

My first office at Cummins was just outside of the entrance to his own, so he often stopped by to chat—in retrospect, to mentor. On one occasion over coffee and overlooking the block on Franklin Street that first came to symbolize his commitment to architectural excellence, he shared with me an insight that became a central part of my own thinking about corporate ethics: the idea that being responsible begins with the decision to do business. The responsible company locates a site responsibly, hires a workforce responsibly, manufactures a product or provides a service responsibly, compensates its employees and distributes the return on investment responsibly, sets prices responsibly, deals with its communities responsibly, and works with governments responsibly.

In an era when others were beginning to speak of the social responsibility of business—but as something separate from the central activities of the company—Miller argued that the so-called soft stuff contributes to the bottom line and could not be divorced from the hard stuff. He had detractors among his colleagues in business as well as scholars like the University of Chicago economist Milton Friedman, but he stood his ground in the company and in public discourse. The architectural support program in Columbus soon became a showcase for how a company contributed to the quality of local education. Miller often quoted Winston Churchill, who said, "We shape our buildings; thereafter they shape us."

He wanted to enhance the quality of life available to all of the citizens of Columbus rather than just Cummins employees, so the company supported the arts and encouraged creative expressions in varied forms because of the belief that a company is likely to be healthier when it operates in healthy communities. A special effort was made to bring to Columbus some of the best minds and best managers in the world, so support was provided for a public lecture series to raise the level of discussion of public issues. Many in Columbus were doing well, but the company also supported those who were not, helping to fund their institutions and to ensure that the public life of the community reflected their thinking and concerns.

Not only did Cummins Engine Company become a prototype of a responsible company, but the Cummins Engine Foundation became a model of the best of corporate giving. Cummins was one of a small group of companies giving away the maximum charitable dollars for which a tax deduction was allowed. People from around the country, literally around the world, beat a path to Columbus, Indiana, to find out more about Cummins and how it defined and met its responsibilities to its communities.

On most social issues, Miller could be as outraged by the wrongs he saw around him as those whose voices were much louder, but while he worked quietly behind the scenes, he was prepared to go public when that seemed necessary. I especially remember a dramatic appearance before the Columbus City Council to appeal for passage of a fair housing law.

When my family and I arrived in Columbus in the summer of 1967, our attempt to buy property in a neighborhood that had always been exclusively white caused quite a furor. The city was earning a reputation as the Athens of the Prairie because of Irwin Miller's support for contemporary architecture, quality education, and the arts. But it had not yet been tested on open housing. The company used its clout to ensure that I was treated like any other wage-earning newcomer, but it did not stop there. As head of the family and company foundations, I was encouraged to work for a more open community. After collaborating with the city's Human Relations Commission and experts on my staff, we developed and proposed an open housing ordinance. When we discovered that the proposal was about to be defeated in a close city council vote, I asked Irwin Miller to make a statement at the council's public meeting. He agreed and was placed on the agenda. It was a memorable statement, with Irwin Miller reminding them of his local roots and loyalty and, without making any direct threats, suggesting that he might need to consider relocating the Cummins corporate office if he could not guarantee employees the opportunity to live wherever they could afford. The ordinance was passed and is still on the books.

A remark Miller made in 1983 illustrates his personal philosophy about the equality of all individuals: "In the search for character and commitment, we must rid ourselves of our inherited, even cherished biases and prejudices. Character, ability and intelligence are not concentrated in one sex over the other, or in persons with certain accents or in certain races or in persons holding degrees from some universities over others. When we indulge ourselves in such irrational prejudices, we damage ourselves most of all and ultimately assure ourselves of failure in competition with those more open and less biased."[2]

Irwin Miller was in many ways ahead of his time, but he shaped his time in ways that still stand as an example for other corporate executives to study or emulate. He had supported the National Labor Relations Act when this was heresy for businessmen, and he had committed the company to giving away 5 percent of its pretax profits for charitable purposes. When pollution became a national issue, the company acknowledged that diesel engines were a contributing factor and joined with the Environmental Protection Agency, the California Resources Board, and other key agencies to develop sensible and effective national standards.

Miller was also known for his commitment to diversity. The company's recruitment and hiring practices caught the attention of the *New York Times*, whose editors dispatched a reporter to Columbus, Indiana, to find out what was going on. Here was a large transnational company and other related Miller enterprises with a global reach attracting large numbers of African Americans, not as window dressing but as central players in the management of very successful enterprises.

Some remained with the company through retirement, moving up the management ladder in the process, while others took the experience gained at Cummins to other sectors of American life. Ulric Haynes, an international vice president I helped recruit, was the U.S. ambassador to Algeria during the Iran crisis who played a central role in negotiating the release of the American hostages. Eddie Brown, who worked in investment for the Miller family, helping to make some of the money I was responsible for giving away, later founded Brown Capital Management, a Baltimore-based firm that amassed more than $6 billion under his management. Like Miller, Brown also became a major philanthropist, giving away millions to charitable causes under the aegis of the Eddie and Sylvia Brown Foundation. William Mays, who remained in Indiana but founded his own chemical company, grew it from a one-person operation to an enterprise with 160 employees with revenues of $150 million. William S. Norman left Cummins to become executive vice president and chief operating officer of Amtrak, the National Railroad Passenger Corporation, and later served as president and CEO of the Travel Industry Association of America.

Black alumni of Cummins can be found in leadership roles across a broad spectrum of American life. The company has also been a leader in employing, deploying, and supporting other population groups. The Latino former mayor of Denver, Federico Pena, in welcoming Irwin Miller to his city, told a national audience of philanthropic leaders that if it were not for the support of Miller and Cummins during his days as a community activist, he would not have become mayor. Pena went on to become secretary of the Department of Transportation in the Clinton administration. Ladonna Harris, a Comanche social activist, served for a time on my staff at Cummins while she was developing Americans for Indian Opportunity, a leading advocacy and training organization for Native Americans. There are many other political, economic, religious, and community leaders who attribute their success to Cummins and the Miller family.

## Beyond Grantmaking

While we saw corporate giving as one of the many options available to improve the quality of life in our communities and in the larger society, Miller and the senior officers encouraged me to make a special effort to ensure that the Cummins Foundation was more than simply a traditional corporate giving program. Long before I sought to urge foundation trustees and staff nationally—during my years as president of the Council on Foundations—to think of the foundation as more than a grantmaker, we at Cummins had come to see this philanthropic arm of the company as a social enterprise with myriad forms of capital that went far beyond fiscal assets.

This was before Robert Putnam, who wrote the book *Bowling Alone*, highlighted the importance of "social capital"—a term that refers to the fabric of our connections with each other as individuals and social networks, and the norms of reciprocity that arise from them. But instead of simply lamenting the collapse and decline of old networks of neighborliness, we set out to revive, reform, and in some instances reinvent the way in which business serves a public as well as a private good. Having decided that a major focus of Cummins philanthropy would be equity and inclusion, we developed a program to deploy program officers in five major cities. Their role was not simply to use Cummins funds to help empower those on the margins of society, but to use their own presence in the field of organized philanthropy as an opportunity to serve as a resource to other foundations and corporations who shared our commitment but did not have experienced staff with a history of working in marginalized communities.

Walter Bremond had founded the Brotherhood Crusade in Los Angeles in the aftermath of the Watts uprising. He became our Los Angeles program officer, whom we later loaned to the National Black United Fund to serve as its first CEO, leading the successful effort nationally to gain access to the payroll deduction systems used by the United Way. Ivanhoe Donaldson had been arrested more than thirty times in the 1960s as a key member of the staff of the Student Nonviolent Coordinating Committee. He was our program officer in Washington, DC, and before he became deputy mayor we loaned him to candidates seeking office in Atlanta, Gary, Indiana, and elsewhere. Richard Lawrence, our program officer in Chicago, had been a key ally of Jessie Jackson in the formation of the predecessor organization to Operation Push. Walter Lively was the youngest member of the city council in Baltimore before he joined us as a program officer for that city. He also worked with me on a variety of projects across the country. Stanley Wise, our program officer in Atlanta, had once been head of the Student Nonviolent Coordinating Committee. He was our major contact with nonprofit organizations promoting social change throughout the South.

At a time when most foundations had rather limited racial diversity on their staffs, the Cummins Foundation had a CEO and five program officers who were black; so when Allen Green, a former professor at the University of California, Riverside, joined us as an associate director, a member of the staff of another foundation said to me, "I am glad to see that you guys hire white people too." The reality is that some of our most successful grants and programs were developed under the leadership of Phil Sorensen before I succeeded him as head of the foundations. We continued to have very good white staff who were equally committed to the goals we were pursuing, but at a time in which one rarely found people of color in organized philanthropy, our black program officers stood out. When I attended my first annual gathering of foundation executives and trustees in 1968, only one other black person was present. It was then that I decided I would urge my board not only to make the two foundations I helped staff more diverse, but to make increasing the diversity of organized philanthropy a grantmaking priority of the foundations.

In addition to providing support and technical assistance to many of the newly formed nonprofit organizations seeking to promote social justice in the regions to which they were assigned, the program officers served as a resource to nonstaffed and understaffed foundations across the country. They helped community groups develop programs and write proposals later funded by other foundations. In addition to the networks established by the program officers, we provided assistance to board members to help them make the case for equity and inclusion in their own networks. J. Irwin Miller, the chair of the board of both Cummins Engine Company and the Cummins Foundation, was not only a member of the board of the Ford Foundation and Yale University but chair of the National Council of Churches during the years of its strong support for the civil rights movement in the South. Miller also advised both President John F. Kennedy and President Lyndon Johnson on national civil rights policy. The program officers also supported other board members who used their networks to promote equity and inclusion in other organizations and communities.

It is thus no surprise that I became a strong advocate nationally for foundations to strategically use their social capital to achieve their mission and support a public good. The same was true of intellectual capital. When Charles Bannerman and his colleagues from MACE, a civil rights group in Greenville, Mississippi, visited us in Columbus, Indiana, in search of a grant to grow their community development organization, we persuaded them to take a look at economic development options that could use profit to support their nonprofit activities. We helped them develop feasibility studies that led to the formation of the Delta Enterprises, which soon became one of the largest black-owned companies in the South. We also provided an advisory group from Cummins management who met regularly with their management team. At the same time, we supported studies that led to the expansion of the National Black United Fund, even providing the legal fees to bolster the gathering of information for litigation that led to the opening up of payroll deductions systems to nontraditional organizations.

We added reputational capital to our strategic use of assets by enlisting Irwin Miller to help Delta Enterprises gain access to major markets by providing introductions to his peers in other companies. We continued, of course, to use our moral capital by working through the Council of Churches and seminaries to make the case for inclusion and equity as moral imperatives. We did not neglect the use or minimize the importance of financial capital, but we sought to go beyond grantmaking. Cummins was among the first to move into what became known as program-related investment, using our financial capital not only to make grants but to provide loans to groups like the National Housing Partnership (NHP) Foundation, which specialized in housing for low- to moderate-income families, the handicapped, and the elderly. The NHP Foundation was founded in 1989 by Gabe Mehreteab, who quickly developed it into a leading national nonprofit provider of multifamily housing for low-income Americans. The Cummins loan, which was later turned into a grant, helped Gabe to grow its portfolio to forty-six properties in fourteen states, totaling more than ten thousand units. A few years after leaving Cummins, I became chair of the NHP board.

It was at Cummins, therefore, that we pioneered what came to be known nationally as SMIRF, the strategic use by foundations of social, moral, intellectual, reputational, and financial capital. The idea of SMIRF as a strategic planning tool was further developed and refined by David Dodson and his staff at MDC, the successor to the North Carolina Fund. Not surprisingly, David was also a Cummins alumnus and went on to a career of great distinction as president of MDC.

### Institutionalizing a Process

If the early years at Cummins were driven by the values of the remarkable man at the head of the company, incorporating his corporate philosophy and values, the middle years saw the institutionalizing of a process that went far beyond what other companies were calling corporate social responsibility. As the directors turned to professional management in the operation of the company, so it was that the company turned to people with a different, but complementary, set of experiences to cultivate and coordinate its commitment to a set of corporate values. While still serving as head of the Cummins and Irwin-Sweeney-Miller foundations, Henry Schacht, Irwin Miller's successor at Cummins Engine Company, initiated a series of conversations with me about the responsibility of business to its stakeholders. While the company was shaped largely by the examples and expectations set by Irwin Miller, Schacht felt that the time had come to more formally institutionalize those values. To my surprise, he invited me to lead a company-wide effort to formalize a process for ensuring that the emphasis on being efficient was matched by an emphasis on being responsible. My new assignment was that of vice president for corporate action worldwide.

One of my first acts was to lure an ethicist named Chuck Powers away from Yale Divinity School and a naval officer named William Norman away from the staff of Admiral Zumwalt, the chief of U.S. naval operations. Powers, who had written a book on corporate ethics, was asked to head a public responsibility unit that helped define and oversee the company's responsibilities to its public stakeholders. Norman, whom Zumwalt gave credit for his pioneering efforts in integrating the navy, was asked to lead our efforts to ensure that we met our corporate responsibilities to the private stakeholders. Schacht assigned to the Corporate Action Division the following tasks:

1. Work with management at all levels to ensure that all business analyses—new plant sites, new ventures, market penetration, product development, functional planning, setting prices, and so on—include corporate responsibility considerations
2. Serve as an in-house resource for understanding the social and political context in which the company does business
3. Interpret political and social issues, propose corporate policies, and coordinate public affairs, community relations, and philanthropic programs

While some executives looked at our new organization and its mission with skepticism, it was not long before executives in other companies wanted to know more about how we operated. One CEO even asked Henry Schacht to loan me to his company to set up a similar organization.

Two decades later, the title of ethics officer was as familiar as information officer. By the end of the 1990s, there were enough ethics officers to form their own professional association, with the trade group reporting that its ranks had soared to a membership of more than seven hundred. Unlike the earlier position at Cummins, however, where we looked at every corporate activity and asked, "What does it mean to be responsible?," most of these ethics officers were corporate guides and advisors whose orientation was primarily legal and regulatory. Being responsible involves far more than that.

Ethical considerations must be a part of a culture of responsibility that integrates normative standards of ethics and corporate responsibility into all corporate activities. Miller was known for his commitment to the communities in which the company operated, his concern for the well-being of employees, and his vigorous support of those who fought against segregation; but he saw the primary moral issue for business as how profits were made rather than simply how much was given away—even for noble purposes.

The concern with corporate responsibility in American society and in the worldwide corporate community seems to go in cycles, but what is consistent is the tendency to narrow the focus to a very thin slice of corporate behavior. In the 1960s, the emphasis was on social responsibility, what corporate executives called the soft stuff of business. Some responded with corporate giving programs. Others provided incentives for employee voluntarism and even loaned executives to struggling nonprofit groups. Some of the most enlightened went one step further and initiated supplier development and other economic programs to help bring economically marginalized groups into the mainstream.

The 1970s saw the beginning of the integration of corporate responsibility concerns into the hard stuff of business as a wave of corruption scandals caused anxiety and alarm. Well over a hundred companies admitted to paying overseas or domestic bribes. Nearly half of these companies indicated that they had also violated U.S. and foreign tax laws. Many admitted that at least some members of senior management had knowledge of, approved of, or participated directly in the bribes. And most of these corporations admitted that they falsified financial records to cover up their practices.

Most people were predictably dismayed by these revelations, since many of the practices, like the accounting and auditing scandals at the dawn of the twenty-first century, interfered with the formation of market prices, thereby distorting the flow of trade and investment. At Cummins, we argued that they undermined confidence in the market system and adversely affected U.S. relations with foreign countries. Worst of all, they reflected a deeply troubling ethical insensitivity in those institutions that were obliged by their power and size to observe the highest standards of ethical behavior and corporate responsibility.

Not only was Cummins out in front in support of ethical standards, but as an example of good corporate practices we were often on the firing line as well, explaining our beliefs and practices to a curious press, concerned business colleagues, and a U.S. Congress eager to find an appropriate role for public policy. There were some defenders of the practices we considered problematic for an ethical corporation. Not much, admittedly, could be said in defense of domestic bribery or political payoffs. For international bribery, however, an array of defenses was put forward that centered on three propositions: (1) the ethical ambiguity argument, the proposition that in many foreign contexts bribes are indistinguishable from legitimate commissions and that in the face of such ambiguities ethical judgments are arbitrary and presumptuous; (2) the ethical imperialism argument, the proposition that to insist on straight commercial dealings with foreign customers would be an imposition of American values on others who do not share them; and (3) the competitive pressure argument, in which many business executives had concluded that without engaging in bribery a firm operating abroad would suffer a severe competitive disadvantage.

These propositions failed to carry the day at Cummins. We argued that it was indeed possible to be clear about what bribery is. There are, no doubt, gray areas between the realm of bribery and the realm of legitimate commissions; but we used some elementary guidelines to help make the distinctions we considered important. Is the payment secret? Is the payment intended to distort a judgment that should be made on other grounds? Is the payment wholly unrelated to any legitimate service rendered the recipient? Would the company be negatively affected if a payment became a headline story in a local newspaper in a present or potential market? If the answer to any of those questions was yes, then the payment probably should not be made.

The proposition that ethical behavior by American corporations would unjustifiably impose American values on members of diverse cultures was, and still is, clearly fallacious. Aside from the condescending assumption that honesty and trustworthiness are peculiarly American values, the major defect of the argument was the notion that declining to do business with another party except on certain terms is somehow an imposition of those terms on the other party. It is nothing of the kind; it is a mere statement of conditions necessary for contractual relations. Such conditions are objectionable or not according to their content. It was ironic to hear businessmen accustomed to driving hard economic bargains professing a modest sense of delicacy at the very idea of insisting on honest, uncorrupted dealings.

The proposition that American business could not compete abroad without bribery was equally suspect. It was indeed true that in the short run, refusing to pay bribes could lose some business opportunities. But we were convinced that in the long run, much more could be lost with the use of corrupt practices. Ironically, those corporations that argued that such practices were common and accepted, indeed demanded, in other cultures were the same corporations that took great pains to conceal the existence of those practices. Double bookkeeping, off-the-books accounts, dummy corporations set up in Switzerland and Liechtenstein, numerous secret agents and intermediaries, code names and code books belied that payoffs were part of the accepted rules of the game. Nor was straight commercial dealing regarded as a virtue only in the industrial world.

While we were making the case to policymakers (I testified before a Senate committee), opinion leaders, our own employees, and business colleagues and competitors, my staff and I worked with Henry Schacht to prepare a memo on ethical standards that went out to all Cummins employees informing them that ethics at Cummins rested on a fundamental belief in people's dignity and decency. Our most basic ethical standard, the memo stated, is to show respect for those whose lives we affect and to treat them as we would expect them to treat us if our positions were reversed. We ended up summarizing this kind of respect as follows:

1. Obeying the law—in every community, in every country in which we operate, and obeying the law in spirit as well as letter; never taking advantage of a loophole in the wording to avoid complying with the intent
2. Being honest—unqualifiedly honest—always presenting the facts fairly and accurately
3. Being fair—giving everyone appropriate consideration
4. Being concerned—caring about how Cummins's actions affect others and trying to make these effects as beneficial as possible
5. Being courageous—treating others with respect and being willing to observe these ethical standards even when it means losing business

This was not a grand statement simply to be posted in public places or to be trotted out for public relations purposes. Each word was carefully considered and chiseled out of actual business practices. We circulated the statement to all employees and announced to the public that we would compete only on a straight commercial basis—that if something more was required, we were not interested.

### The New Ethics Movement

Meanwhile, a new focus on capitalism with an ethic was dawning. Many countries once suspicious or downright hostile to business were beginning to develop business-friendly environments with business-friendly policies. There was a feeling that democracy was good for markets and markets good for democracy. This was a great social moment for business, but there were also reasons for caution. The public perception of the social utility of private enterprise in many emerging markets was directly related to the expectation that business would contribute to the public good.

I logged many miles traveling to countries in Europe, Latin America, Africa, and Asia to make the case to employees, distributors, and others with whom we worked that being an ethical company was part of enlightened self-interest. In some places I met resistance, but it was not long before our reputation for producing the best heavy-duty diesel engine was matched by our reputation for the way we treated our employees and helped improve the quality of life in our communities. Instead of limiting business, the company grew enormously, becoming an $18 billion business with 44,000 employees.

Many years later, the debacle of deception at Enron and the revelations regarding the auditing firm Arthur Andersen validated our earlier contention that ethics contributes to the bottom line. In an era when consumer choice is increasingly as dependent on ethically responsible corporate behavior as it is on quality, those companies that have developed a reputation for being responsible can often have a competitive advantage in some areas. Others who have more recently joined the ethics movement are increasingly elevating the conversation about ethics and social responsibility to the board level. A Conference Board study of 122 companies in twenty-two countries found that directors are now much more involved in the creation of ethical standards.[3]

Even before the scandals of the summer of 2002, companies were joining the ethics crusade for some very practical reasons. In 1991, the U.S. Justice Department issued sentencing guidelines that in effect promised more lenient treatment of convicted corporate executives if their companies had established good-citizenship ethics programs. The federal government was followed a few years later by the Delaware Court of Chancery, who warned that corporate directors could be held personally liable for subordinates' wrongdoing if they had failed to establish programs to ensure compliance with the law.[4]

Public opinion was also pushing business to focus more attention on standards for corporate behavior. At the beginning of the twentieth century, the public simply expected business to provide jobs, services, or products. By the beginning of the twenty-first century, public groups concerned with business behavior proliferated. Daniel Yankelovich, chairman of DYG Inc., a market research firm, found that there was an increased readiness to believe negative things about corporations. "Executives," he reported, "haven't had to worry about social issues for a generation, but there's a yellow light flashing now, and they'd better pay attention."[5]

Even prominent business leaders who once enjoyed celebrity status suddenly found themselves and their companies greatly diminished in stature because of the scrutiny of the new ethics movement. It was not just investors who were greatly disillusioned by the house arrest of "DeDe" Brooks, the former chief executive of Sotheby's; the fall from grace of Kenneth Lay, the well-connected CEO at Enron; and the diminished reputation of Jack Welch at General Electric, probably the epitome of the cult of the all-powerful chief executive. Many other stakeholders, including employees and consumers, demanded that the standards to which management is held accountable become less focused on a single bottom-line number such as profits. Rush Kidder, who was president of the Global Ethics Institute, reported at a forum I led at the Graduate School of Business at the University of Cape Town that he had been engaged to help determine what questions should be raised when interviewing future managers to determine not simply whether they are likely to be effective as managers but whether they will be responsible as custodians of values.

This renewed concern with corporate responsibility and ethics was a welcome development, but the focus was primarily on what it means to be responsible in the financial arena. It would be most unfortunate if this new spotlight on accounting, auditing, and financial reporting took the eyes of the public away from the need for similar standards and scrutiny in other areas such as human resources, marketing, community relations, and so on.

Every business corporation needs to put systems in place to promote and support a values-based corporate culture. All the new rhetoric about values (integrity, trust, respect, honesty, excellence, and accountability) will mean little unless the reward systems reflect those values. J. Irwin Miller understood the connection between affirming good values and practicing them, between advancing promising managers and rewarding them for being not just efficient but responsible. It is instructive that what we tried to do (the systems we put in place, the values that employees were expected to practice) at Cummins in the 1960s is now being touted as paramount for sustaining the foundations on which market capitalism thrives.

### Can Capitalism Be Made More Moral?

I was sometimes complimented and sometimes criticized for my efforts to make capitalism more moral, but there was a growing recognition that Cummins was a different kind of company. The economic downturn of 2008–9 gave rise to new questions about whether capitalism can be made more moral. What surprised many is that a large number of these questions came from businesspeople. George Soros, a billionaire investor, told a group of economists and bankers in 2009 that the philosophy of market fundamentalism was now under question. The economic crisis, he said, has brought an end to the free-market model as we have known it.[6] Bill Gates, like Soros one of the world's richest men, called for a "creative capitalism" in his 2008 speech at the World Economic Forum in Davos. He used the term to emphasize the need to expand capitalism into new areas and to use it to solve problems that previously were assigned to government and philanthropy. The man who is arguably the most successful capitalist of all time and potentially the greatest philanthropist of all time—at least if success is measured by dollars—concluded that since corporations dominate our economic landscape, they must be included in any attempt to solve social problems or contribute to the larger public good. Both Soros and Gates are calling for modern capitalism to integrate doing good into the way corporations do business. They are not suggesting the end of capitalism. They are only arguing that the genius of capitalism lies in its ability to make self-interest serve the wider interest.

Even before the financial crisis exploded in 2008, key government leaders were calling on business to be more moral. French president Nicolas Sarkozy called for the moralization of capitalism, by which he meant a greater sense of social and personal responsibility on the part of business. "I believe in the creative force of capitalism, but I am convinced that capitalism cannot survive without an ethic, without respect for a number of spiritual values, without humanism, without respect for people," the French president said in a February 2007 speech that articulated a critique he subsequently strengthened.[7] The Japanese economic minister introduced the language of tenderhearted capitalism while Gordon Brown, the British prime minister at that time, spoke of the need for free markets that are not value-free markets.

Journalists also joined the debate. The February 16, 2009, issue of *Newsweek* screamed loudly on its cover, "We Are All Socialists Now." At about the same time, the cover of *Time* asked, "What Would Marx Think?" In the latter issue, there was an acknowledgment that while Karl Marx's utopian predictions about revolution and the triumph of socialism were dead wrong and, indeed, many of his policies brought misery to millions, his diagnosis of the underlying problems of a market economy are nevertheless surprisingly relevant today. Even his analysis of globalization's costs and benefits are described as uncannily prescient.

The intellectual debate about how to fix or modify capitalism is not about how to end it. What is emerging is the demand for the new form of moral capitalism we espoused at Cummins years ago. The public is demanding that government play a larger role in guiding the economy toward ends the state deems healthy for the overall well-being of society. Yet what is happening is not a call for new socialism, as some feared, but a rebalancing of the relationship between the market and the public sector. It is not the "compassionate conservatism" we were told reflected a new kind of Republican, but the compassionate capitalism of a new kind of realist. The world is searching for the next economy. Capitalism is entering a new phase in which the major issue has to do with the relationship of the democratic state and the private sector.

Our sense in the 1960s that determining what it means to be responsible should not be left exclusively to the private sector is now winning wide public support. A large number of probusiness policymakers and opinion leaders now confess that while they have long opposed unnecessary regulation of business activity, they are now convinced that only a restoration of the system of checks and balances that once protected the American investor—and that has seriously deteriorated over the years—can restore the confidence that makes financial markets work.

We at Cummins were also ahead of our time in arguing at congressional hearings and public conferences that both government action and corporate self-interest have a role to play in fostering a culture of corporate responsibility. There is now wider recognition of the need for a new generation of managers who understand that being responsible contributes to the bottom line, but we also need public officials who understand that there can be no such thing in a democracy as an unrestrained market.

Benjamin Barber wrote in a *New York Times* op-ed article that business malfeasance is the consequence neither of systematic capitalist contradictions nor private sin. It arises instead from what he describes as "a failure of the instruments of democracy, which have been weakened by three decades of market fundamentalism, privatization ideology and resentment of government."[8] "We have grown too timid as citizens," he argues. There is far too much acquiescence "to deregulation and privatization (airlines, accounting firms, banks, media conglomerates, you name it) and a growing tyranny of money over politics." And thus Barber's summative claim: "Capitalism is not too strong: democracy is too weak."[9]

Are we witnessing the decline of the cult of business, with its prosperity gospel and its worship of wealth? The answer is not altogether clear. Most people would like to acquire wealth for themselves and their families. Yet there is no question that they seek a new social bargain that would see government holding business more responsible for contributing to the public good. The present mood favors the tenderhearted capitalism proposed by the Japanese economic minister and the capitalism with an ethic proposed by the French president. We have come a long way from the 1925 best seller by Bruce Barton titled *The Man Nobody Knows*, which depicted a hard-driving Jesus Christ as "the world's greatest business executive." The mood has changed, and the world is searching not only for the next economy but for a new kind of capitalism and a new kind of capitalist.

## A Market Society

We were ahead of our time in the 1960s in raising questions about the moral limits of markets, but we were responding to one of the most significant changes in American values in the last century. American democracy was changing from having a market economy to being a market society, in which almost everything is for sale. All that is needed is a willing seller and a willing buyer. As Michael J. Sandel points out in his book *What Money Can't Buy*, the difference is this: "A market economy is a tool—a valuable and effective tool for organizing productive activity. A market society is a way of life in which market values seep into every aspect of human endeavor."[10] While there are still some things money can't buy, they are fewer and fewer. Consider these examples identified by Sandel:

- In Santa Ana, California, and some other cities, nonviolent offend-ers can buy a prison cell upgrade. They can pay for better accom-modation—a clean, quiet jail cell away from the cells for nonpaying prisoners.
- There are now concierge doctors, whom patients can pay $1,500 and up per year for their cell phone number.
- The right to immigrate to the United States is being legally sold to those who can afford to pay. Foreigners who invest $500,000 and cre-ate at least ten jobs in an area of high unemployment are eligible for a green card that entitles them to permanent residency.

Sandel has concluded that the reach of markets, and market-oriented think-ing, into aspects of life traditionally governed by nonmarket norms is one of the most serious moral developments of our time. In many places, public police forces are being eclipsed by private security firms ensuring that those with money are the best protected. The proliferation of for-profit schools and the decline in the quality of public education ensures that those with money are the best educated. The outsourcing of war to private military contractors ensures that low-wealth nations are doomed to defeat in violent conflicts, and the sale of naming rights to parks and public spaces has greatly diminished the number of authentic heroes we honor. We are even seeing the outsourc-ing of pregnancy to surrogate mothers in the developing world, and compa-nies and countries buying and selling the right to pollute. Here in the United States, a system of campaign financing that comes close to the buying and selling of elections is eroding our democracy.

We need a debate about public values that allows us to think through the public role of money and markets in our society. We need to ask to what extent it is in the public interest to allow markets to allocate health, education, security, criminal justice, environmental protection, procreation, recreation, and other social goods.

The ends I have long fought for in demanding responsible behavior by business corporations were not just private but also public ends, and should now be the purview of citizens acting publicly through their government as well as business executives acting privately through their corporations. What is being asked of the business community, according to both its critics and those in its ranks who are committed to managing a responsible corporation, is neither extraordinary nor excessive: a decent product at a fair price; honesty in advertising; fair treatment of employees, customers, suppliers, and competitors; a strong sense of responsibility to the communities it inhabits and serves; and a reasonable profit for the financial risk-taking of its stockholders and owners.[11] Robert Wood Johnson, the founder of Johnson and Johnson, argued on behalf of some of his most enlightened colleagues that "the day has passed when business was a private matter—if it ever really was. In a business society, every act of business has social consequences and may arouse public interest. Every time business hires, builds, sells or buys, it is acting for the people as well as for itself, and must be prepared to accept full responsibility."[12]

It was at Cummins that I learned the importance of institutionalizing values that might once have been ad hoc based on who was leading the institution. When Ethisphere Institute named Cummins in 2013 as one of the world's most ethical companies, it was validating not just the values I had helped Irwin Miller and Henry Schacht to inculcate, but all those who have worked over the years to sustain those values.

# CHAPTER 8

# Debating Disinvestment

*A Visit to South Africa*

The calls for capitalism with an ethic were nowhere more pronounced or more passionate than in the 1970s debate about economic disengagement from South Africa. It was a debate that took me to South Africa in 1973 for the first time. The purpose of the visit was to hear directly from those blacks living under apartheid how we in the United States could best support their struggle. Activists inside the country, exiles on the outside, and their allies in both places had tried myriad strategies to bring apartheid to an end, but the entrenched leadership of the apartheid state refused to budge.

Under a state policy of separate development, all members of the African majority were legally regarded as foreigners in their own country, with separately designated areas for each population group. The black African and colored people primarily of mixed race who composed 90 percent of the population were relegated to 13 percent of the land, much of it barren, isolated, and underdeveloped, while the remaining 87 percent was reserved for whites. Blacks and coloreds living in white areas were forcibly removed and resettled in tribal reserves or townships specifically set aside for them. Those entering urban areas for work were regarded as "temporary sojourners" and required to carry a cumbersome passbook at all times. More than two hundred laws were passed to implement this policy of separate development in all areas of South African life.

It was during my freshman year in college that I first heard from one of my professors about the Defiance Campaign in South Africa and the calls for international support. But it was not until much later that I started to take note of the similarities between the young civil rights movement in the Southern United States and the increasing efforts to liberate blacks in South Africa. I was fulfilling my military obligation at Fort Devens in Ayer, Massachusetts, where I had been largely out of touch, when I met students in Boston advocating an economic boycott of South Africa. As I began to ponder the issues under debate, especially who would be helped and who would be harmed, I learned that the local people who would be affected were debating the same issue. Many of them agreed with Nobel Peace Prize laureate Albert Luthuli, the head of the African National Congress (ANC), in his call for an international boycott. Luthuli admitted that an economic boycott would bring about "undoubted hardships for Africans." But he went on to say, "We do not doubt this. But if it is a method that shortens the day of bloodshed, the suffering to us will be a price we are willing to pay."[1]

By the time I joined Cummins in 1970, the debate about disinvestment was heating up, and I was being asked to help inform the debate, both inside the company and in the larger society. The antiapartheid divestment campaign was growing and was often led from the campuses of American universities. Students at Michigan State University in the Midwest, Stanford University on the West Coast, and Columbia University on the East Coast gave the new movement a national focus from the very beginning. Following the divestiture by Michigan State University, the legislature of the State of Michigan voted for divestiture by all of the more than thirty State of Michigan colleges and universities. A Michigan court later struck down the legislation as unconstitutional, but a movement had been launched that came to include colleges and universities in every state. Some built shantytowns on campuses. Others staged protests at trustee meetings, and some occupied the offices of university presidents. The first educational institution to divest completely was Hampshire College in Massachusetts.

National organizations also played a significant role in the divestment campaign. One such organization was TransAfrica, with which I was involved from its founding. The idea of a foreign policy advocacy organization led by African Americans and focusing on the black diaspora was first vetted at a meeting convened in Puerto Rico and funded largely by the Cummins Foundation to discuss support for the liberation movements in South Africa. It was again discussed at a black leadership conference convened by the Congressional Black Caucus in September 1976. Almost a year later, on July 1, 1977, the new organization TransAfrica was formally launched in Washington,

DC, and I was able to provide another grant from Cummins to help the new group to hire Randall Robinson as executive director.

The primary human rights issue that brought us together in Puerto Rico and later in Washington, DC, was the unjust treatment of blacks in South Africa. TransAfrica's activism, legislative campaigns, and strategic media work helped spark and support antiapartheid movements on campuses, in corporate board rooms, and in government centers. The Free Mandela movement in the United States was largely led and kept alive for many years through the work of Randall Robinson and TransAfrica.

My interest in South Africa caught the attention of many of the supporters of the antiapartheid movement in the United States as I became increasingly involved in the debate about disinvestment. It was somehow surprising to many that a black executive at a large Fortune 500 company was taking the disinvestment side of the debate rather than joining the internationally respected Leon Sullivan in calling for companies to remain engaged, but to sign a statement of what became known as the Sullivan Principles. Leon Sullivan was a black minister who served on the board of General Motors. His opposition to disinvestment made him very popular in much of the business community.

I was invited to South Africa in 1973 by the United States–South Africa Leadership Exchange Program (USSALEP) because of my efforts as a foundation executive to interest other foundations in helping to develop a new generation of leaders for the region, rather than because of my public statements about disinvestment. As it turned out, the position of the organization and many of the leaders invited seemed to be in support of "constructive engagement," not disengagement. I suspect that there was some hope that I would have second thoughts after meeting with prominent South Africans like Helen Suzman, the liberal member of Parliament, and Chief Buthelezi, the head of the KwaZulu homeland, who both opposed separate development but supported the government's position that divestment would hurt the people we were trying to help.

At about the same time, Cummins was invited to submit a tender to manufacture or assemble diesel engines in South Africa. After some discussion with Henry Schacht and other senior executives at Cummins, it was decided that I should add some extra days to my itinerary and use them to examine and report back to Cummins on whether it was possible to operate in South Africa without violating company values. In my position as head of the Corporate Action Division, my staff and I were frequently dispatched to other regions of the world to examine whether the political, economic, and social climate would enable the company to operate in accordance with its corporate values if we chose to enter that market.

At the time of my visit to South Africa, July 25–August 10, 1973, a great debate was also taking place in the African American community about whether blacks should visit South Africa in any capacity, whether as athletes, entertainers, or activists. My credentials as an activist who not only actively opposed apartheid but who raised money to support the liberation struggles in South Africa were well known; so I decided that my ability to make the case to policymakers and opinion leaders for changes in U.S. policy toward South Africa would be enhanced by direct interaction with the people of South Africa.

Official statistics and scholarly analysis of how South Africans were living, where they were working, what they were earning, even the political reports of exiles, were readily available, but the state of the collective psyche, the country's sociological state, and the myriad components that constitute culture, shape the national ethos, and lead to resistance and resilience among the most oppressed were not to be found in either published or private reports. It needed, for me at least, to be grasped both intellectually and intuitively, observed from within as well as studied in detachment. I knew that this was not what the South African government had in mind in granting me a visa, but I decided to see for myself whether real listening and learning were possible, knowing full well the professional risk and personal dangers this implied.

I did not know many of the people with whom I would be traveling nor the positions they took on the issues under debate in South Africa and the United States, so I added an additional week and more interviews to my visit to ensure that I would not be treated to only one side of the debate. Since I was traveling under the umbrella of USSALEP and as a vice president of a diesel engine manufacturing company, the representatives of the apartheid state agreed, probably reluctantly, to grant me additional travel and interviews.

### Arriving in Johannesburg

The arrival at the Johannesburg airport was my first introduction to what I could expect. On the plane I had been reading a report on economic engagement with South Africa that concluded foreign trade was propping up the system of apartheid and exploiting black labor to maintain the wealth, power, and prestige of whites. The report concluded also that sanctions and divestment were the only way to undermine the exploitation of blacks under apartheid.

The face of the customs agent who fingered through my luggage suddenly turned red when he saw what I had been reading. He took the report out and called several nearby agents to show them what I was bringing into South Africa. They laughed and spoke to each other in Afrikaans. The report was confiscated, which was standard practice, to keep outside critiques of the apartheid system far away from both black and white South Africans. But after double checking my visa information, they let me go, much to my relief.

Once outside the airport, I saw a land of unusual beauty, a place of gracious living and hard work—with the former enjoyed by whites and most of the latter provided by blacks. During the weeks that followed, I talked to a wider cross-section of people, toured more industrial plants, visited more universities, and saw more places than most South Africans do in a lifetime. It was a widely accepted practice, often supported by legal requirements, for white South Africans to restrict their social contact to members of their own group and to relate to other groups only on a circumscribed basis. To my surprise, there was minimal contact between Afrikaners and English-speaking citizens as well as black and colored Africans. The English driver transporting us through an Afrikaner area made comments as disparaging of the Afrikaner culture and traditions as any I heard about Africans.

Of course, insulting comments about black Africans were infused into the narrative of some of our hosts in language they apparently did not consider offensive. Sadly, it was too easily tolerated by some members of the USSALEP delegation. After hearing a resource person, considered progressive by some in our group, repeatedly refer to the "natives" as "kaffirs," I objected and threatened to walk out of the meeting. I was later criticized by some of my American colleagues for violating the hospitality of "these fine people." But the speaker later apologized and invited me to his room to continue the conversation. Overhearing the invitation and realizing I was about to accept it, an African American member of the delegation who was tall and muscular said he would accompany me. He said nothing during our conversation upstairs in the hotel, but his imposing presence kept the conversation civil (and me safe).

The best description of South Africa as I saw it in 1973 was "pigmentocracy," a racial autocracy in which rights and responsibilities are apportioned in accordance with the pigmentation of the skin: whites had exclusive power and privileges; the coloreds and Asians had a very few; and the Africans had none. This system of minority rule was distinguished by its ban on the majority from rising above a dependency status, no matter what their gifts or qualifications, while ensuring to all whites certain automatic privileges.

The visits to the universities reminded us that population groups were also educated separately, and with the same inequalities found in other sectors of the society. There were four university centers of influence among Afrikaners, but Stellenbosch University was considered the cradle of their political party and a critical think tank for refining and defending their public philosophy. Afrikaners tended to look up to intellectuals. The title of professor was probably the most revered in the Afrikaner community. At the same time, intellectuals were often accused of not being practical in political affairs, especially if they suggested tinkering with apartheid to make it less oppressive. I found this to be especially true of those who put more emphasis on development and less on separation. There seemed to be little inclination toward agitation for complete change in the policy of racial domination.

I met with faculty members from the University of Natal, one of the major English universities at the time. In 2004, it merged with the University of Durban-Westville, but at the time of my visit, the most outspoken and one of the most prominent faculty members was Dr. Fatima Meir, an Indian sociologist. My public visit to the Indian university near Durban was unproductive. I was not allowed to see any students, but this was just one of several times I made alternative private arrangements. I met a faculty member who agreed to set up a late evening meeting with some of the more outspoken students. Many of them were beginning to identify with other blacks, and I heard considerable talk of trying to revive the Indian National Congress, which was a product of Mahatma Gandhi's passive resistance campaign in Natal some years earlier. I was not surprised when later, during our visit elsewhere, we learned that the students at the Indian university had staged a mass protest in support of students at the colored university who were being harassed because of their involvement in the black consciousness movement.

The faculty members with whom I met at the University of the Western Cape, established for colored students, were mostly white. One exception was Jakes Gerwel, a colored lecturer who wore an Afro and liked to quote Malcolm X. He referred to a rise of black consciousness "among the bruin [brown] Afrikaner" as a new phenomenon to be reckoned with in the society. This seemed somewhat surprising, even disturbing, to some of our hosts, who were trying to persuade us that the nonwhite groups disliked each other and liked the idea of separate development. The high priest of black consciousness among the colored population was Robert Small, who along with Jakes was a colored lecturer at the so-called colored university controlled and dominated by Afrikaners.

Jakes Gerwel went on to later become the head of the University of the Western Cape and was recognized internationally as one of the foremost scholars on Afrikaans literature. When I returned to South Africa in 1996 as the new U.S. ambassador, I was pleased to see him again, but this time he was the chief of staff to President Nelson Mandela and one of the architects of the new democracy. Jakes grew up in the Cape Province where most coloreds still live. Under apartheid it was designated a colored preference area and enjoyed more benefits than areas reserved for blacks. Most of the so-called coloreds originated in miscegenation between the earlier settlers and slaves, but their race classification included Malays, Hottentots, and the group referred to, often disparagingly, as Bushmen. Some of the Afrikaners I met admitted privately that they felt more in common with the coloreds than the English South Africans they despised. While the younger coloreds we met at the University of the Western Cape tended to identify with the black consciousness movement, the colored community was divided, publicly, right down the middle, between those who wanted to be accepted as brown Afrikaners and those who insisted on identification with their "black brothers and sisters."

Each major city in South Africa was surrounded by African townships that were in reality black dormitories to provide cheap labor for whites living in urban areas. The largest was Soweto, where I made several visits. The first was with the USSALEP group, when we met with township counselors, who were elected by the people in elections conducted in accordance with ethnic groupings. They served three-year terms but had no executive powers, serving in an advisory capacity as intermediaries between the white government and the people of Soweto. While some of our hosts expected them to brief us on how well this worked, the counselors rose one by one to reject the concept of separate development and of the dividing of black groups according to tribal heritage. The mayor of Soweto, whose position was not to be confused with real executive power, pointed out that "the idea comes from white people."

My general impression of life in Soweto was that it was a refined system of oppression of the worse kind, a highly regulated existence of more than a million people. And while the counselors had taken some risks to tell us what they thought of apartheid, I wanted to find out how much further a private conversation without the Afrikaner overlords present would go, so I made arrangements to sneak out of my hotel later that evening to meet with a different group of leaders. Twenty-four blacks showed up who were more militant and very articulate. Their spirits clearly had not been broken by the system of apartheid. They were warm and cheerful, and like the blacks I met elsewhere were eager to speak to a black American. There was always a clear identification with our struggle in the United States.

As we moved to the issues that concerned them, members of the Soweto group were especially angered by the fact that parents had no say in the education of their children. Their greatest complaint, even greater than the concerns about a curriculum designed to stifle rather than promote intellectual growth, was the whites' insistence on the use of ethnic language as the medium of instruction in elementary schools. Several emphasized that English was the language of the modern world, and without it their children would have no possibility of competing successfully in the marketplace. They lamented the absence of land tenure rights and the prohibition of ownership of even the land on which they lived, even though they lived in an all-black township. All housing was on a rental basis, keeping in line with the conceptual fiction that they were foreigners and, therefore, temporary sojourners.

I was told that while education was free for white children, the parents of African children in Soweto had to pay a school tax as well as provide funds for uniforms for school-aged children. Since it was government policy that high schools and colleges should be established only in the homelands, thousands of children were deprived of the opportunity to further their education.

The government made every effort possible to discourage the development of a cross-tribal black nationalism in places like Soweto while encouraging a nationalism based on tribal identity in the black homelands, where they hoped it would be easier to guide and control. Until 1948, white South Africans had regarded Africans as one race set apart, but with the coming of an official and more rigid apartheid they insisted that there were seven to eight different nations, and they should therefore live in homelands according to ethnic or tribal groupings. The three most advanced of the so-called homelands at the time of my visit were KwaZulu, Bophuthatswana, and the Transkei.

I had numerous conversations with Chief Buthelezi of KwaZulu, Chief Mongope of Bophuthatswana, and Chief Mantanziamia of the Transkei. Each appeared to be trying to make the best of artificial political constructions by the white apartheid government, but they also had other agendas that led to a personal investment in the system. The residents of Bophuthatswana, for example, were of the same tribe as the people living in the independent country of Botswana north of South Africa, and Mongope expressed a desire for the national unity of all Swana people. He supported the apartheid-sanctioned homeland as a step he hoped would lead to a union with Botswana.

I was able to travel across KwaZulu with Chief Buthelezi, who at that time enjoyed a close relationship to the apartheid government leaders, who saw him as a potential ally in seeking to make the artificial institutions of separate development work. Officially, however, Buthelezi was clear in his opposition to separate development, an enigma to those of us trying to find out what he really thought and felt about the issues under debate. When I was attacked by white South Africans in response to a speech I made in Durban about black empowerment, a well-dressed black man stood up and commented, "I agree with everything my brother has just said." That was how I first met Buthelezi and also how I came to be traveling with him to see his homeland.

His so-called homeland was made up of twenty-three townships with more than two hundred fragments of land. Each fragment was surrounded by white areas. While Buthelezi bragged of having a legislative assembly since 1972, authority was very much entrenched in the white minister of "Bantu affairs." As part of the attempt to cultivate a good relationship with Buthelezi, KwaZulu was reasonably well served with roads and public transport facilities. While the population was not self-supporting, many were engaged in productive work that took advantage of KwaZulu's rivers, fertile lands, and other natural assets.

With South African business dominated and largely controlled by English-speaking whites, I found it useful to meet with some of the most distinguished and wealthiest, including Harry Oppenheimer, chairman of Anglo American Corporation. Oppenheimer symbolized the dual realities of those sometimes described as progressive businessmen. A regular critic of formal apartheid, he had probably done more than anyone else to fuel the economic machine upon which the strength of white supremacy depended. He was a driving force behind the Urban Foundation, which described its goals as "contributing to the establishment of a society founded on justice and the explicit recognition of the dignity and freedom of individuals." Yet in private one of the black leaders with whom I met criticized his philanthropy as "a pacifying cosmetic, seeking greater flexibility in the apartheid system so as to make more effective use of black labor." Anglo American employed more than 150,000 blacks, who helped the country control the world's diamond market, but even the best intentions of Harry Oppenheimer were often frustrated by the system of apartheid, which controlled what black workers earned in wages, how they lived as so-called foreign workers, and even, to the dismay of many, the environment in which they worked.

In addition to meeting with business executives in elegant settings not normally available to blacks, I visited eight different plants to talk directly with plant managers, human resource executives, and people on the floor (where I could) to help determine whether Cummins could operate in accordance with its values in this social, economic, and political milieu. The first and most obvious impediment was a system of job reservations. Certain categories of jobs were reserved through agreements with white labor unions for members of their unions only. The shortage of skilled white labor led some companies to use deceptive practices to train and utilize black workers in prohibited jobs, many specifically identified by government regulations. I met with one company manager who had been fined by the government on two separate occasions in the last year, but who continued deceptive practices for work assignments, although not for wages, because he needed black labor in order to be productive and profitable.

A second impediment was in education, where black institutions were prohibited from teaching math and science. Moreover, students studied European history while their own history was either ignored or stereotyped and ridiculed. I visited one of the remote black universities where almost 100 percent of the graduates majored in biblical studies. The one notable exception, based on a tradition that preceded formal apartheid, was Fort Hare, located in a rural area so isolated that even representatives of the Ministry of Bantu Affairs rarely visited. Founded in 1916, it had a long history of offering Western-style education, with its own shortcomings of course, to students from across sub-Saharan Africa, creating an African elite until it was more closely controlled and regulated by the apartheid state beginning in 1959. But even with its reclassification as a Bantustan college in the black homeland of Ciskei, there was much antiapartheid activity during the struggle years, including the black consciousness movement led by Steve Biko.

A third impediment to Cummins practicing company values was the restriction against integrated gatherings. This controlled how and where black workers were fed as well as their ability to participate in the social outlets often used to provide extra meaning and fulfillment to work.

The English-speaking white South Africans I met did not share the Afrikaners' political passion. Their enthusiasm was for financial success, material comfort, and sports. There was a sports nationalism, with the English preferring cricket, the Afrikaners rugby, and the Africans soccer. This closely matched the division in politics, where it was frequently said that the English-speaking white South African thinks Progressive Party, votes United Party, and gives thanks to the National Party for controlling the political sector while allowing the English to dominate the business sector. But like the Afrikaner, the English had three basic fears, sometimes acknowledged but even when unacknowledged clearly evident: the black threat, communism (often described as terrorism), and those they simply called thugs. As a group, the English formed the upper level of the white aristocracy, an elite of the most privileged. They predominated in urban areas and looked down their nose at the rural Afrikaner, whom they despised.

I found South Africa to be a living monument to the errors of Karl Marx's analyses about where power lies in a society. The key "means of production, distribution and exchange" were in the hands of white English-speaking South Africans, who were said to control more than 85 percent of industrial capital and an even larger percentage of the private sector. Yet they had no chance of wresting political power from the Afrikaners. After a number of years of ineffectual disquiet about apartheid, especially job reservations, English leaders had come increasingly to "mind their own business," which was, of course, the economic activity of the country. It had become the nature of business to make accommodation with the government for its own well-being. Some expressed privately a fear that African politics might be far more disruptive of their economic interests than apartheid.

The political center and controlling political power in the 1970s may have seemed to outsiders to be the National Party, but there was a smaller group called the Broederbond who developed and sustained the policies the party implemented. Every prime minister and state president in South Africa from 1948, the beginning of formal apartheid, to the final abandonment in 1994 when Nelson Mandela became president, was a member of the Afrikaner Broederbond, an Afrikaans term meaning "league of Afrikaner brothers." I met with several members of the group, who sought to portray themselves as more like a think tank in the United States, but the organization's main aim was to further Afrikaner nationalism in South Africa, to maintain Afrikaner culture, develop an Afrikaner economy, and maintain Afrikaner control of the South African government. The group sought to operate quietly and secretively through public front organizations, but in some circles even to mention the word Broederbond was to raise great fear.

While blacks had no political power, it was clear that they were politically active in ways that caused great concern to even those whites most critical of separate development. With the ANC and all of the politically active groups banned, some of the whites with whom I met referred to the newly formed Black People's Convention as an organization catering to the interest of black people. It was formed as an umbrella organization of existing member groups and announced in its initial press statement that false impressions had been created that it was unlawful for blacks to form political movements and to engage in political activity unless such political activity had been approved by white society and its government. The committee argued, therefore, that it was working toward the formation of a black people's political movement whose primary aim was to unite and solidify black people (African, colored, and Indian) with a view to liberating and emancipating them from both political and physical oppression.

The Black People's Convention turned out to be primarily an educational group, but in bringing blacks together it helped make the transition to the more militant groups that increased the intensity and scope of the opposition to apartheid in later years. The student embrace across the color divide of apartheid was most evident in the work of the South African Student Organization, and while the ANC was banned, many of those seeking changes inside South Africa were closet supporters and sympathizers. At the same time, the ANC was gaining increasing traction outside South Africa as a legitimate representative of black South African aspirations and a strongly supported voice for conveying the will of the people. While many of the South Africans I met seemed unaware, or pretended to be unaware, of the winds of change blowing through the townships, the so-called homelands, the black universities, and the churches, it was clear to me that time was running out for separate development, both as a political philosophy and as a public process for governing.

### Back in the United States

I left South Africa persuaded that I had made the right decision to visit the country and that I was now better equipped to fight for policy changes by the U.S. government in its relationship to this pariah state now condemned by most of the world. I had traveled widely and met with a cross section of black, white, Indian, colored, and white leaders and it was clear that despite the many intentional violations of the humanity of the black population, the spirit of black South Africa had not been broken. I could now report that everywhere I went, blacks were outspoken in their opposition to apartheid, and aggressive in affirming their own self-consciousness and pride in their heritage. It was also clear that the so-called homelands were artificial constructions with no chance of ever becoming economically viable under apartheid and that while most of the blacks I met acknowledged that economic sanctions against South Africa could be painful, it was a price they were willing to pay.

In a written report and briefing for the board and management of Cummins, I argued that South Africa was on a collision course that the cosmetic changes under way could not help avoid, and that should a collision come, a major battleground was likely to be industry; for one of the only real powers of blacks was the ability to withhold their labor. I analyzed the conditions that Cummins would have to meet and the values we would have to violate if we chose to operate in South Africa, and the board decided that this was not a business we wanted.

South Africa was now in my blood, and I took advantage of every opportunity to support the antiapartheid movement and to educate the American public about why it was not in the national self-interest to continue to be engaged. Constructive engagement had been tried but failed to change either white attitudes or government practices.

Cummins had another encounter with South Africa that strongly tested its principles. This time it was through the corporate giving program. I was approached by a representative of exiles living in the United States requesting foundation support for a documentary film that was to be made clandestinely in South Africa about business exploitation of African workers. As head of the Cummins foundation and an officer of the company, I carefully considered whether this was the best way to expose apartheid to the American public. In order to minimize controversy and yet do the maximum good, I decided that while a grant could help greatly in educating the American people about South Africa, it should be anonymous. When the documentary *Last Grave at Dimbaza* was completed and shown on PBS, the public television network in the United States, the Cummins Foundation was given bold credits at the end of the film. This caused quite a stir in the business community, with powerful influences arguing that I should be fired. Representatives of the South African government even contacted company executives to suggest that I was a discredit to the company. Irwin Miller not only stood behind the grant but replied that I was a credit to both the company and the United States. His sister, Clementine Tangeman, who owned a large share of the company, even called to say that if her brother gave me any grief to let her know. She assured me that she was 100 percent behind the grant.

The knowledge gained from my visit to South Africa and the passion of my argument for actively opposing apartheid led to many invitations to share my thoughts with foundation boards and staff as well as religious and civic groups. On one such occasion, after speaking to the board of the Kaiser Family Foundation shortly after the release of Nelson Mandela from prison, Barbara Jordan, a member of the board who had been widely respected as a member of the U.S. Congress, said to me, "You should be our ambassador to South Africa."

Over the succeeding years, the pressure from campuses and constituencies mobilized by civic activists helped generate major victories, with decisions by many private and public institutions not to invest in financial institutions doing business in South Africa. In 1986, Congress passed the Comprehensive Anti-Apartheid Act. President Ronald Reagan vetoed the legislation, but a coalition of both Republicans and Democrats overrode his veto, and the legislation banned all new U.S. investments in South Africa, bank loans, and sales to the police and military. The act also prohibited the import of agricultural goods, textiles, shellfish, steel, iron, uranium, and the products of state-owned corporations. In 1987, the Budget Reconciliation Act included an amendment by Representative Charles Rangel, ending the ability of U.S. firms investing in South Africa to claim tax credits in the United States.

President Ronald Reagan continued to advocate for constructive engagement. John Major, the British leader, agreed with opponents of disinvestment strategies who argued that these strategies would feed white consciences outside South Africa, not black bellies within.[2] But the tide had turned. Both the demands from inside South Africa and the pressures from outside caused a rethinking of separate development as state policy. Nelson Mandela was released after twenty-seven years of incarceration in 1990, and four years later he was elected president of the new democracy. In 1996, as I describe in chapter 11, I was nominated by President Bill Clinton and confirmed by the U.S. Senate as the U.S. ambassador to South Africa.

......................

# CHAPTER 9

# The Carter Administration

*Private Wants and Public Needs*

Nowhere is the interplay between public values and private virtue reflected more clearly than in the competing demands for the use of the resources of the earth. Much of my four years (1977–1981) as the undersecretary of the interior in the Carter administration were spent trying to reconcile the competing claims of myriad stakeholders to our natural resources. Indians on the reservation and non-Indians upstream wanted the same water. Coal miners and park enthusiasts wanted the same mountain. Oil drillers and fishermen wanted control of the same stretch of the ocean. Historic preservationists and urban developers wanted title to the same historic landmark. Eskimos wanted to hunt the bowhead whale as part of a ritual to preserve their culture, while environmentalists wanted to greatly limit the hunt in order to preserve an endangered species. These were major public policy issues having to do with our stewardship of the earth's resources, how decisions are made about their use, and who benefits.

It was partly to help resolve these largely ethical issues that I accepted the invitation of the newly elected president, Jimmy Carter, to join his administration at the beginning of 1977. As a candidate, he had promised, if elected, to bring new faces to government. I had not expected to be one of those faces. But here I was a few months after his inauguration at a confirmation hearing in the hallowed chambers of the U.S. Senate as the president's nominee to be a senior executive in his administration.

It was a time of considerable public concern about ethics in government. Ministers were preaching about it. Journalists were writing about it. Congress was legislating about it, and citizens of all political persuasions were demanding it. It seemed like just the right time for someone with my concern about public values to enter government.

The hearing went smoothly. I was queried on the many aspects of public policy for which I would be responsible, but I soon found my nomination embroiled in a controversy between some members of the Senate and the president about water projects in the West. It was an illuminating welcome to Washington and my first introduction to an issue that was to hang over my head for all of my four years in the Carter administration. In February 1977, just before I joined the administration, President Carter had announced that he planned to veto nineteen federal water projects in a dozen Western states. He found, however, that water politics was more powerful in Washington, DC, than it had been in Georgia, where as governor he had vetoed one of them.

The threat of a veto galvanized some powerful Western senators against him and made life uncomfortable for those of us in the Interior Department who had oversight of water affairs. House Speaker Tip O'Neill proposed a compromise—to suspend the projects rather than veto them—but it was a year later before the president signed a bill canceling some of the most egregious projects.

It was at the early stage of the debate that I was confirmed, was sworn in, and took office as the number two executive in a department with 80,000 employees, a $6 billion budget, and some of the most intriguing questions in government about how to determine the public good. For four years, ethics and values would inform what I did and how I did it.

As the new undersecretary, I was asked to share responsibility with Cecil Andrus, the former governor of Idaho and newly confirmed secretary, for managing almost one-third of the land area of the United States with huge coal, oil shale, and alternative energy resources; for overseeing the exploration and development of petroleum on approximately one billion acres of submerged lands in the ocean; for providing services to more than four hundred Indian tribes and Eskimo villages as well as people living in the Virgin Islands, Guam, Samoa, and the two thousand Micronesian islands scattered over three million square miles of ocean in the South Pacific; for administering several hundred parks and recreation units; and for managing water projects that served as the lifeblood of many Western states.

Among the issues waiting for me after confirmation were the now infamous water projects. The Department of the Interior had been given lead responsibility for the presidential review with assistance provided by the Army Corps of Engineers, the Tennessee Valley Authority, the Office of Management and Budget, and the Council on Environmental Quality. The decision-making process was my introduction to how extensive public reviews can be. Thirty-two projects were subjected to public hearings that were both contentious and illuminating. The analysis and interaction among government agencies were sometimes equally contentious, but in the end the president was able to announce his decision. He recommended the deletion of funds from the federal budget for eighteen projects, at a total savings of $2.5 billion, and the modification of five projects at a total savings of $1.5 billion.

I learned from the water project analysis how much I would have to work with others in the Carter administration to develop or implement policy. The newspapers were often full of disparaging commentary about the Carter staff, especially isolated incidents like the president's chief of staff pouring amaretto and cream down the back of a female companion. But the people with whom I worked at the White House were very serious, hard-working public servants. One of my favorite and most respected was Stu Eizenstat, who was President Carter's chief domestic policy advisor. He was the man through whom all domestic policy had to flow. He came to Washington with a strong track record in supporting liberal causes and liberal candidates, but it was his impressive combination of intellectual gifts that stood out. He was a part of the Georgia mafia that came to the White House with the president, but he was a Phi Beta Kappa graduate of the University of North Carolina and a graduate of the Harvard Law School who had cut his teeth in politics in the campaigns of two of my personal friends, Andrew Young and Maynard Jackson, two black mayors of Atlanta. He brought with him the ability to comprehend and assimilate huge quantities of information and to integrate them into very pragmatic, value-driven recommendations.

There were many internal debates in the administration about public policy, but Stu always seemed to understand the needs of those population groups who had been traditionally left out of policy deliberations at his level of engagement. His policy recommendations seemed always to be grounded in a highly developed ethic that understood the imperatives of justice, fair play, and equal opportunity. Nowhere was this more evident than in the internal administration debate about what came to be regarded as one of the most important issues to be brought before the U.S. courts in the twentieth century. In 1977, many Americans were moving toward the political right and there was talk of a new conservatism fueled largely by issues of race. African Americans had voted overwhelmingly in favor of President Carter, and many religious and political leaders in the black community had gone far out on a limb urging their constituencies to support this Southern governor. So when the famed Bakke case challenged affirmative action at the University of California, many voices demanded that the Carter administration submit an amicus brief on the side of the university. None of us regarded Griffin Bell, the attorney general, as a likely champion for racial equality, so we were greatly pleased when we learned that Vice President Walter Mondale and Stu Eizenstat were very involved in briefing the president and preparing a recommendation.

Bakke argued that he had been the victim of reverse discrimination because of race, because the medical school had accepted minority students with lower grades. Jewish groups, who had long been our allies on civil rights, came out in support of Bakke. Some argued that the practices used at the University of California would greatly damage the fabric of the American society. Black groups countered that taking the side of Bakke and portraying affirmative action as racial quotas would sabotage black advances far into the future. The case heightened public consciousness of the government's commitment to affirmative action, although polls were showing that an overwhelming majority of Americans regarded affirmative action as reverse discrimination and were opposed to it. Showing leadership on an issue at the very heart of American values, the president personally entered the discourse, pledging that he would not turn his back on two hundred years of discrimination against blacks. He sought also to make it clear that affirmative action and quotas were two different approaches to equality of opportunity and that while he was against quotas he was strongly in favor of affirmative action, which ironically was put in place by Republican president Richard Nixon.

The strained relationship between blacks and Jews led to disappointments and even dismay by some on both sides, but most continued to work together to tackle other issues of mutual concern. As someone who had not known Jimmy Carter or any of his key staff before my appointment, I was now proud to be a part of his administration and to be able to support the public values we shared in common. But this emphasis on public values was very different from the regulatory ethics of government, mostly paperwork designed to control individual behavior.

When I arrived in the Department of the Interior, I received a letter from the "ethics counselor" reminding me of the Ethics in Government Act of 1978, which mandated certain procedural requirements for federal executives. Enclosed were Standard Form 278 and Supplemental Form DI-278, as well as Form DI-211 (revised) and DI-211(b), each to be filled out in at least six copies. I was also informed that as undersecretary I would be required to annually assure the public that I was meeting the requirements of the Sunshine in

Government provisions of the Federal Land Policy and Management Act, the Outer Continental Shelf Lands Act, the Mining in the Parks Act, the Energy Policy and Conservation Act, and others.

In making decisions about what serves the public good, the regulatory ethics of public management are obviously necessary but severely limited. Ethicists like Aristotle, Aquinas, and the Niebuhr brothers would have difficulty relating this formal institutional process to their concern for discovering and serving a universal good. Yet my theological training and my exposure to the moral teachings of some of the great men and women in moral philosophy did not seem to help very much either. As I started to tackle the issues of the department and the political controversies they spawned, I began to wonder whether I had made a wise decision to leave the comforts and the far more lucrative incentives of the private sector for the rough-and-tumble world of national government.

How did all this happen? Had I been seduced by the trappings of power, the intrigue of early morning cabinet meetings at the White House when Cecil Andrus was out of town, the glamour of my large paneled office at Interior built by Harold Ickes, a powerful secretary of the interior in earlier times? No, it was simpler than that. Andrew Young, a good friend who was at that time a congressman from Georgia, and I were having breakfast at a conference in Lesotho in December 1976 when the subject of the Carter election came up. He asked if I would consider serving in Washington if invited. My response was an unequivocal no. I asked him the same question. He said no also. A few weeks later we were both in the Carter administration.

Our being in South Africa together was a coincidence at the time, but our interest in the region was to play a large role in our future work. We were in Lesotho just a few months after the 1976 rebellion in Soweto that saw very young children leave their homes for a life in exile. Some headed to this landlocked country surrounded by South Africa and nicknamed the Kingdom in the Sky. It was in reality a kingdom of hills, plateaus, and mountains, a place where chilly skies linger over snow-covered mountains as well as lush green and barren mountains. While the breathtakingly beautiful mountains were obviously a tough place to live, some of the young exiles found their way to remote highland areas where herd boys as young as five spend long periods away from home tending sheep and cattle. Most were simply passing through, however, in hopes of finding safety from the South African police and support from antiapartheid activists who might help them make the transition outside South Africa.

I had not known nor campaigned for Jimmy Carter, so I was somewhat surprised when I was invited to Washington by his transition team to discuss a position in his administration. I respectfully declined, but Leo Krulitz, my neighbor in Columbus, Indiana, who was soon to become solicitor of the Department of the Interior, urged me to talk to his friend Cecil Andrus, the governor of Idaho who had been tapped to be secretary of the interior. I agreed to meet with Andrus (Cece, as he was affectionately known in Idaho) and liked him immediately. I was flattered when he said he would like to recommend me to the president for the job as undersecretary (now called deputy secretary). After the usual vetting by the White House and intelligence units, a formal offer was made and, after much research on the public issues with which I would be dealing and the department I would be helping to manage, I accepted. Following official nomination, a comprehensive security investigation, and a confirmation hearing before the U.S. Senate, I was confirmed and sworn in. It was the first of three presidential appointments requiring Senate hearings over the next two decades, so I was a little anxious about what in my past (especially my antiwar activities in the 1960s) might surface. I was introduced at the hearings by two senators whose conservative credentials blunted any allegations that I might be too liberal. The highly regarded Richard Lugar, a conservative Republican senator with whom I had worked in Indiana, and Bennett Johnston, a conservative democratic senator from my home state of Louisiana, introduced me at the hearing and vouched for my fitness and competence. The rest was history.

The only problem to surface was from a liberal senator who wanted to know why I was going into the Department of the Interior rather than one of the social service agencies where I could do more good "for my people."

I came to realize soon after assuming my responsibilities that while government regulations as microethics had serious drawbacks, they were, nevertheless, an important form of social discipline when developed openly and implemented fairly. While we are in continuing need of an ethic that bases our uses of the earth's resources on qualities of prudence, moderation, and responsibility to the future, we also need nationally enforceable standards. The inquiry at my hearing about the social good of those disadvantaged because of race or economic marginalization had helped to more finely tune my sensitivity about who benefits from the policies governing the use of natural resources, so this was always a major consideration in my approach to the making of public policy. The role of government in shaping environmental policies is primarily to provide authority, to set standards, to ensure fairness, and to raise the level of consciousness about natural resource conflicts and their resolution.

There were some Americans who argued that public policy and the management of water affairs as well as natural resource extraction should be the responsibility of local governments rather than federal agencies. The debate became so intense that it led to a movement called the Sagebrush Rebellion. At the height of its intensity, I was invited to appear on the television program *60 Minutes* to present the Carter administration view that these resources as well as the crown jewels set aside for national parks belonged to all Americans and should be administered on behalf of all Americans.

The need for a higher authority arises not only because multiple publics assert different views of the public interest but because different claimants often appeal to the same authority. Each may argue that nature, science, patriotism, or even God is on their side. It is to adjudicate these competing claims that public policies are developed that set limits, prescribe behavior, and define social balance. Closely related to the need for authority is the need for legitimacy. Regulations are not usually developed by fiat. In the Carter administration, we subjected them to various forms of regulatory analysis to determine economic and social impact as well as consistency with legislative intent. Public hearings were held and proposed regulations made available for public comment while still in draft form.

I found the 1977 executive order reforming the process of issuing regulations especially useful in meeting the regulatory responsibilities of the Department of the Interior in managing natural resources and setting environmental policy. The order required each agency to write in plain English (no small accomplishment), facilitate public participation, analyze the economic and environmental impact of costly regulations and assess alternative approaches, and subject key regulations to sunset review each year.

My encounter with the limitations of regulatory ethics became even more intense when I discovered that it was my responsibility as undersecretary of the interior to identify and implement appropriate safeguards for the exploration and transportation of oil in Alaska. Passions were aroused and many different groups sought to argue that they alone represented the public interest. While the focus came to be on the Arctic National Wildlife Refuge, the issue of oil—protecting the environment and ensuring broad public benefit—was at the top of the pile of papers waiting for me on my first day as the new undersecretary. When told that I had direct responsibility for the Alaska pipeline office and was expected to appear before a congressional oversight committee in two weeks to verify the integrity of the newly constructed pipeline, I requested a briefing from Interior Department experts.

I was dismayed to learn that in the clearing of the decks of political appointees that occurs during times of transition from one political party to another, one of the major authorities on the subject had been given his walking papers. I immediately called him back and over time he became one of my senior deputies. My next step was to talk to both the environmentalists who were worried about the impact of the pipeline on the delicate tundra and the huge caribou herd, and representatives of the oil industry who were confident that sufficient precautions had been built into the construction of the pipeline.

When neither group provided the assurance I needed, I decided to go to Alaska to find out for myself. It was winter and my preference would have been to traverse the treacherous terrain of ice and snow at a time more fitting to my Southern temperament. I did not have that luxury, however, and went to Alaska anyway. While I thought I had seen cold weather as a young military officer at Fort Devens in Massachusetts and Camp Drum in upstate New York, it was in Alaska that I found out what it really means to be cold.

Dressed with every piece of cold weather apparel I could find for temperatures forty degrees below zero, I traveled the pipeline from Prudhoe Bay to Valdez, stopping at critical points of pipeline control and crew camps for observation and briefings. I also met with the governor of Alaska, local business leaders, environmentalists, and representatives of the Alaska Federation of Natives. I learned enough to conclude that it was indeed possible to balance the conflicting claims of two important stakeholders of the department, the petroleum industry and environmentalists. I went before Congress and testified that the necessary safeguards were in place to now permit the flow of oil through the new pipeline.

The Alaska pipeline issue turned out to be merely a dress rehearsal for the storm that came to center on the Carter administration's efforts to preserve and expand the Arctic National Wildlife Refuge. Once again the battle lines were drawn and the Interior Department was charged with navigating politically dangerous waters. In 1960, the year after Alaska became a state, President Dwight D. Eisenhower had designated an area of 8.9 million acres as a wildlife refuge. President Carter wanted not only to keep the area protected but to double its size.

Cecil Andrus, the secretary of the interior, was given the responsibility for putting together a coalition both within the administration and among concerned citizen groups to pursue this top national priority. Those who wanted to open the area to oil drilling argued that drilling in the refuge would lessen the nation's dependence on foreign oil, which accounted for 57 percent of domestic consumption. Opponents led by Cece Andrus and a special working group that filled the offices surrounding the beautiful executive suite where Cece and I were located, responded that this crown jewel of the American ecosystem must be viewed from a larger perspective than our insatiable appetite for oil. It belonged not simply to the present generation but to succeeding generations who would not forgive us for spoiling this national treasure rather than seriously pursuing other energy policy options such as conservation, efficiency, and the development of alternatives to burning fossil fuels. Moreover, 95 percent of the North Slope of Alaska was already open to oil drilling.

In 1980, after considerable debate and hard work by all of us involved, President Jimmy Carter was able to sign a bill continuing the protections and more than doubling the size of the Arctic National Wildlife Refuge. The 1980 consensus that Cecil Andrus put together held throughout the 1990s and at the beginning of the new millennium, when the Senate defeated a Bush administration proposal to open the area for oil drilling. The use and significance of the Arctic National Wildlife Refuge continues to be a matter of legitimate policy debate. But it is important that both sides make their case in terms of competing public goods—not only the high cost of fuel, but the 68 million federal acres already under lease but unexplored, the impact on native communities, the health of our planet, and our obligation to future generations.

Environmentalists alleged that our decision on the oil pipeline was in favor of the oil industry. The oil industry maintained that our decision on the Arctic National Wildlife Refuge was in favor of environmentalists. In both cases, we carefully considered the conflicting claims of divergent stakeholder groups and carefully navigated our way through the passions of the moment to identify and defend the long-term public interest.

Much of today's debate more than thirty years later about offshore leasing, the potential of oil shale as a source of energy, and the development of areas already leased sounds like the debates of the 1970s. In my own remarks in 1979 before the national Outer Continental Shelf Advisory Board in Norfolk, Virginia, and before 450 representatives of the oil and gas industry meeting in New Orleans, I had joined the debate, arguing that a nation as rich in resources, technology and ingenuity as ours should not find itself in the position of bartering our self-esteem for barrels of oil.

As chairman of President Carter's Task Force on the Potential of Oil Shale, I also addressed a special sitting of the Colorado legislature. After what seemed like a very warm acceptance of my speech, I read a business card that had been slipped into my hand. It said, "I am in business for myself. I make the front end of horses and ship them to Washington for final assembly."

Another form of microethics surfaced in the 1970s—the microethics of parochialism. It grew out of the fragmentation of the public interest into a focus on private wants. This contributed to the rise of single-issue political candidates who became single-issue officials who sought to serve single-issue constituencies. Members of Congress who might have been expected to be statesmen in the past were acting more like ward councillors in a metropolitan area preoccupied with the interest of their particular districts rather than the state or region. They were the ones who seemed particularly vulnerable to the litmus test of one-dimensional groups such as the gun lobby and the antiabortion crusaders.

When I left Yale Divinity School in the 1960s, many of the dominant moral voices in society were those of social ethicists in seminaries and social activists in universities and churches. Their goal was a new vision and a higher reason. They sought to build a society that was just and humane. Government was asked to play a leadership role, to take the initiative and call Americans to a higher sense of purpose.

But in the 1970s the mood began to change. Many Americans concluded that far too many government programs had failed. They called on business and the voluntary sector to take the leadership in charting a new course. This narrowing of the role of government was to be expected, given the public mood, but with no other sector powerful enough to fill the leadership vacuum, the opportunity for genuine partnership was missed.

This confusion about the private role of the public sector and the public role of the private sector led to both a compassion gap and a great distrust of government. President Carter decided that the time had come to address these issues as a national problem deeper than the gasoline lines, energy shortages, inflation, and recession facing the American people and plaguing his administration. So he invited people for a conversation at Camp David from almost every segment of American society—business and labor, teachers and preachers, governors, mayors, and private citizens. He said he wanted to listen to the people even more broadly, so he left Camp David to listen to others. On July 15, 1979, in an Oval Office speech, he crystallized his reflection on what he had been hearing in what became known as the "Malaise Speech." While he was both misunderstood and maligned, we may need to take a second look at some of what he said: "What you see too often in Washington and elsewhere around the country is a system of government that seems incapable of action. You see a Congress twisted and pulled in every direction by hundreds of well-financed and powerful special interests. You see extreme positions defended to the last vote, almost to the last breath, by one unyielding group or another. You see paralysis and stagnation and drift. You don't like it and neither do I."[1]

The prescriptions the president suggested for this malaise were both debated and denounced, but the initial reaction to his diagnosis was more positive than is now portrayed. His polling numbers shot up. His lamentations about a "crisis of confidence" and his calls for sacrifice struck a nerve. But the public distraught about the economy, especially the high price of oil and nearly 9 percent unemployment, provided the lens through which the speech was ultimately viewed. With help from his political opponents, the initial public reaction diminished into a crisis of confidence in the president himself.

I was not a part of the internal discussions or the policymaking that followed, but as I traveled around the country I concluded that what most Americans seemed to want was a government capable of helping people to help themselves. While their leaders debated whether we needed a smaller government or simply a more effective government, many people appeared to have already made a decision. They seemed to want government to provide them with the tools to solve local problems locally, but they also seemed to want a caring society in which leaders see needs, propose solutions, and set out to make them work. So we were led to ask: How are we to determine the public will and the common good? Are there transcendent values and normative standards appropriate for determining public responsibility in a time of increasing privatism?

### Alternative Theories

Seeking to use the conceptual framework I learned at Yale Divinity School, I turned to the moral theories offered by philosophers and theologians about how one determines appropriate moral standards. The first is the so-called teleological theory. It holds that the ultimate criterion or standard for determining responsibility or obligation is the amount of good produced in comparison to the amount of evil. Thus, a political act is morally right if it produces—will probably produce, or is intended to produce—at least as great a balance of good over evil as any available alternative. The emphasis is on the potential consequences of an act.

I tried also to apply the moral standards that come from so-called deontological theories. They emphasize that other considerations may make an action right or obligatory besides the goodness or badness of its consequences. The focus is on what is required. An action may be considered right because the state commands it or because religion glorifies it.

Of course, no consideration of the application of moral theory to the demands of public life would be complete without a situation-based approach. It begins with trying to understand the context, the shifting demands and circumstances that give rise to the need to decide and act. Situation ethics flourished as part of the new morality of the 1960s but is now in disrepute among the new moralists. Yet it can be argued that public policy decisions would be enhanced if policymakers stopped to ask in each situation what is the most loving thing to do.

These concepts never found their way directly into any public documents for which I had responsibility, but they often provided a framework for my own reflection on what was right and what ought to be done. Yet the standards that controlled political action around me usually stemmed from one of three areas of moral development and ethical influence. The first area is instinct. The individual does not ask what is right but simply does what is dictated by a moral impulse or inherent aptitude. This behavior is mediated by reaction below the conscious level. There is no moment of moral choice about which to agonize. There is only the requirement to follow one's instincts.

The second area of moral development and control is custom, long-established practice so common to a place or group that it is accepted as unwritten law. It begins with the community but develops into a form of individual acquiescence to the moral norms of the group. The authority for determining what is right is outside the political actor.

A third area of moral development and control is conscience, the sense of the moral goodness of one's own conduct, intentions, or character together with a feeling of obligation to do right or be good. The public official makes judgments about what is right and wrong based on values he or she has internalized. These judgments may be based on the internalization of customs or the moral norms of religion. Two government officials involved in similar actions in similar situations may relate them to different imperatives. The one who sees himself as merely doing what the public interest requires engages in a good action because he feels it is good for the community. A person committed to a particular religious perspective, on the other hand, may engage in the same action but define it as the requirement of faith. Both are likely to be acting, however, in accordance with a conditioning that emanates from the religious feeling or moral traditions of the community.

### Making Ethical Decisions

My experience in the Department of the Interior caused me to think as much about the decision-making process as the decisions I had to make. In business, I had learned to concentrate on the most important decisions, making them in a deliberate fashion and only after considerable analysis at a variety of levels and after entertaining a variety of views. In government, there were two kinds of decisions: (1) those that were subject to careful and sustained policy review with experts from a wide variety of areas, and (2) those that came at a rapid pace all during the day, often in the evenings as well, and needed to be made with dispatch.

To deal with the first set of more systematic decisions, I followed to a large degree the advice of gurus like Peter Drucker, who described steps they considered important to the decision-making process.[2] But my own checklist was often less elaborate, although equally compelling and controlling. In business, I had learned to ask: (1) Will someone get hurt or, in some cases, which decision will cause the least harm? (2) What does the law require and is it consistent with the national values commonly accepted by nation-states? (3) What public interest will be served, and have I made an appropriate distinction between public good and private want? (4) Do I have all the facts, and have I made a good effort to determine whether anything has been suppressed? (5) Is the decision I am about to make consistent with my perception of who I am and what I stand for?

These questions have come to shape my instincts, intuition, and identity in such a way that I do not always need to engage in a detailed analysis to ensure that they inform my decision. They provide a moral compass that I have come to regard as the ethics of intuition, the marriage of context, spontaneity, and self-expression with grand principles and analysis. This is the approach I found helpful in dealing with the second set of decisions in the Department of the Interior, those that had to be made immediately. It is important to emphasize, however, that the ethical instinct is not just a single, compelling me-istic impulse or a substitute for rational thought, common sense, or a consideration of basic ethical principles. The intuition arises after serious attention to relevant facts, not in place of them. As William James argued in his seminal work on pragmatism, good decisions require us to walk on both sides of the line. "Facts are good," he said. "Give us lots of facts." But so are principles good. "Give us lots of principles."[3]

No individual is an unencumbered self. Each of us is the product of our experiences, beliefs, principles, and visions. It is when all of these come together to shape our instincts and intuition that we are most fully prepared to make a moral decision. Intuition as I use it here is not personal but social, not individualistic but communal. The philosopher Alasdair McIntyre made this point when he wrote, "I am someone's son or daughter, someone else's cousin or uncle; I am a citizen of this or that city, a member of this or that guild or profession; I belong to this tribe, that clan, this nation. I inherit from the past of my family, my city, my tribe, my nation, a variety of debts, inheritances, rightful expectations and obligations. These constitute the given of my life, my moral starting point. This is in part what gives my life its own particularity."[4]

To acknowledge the socializing influences that have shaped my moral instincts is in no way to diminish the uniqueness of intuition as a private moral force. While I am an altogether unique personality, I am at the same time a social being who has been socialized in a particular time and shaped by a particular tradition. This is the moral particularity that provides the foundation of the values I take into the public arena. It is tempered, however, by the awareness that while I have been shaped by my society, I also have the capacity, and sometimes the need, for transcendence. The consciousness that is particular is always pushing the envelope of a consciousness that is universal. Just as there is in each of us an urge to connect with something beyond the self, there is also a persistent disposition to think and act in transcendent moral terms. It is this moral sense that distinguishes human beings from all other creatures.

## Right versus Right

Many of the decisions I encountered in government were right-versus-right decisions where each of the options under consideration was morally defensible, rather than simply right-versus-wrong decisions where only one option could be defended as the right thing to do. I struggled with such a decision when I had to decide whether to support the annual hunt for the bowhead whale by Alaska Eskimos as essential to the survival of their culture or the alternative argument advanced by environmentalists that restriction on the hunt was essential to the survival of the bowhead whale species. For centuries, the bowhead whale hunt was a ritual used by Eskimos in Alaska to signify the coming into manhood of young Eskimo males. The hunt was carefully planned and carried out with great precision and festivity. It was not only an ancient tradition but a signal of the survival of Eskimo culture. The Bureau of Indian Affairs in the Department of the Interior protected this practice and argued against interference by outsiders who did not understand the critical importance of this ritual to Eskimos. Environmentalists who were lined up against the position of the Bureau of Indian Affairs had been very helpful in securing the election of Jimmy Carter as president and had considerable clout in the administration and the Congress. The issue was not just moral and cultural, but political.

The conflict came to a head when powerful environmental leaders met with me to demand that we overrule the Bureau of Indian Affairs and stop the hunt. Eskimo leaders were outraged and demanded that we not abandon them and put the survival of their culture at risk. The idea of quotas, a modified restriction on the size of the hunt, was unacceptable to both sides.

After many attempts to find a compromise, the issue was ultimately defined as whether to support the survival of the bowhead whale or the survival of Eskimo culture.

I came down on the side of the Eskimos. However, the International Whaling Commission went in the opposite direction, placing a ban on the harvest of bowhead whales by Eskimos. The whalers responded by organizing the whaling communities and establishing the Alaska Whaling Commission to fight the ban. They were successful in persuading the International Whaling Commission to replace the ban with a quota both sides found satisfactory. A few years later, scientists improved the methods for estimating the bowhead whale population and concluded that it had been increasing rather than declining. Equally illuminating was the finding that the bowhead population was never as low as estimated in 1977. At the end of the commercial whaling era in the early twenty-first century, the population was estimated at one thousand. Now, it is reliably estimated that there are more than twelve thousand. Annual assessments show a 3 percent growth rate per year.

This issue of what to do when we face a difficult decision where each alternative appears to be the right thing, but there is no way to do both, was even more pronounced in the case of the Bikinians who had petitioned the department to permit them to return to their still-radioactive island, so that they could die in the land of their ancestors. The United States conducted nuclear testing programs at Bikini and Enewetak Atolls from 1956 to 1958. The soil still produced radioactive coconuts and was obviously unsafe, but despite the danger to their health the Bikinians had voted overwhelmingly to return to their ancestral home.

My job as the undersecretary was to decide whether the U.S. government should agree to their request, thus honoring the democratic process in which the elders had voted to return to their island home, or act as guardian for the younger generation who could not vote, but by returning to Bikini would be sentenced to an early death.

The decision was complicated by the fact that my predecessors in previous administrations had not always acted responsibly toward the island. There were both suspicions of our intention and concern about the long history of American paternalism in dealing with island leaders. As undersecretary, my approach to the Pacific territories had been to endorse and accept all recommendations approved through a public vote, although a public referendum had no standing in U.S. law. The approach was beginning to win respect for me and the Carter administration. Should I now play God and overrule the elders, thus preserving their lives and protecting their children, or should I honor the commitment to the democratic process? Every effort had been made, including my visit to the island, to ensure that the elders had access to the very persuasive environmental information that indicated a risk of an early cancer death. But they were determined that I should allow them to return home since their recommendation reflected a consensus among island leaders.

They had reasons to doubt that their personal needs and even unanimous recommendation would be an influential part of the government's decision-making process. When I arrived on Kili in the Marshall Islands for a public meeting, I sat facing these words on the back wall of their meeting house: "Mr. Under Secretary, we must say sadly that our situation is akin to that of the children of Israel who wandered in the desert for forty years. We have wandered for 32 years. But, unfortunately, we will not see our promised land." The words on the banner set the initial mood and content of the meeting.

For three hours I answered questions. The first questioner wanted to know why we did not just go ahead and resettle Bikini. "The radiation was created by a bomb," he said. "The U.S. also dropped atomic bombs on Japan, and you have been able to resettle Japan." My reply that the bombs used in Japan were different from those exploded on Bikini, and the concentration and longevity of the radiation was very different, provided no comfort. The second question was equally disturbing. "You say we should move, that you will move us and take care of us. We were moved once before and we were forgotten after we were moved." He went on to describe that first move from Bikini—how the people were left without food and adequate housing.

The Bikinians had been in fact removed from their first temporary resettlement on Rongerik Atoll to a tent camp on Kwajalein just two years after their departure from Bikini. To my dismay, the reason was listed as impending starvation. As a senior official of the U.S. government, I had to accept the responsibility for the performance of that government, although I was still in college at the time of the first atomic test. I did make the case, however, that those were different times and a different administration. I ended up giving them my personal assurance that the current administration was committed to meeting its obligation.

While it is the values driving the decision-making process that have most concerned me, it is important to note the decisions I made in each of the two dilemmas cited. In the case of the people of Bikini, my travels through the region ended on a life raft after the plane crash described in the prologue of this book, but I considered it important to meet directly with the people who would be affected by my decision. This was not a generic issue that could be resolved through an existing precedent or principle. I had to find out as clearly as I could what I was dealing with and what boundary conditions applied. Finally, I had to decide on the basis of some standard other than simply what was acceptable to the leaders. I had to ask which of the competing values should have preeminence. Was it democratic process or a larger sense of obligation to the community that included the children who did not vote, but who would be doomed to an early death? I offered the leaders other options including relocation to Hawaii, an improved quality of life with increased U.S. support on an alternate island in the Marshalls, and so on, but they refused to budge from their desire to return to Bikini. I decided to veto their decision and not let them return, but I also got an agreement from the Environmental Protection Agency to expedite the cleanup of the radioactive soil and coconuts on the island, and from other agencies of government to improve education and access to health care. The cleanup was successful and a few years later the people of Bikini returned to their island home.

### The Search for an Environmental Ethic

While struggling to apply ethics to the making of public policy, the operation of a large bureaucracy, and the adjudication of the competing claims of diverse stakeholders, I felt the need to think more deeply, and articulate more clearly, some normative principles appropriate for the stewardship of natural resources. I was aided in this regard by some of the very wise tribal leaders I met in fulfilling my responsibility for oversight of the Bureau of Indian Affairs. They reminded me that Native Americans and some other indigenous people have long seen the earth as an all-encompassing community whose members include many species and living forms, only some of whom are humans. For the early tribes, every terrain was saturated with the spirits that were the custodians of the landscape. Every hillside, every valley, and every plain were suffused with sacredness.

The emphasis was on not one environment but three: the natural environment with its meandering streams, flowering trees, and striking wildlife; the social environment in which we human beings work out our relationship to each other; and the moral environment of human values that define and direct our relationship with each other, to nature, and to the world at large. We do not need to accept the view that water and land have spirits, that trees have rights, or that animals are power beings with a spirit to accept and feel a oneness with our world, a need to reconcile conflicting claims on natural resources and to learn to live in harmony with nature.

The search for an environmental ethic led to some complex questions about our ethical obligation to nature. Does the earth exist, for example, exclusively or primarily for the benefit of humanity? Are there other species with an intrinsic right to exist? Aldo Leopold, the legendary forester, wildlife manager, and author, struggled with these issues and suggested the need for a land ethic that enlarges the boundaries of our concept of community to include the soils, waters, plants, and animals or, collectively, the land.[5] In appealing to us to change our understanding of the role of *Homo sapiens* from conqueror of the land community to a plain member and citizen of it, Leopold took us to another level in the consideration of both public policy and the management of natural resource bureaucracies.

My own efforts to place natural resources in a larger context led me to the conclusion that at the heart of the idea of an environmental ethic must be the notion that we humans are an integral part of our environment and have obligations to it. To see ourselves as citizens of both the natural and human order, rather than simply exploiters, means that we have to preserve and protect nature, not just buy, sell, and consume it. As Leopold reminded us, to be a citizen of the land community implies respect for fellow members. It means that acting responsibly refers not just to our individual actions but to our collective action as a nation-state and as members of an interdependent world community. The literature on environmental ethics makes a distinction between instrumental value and intrinsic value. The first refers to the value of things as means to further some other ends, whereas the latter refers to the value of things as ends in themselves. Whether we think of nature as having instrumental or intrinsic value, a prima facie case can be made that we have a moral duty to protect and preserve it, or at a minimum to refrain from causing undue harm.

Our notion of environmental justice rarely includes the whole of the earth community. The Environmental Protection Agency's Environmental Justice home page defines environmental justice as fair treatment for people of all races, cultures, and incomes regarding the development of environmental laws, regulations, and policies. It was certainly my experience in government that the environmental consequences of our use of natural resources fell disproportionately on certain racial, ethnic, and socioeconomic groups. It is thus appropriate that environmental justice groups make the case that hazardous waste sites, for example, are usually located in disadvantaged communities (even disadvantaged nations) while our great parks and other crown jewels of nature are often out of their geographical reach. Is it possible, however, to extend the idea of justice to include nature?

If those who make public policy are to pay due regard to the moral standing of nature, does this mean that trees, forests, mountains, and animals should also have standing in law? In 1972, when Christopher Stone (a professor of law at the University of California) proposed that trees and other natural objects should have the same standing in law as a corporation, he was ridiculed by some and dismissed by others as a kook. Yet his proposal struck at the heart of a real dilemma in California at the time. Walt Disney Enterprises was seeking to develop a major resort complex that would need to be accessed by building a superhighway through Sequoia National Park. When the U.S. Forest Service granted a permit for preparatory surveys, the Sierra Club took it to court, challenging the development on the grounds that the valley should be kept in its original state for its own sake. The Supreme Court determined by a narrow majority that the Sierra Club was unable to prove the likelihood of injury to the interest of the club or its members. Yet in a strong dissent, Justices Douglas, Blackmun, and Brennan referred to Stone's argument that giving legal standing to natural things would allow conservation interests, community needs, and business interests to be represented, debated, and settled in court.

The groups with a stake in natural resource decisions are as diverse as they are insistent that they alone understand and represent the public interest. Environmentalists have been accused both of failing to promote justice in the world and, even more seriously, of contributing to injustice by advocating policies that give priority to protection and conservation rather than development and distribution. Energy entrepreneurs and their colleagues in the natural resource industry, on the other hand, are seen by many as preoccupied with profits with little or no consideration of the public good. While both of these accusations point to a streak of selfishness that is presently troubling American society, they tend to limit the public policy discussion to name calling and appeals to a superficial patriotism. The public policy standard required is a form of stakeholder responsibility that parallels shareholder responsibility in the private sector. Each group affected by natural resource decisions must be treated as a stakeholder with legitimate rights and claims, but no one group, no matter how powerful, should be allowed to transform their private wants into a public need.

The idea of a natural resource ethic is back in fashion. The Andrus administration at the Department of the Interior and our continuing quest for an environmental ethic was succeeded by James Watt, a man who called himself a conservative but who turned out to be a radical determined to turn back the clock in irrational and provocative ways. We had proven over our four years that environmental protection and energy development could both be achieved, that it was possible to find balance in the use of public lands and the ocean, and that different voices with different visions of the public good could be heard with civility and respect. But at a time when the nation was seeking values, James Watt offered them ideology. While he claimed to be representing the public interest in dismantling all manifestations of an environmental ethic, he brought to mind Emerson's statement, quoted often by one of my Republican predecessors whenever he referred to James Watt: "The louder he talked of his honor, the faster we counted our spoons."

Now, more than ever, we need to recognize that humanity is an environmental component, just like plants, animals, and endangered species. As S. Dillon Ripley, a former secretary of the Smithsonian Institution, reminded us, "The future of the human race may depend on the degree to which we come to realize what the evolutionists and the ecologists have long sensed: the biosphere is all one; the realms of species are all finite; the ecosystems interrelated. The quality of life turns out to be not simply a romantic ideal, but a set of standards, still intangible, still highly arguable, but on which survival may be based."[6]

Cecil Andrus and I knew when we arrived at the Interior Department that we were assuming responsibility for a department with a reputation for cozying up to those it was supposed to regulate. Our strongest concerns were about the practices of the oil and gas regulators, who had been accused of favoring the oil and gas industry. Few people know the extent to which the Interior Department is a revenue generator as well as a manager of public lands. In 2008, the department's Minerals Management Service (MMS) collected about $12 billion in revenues from oil and gas production on federal property, onshore and in waters like the Gulf of Mexico. That same year, the department's inspector general told Congress that MMS officials accepted gifts, steered contracts to favored clients, partied with industry officials, and engaged in drug use and sex with oil company employees as part of what he called "a culture of ethical failure."[7]

This certainly helps explain why our policies of strong, transparent standards did not sit well with industry critics who tried so hard, but failed, to persuade us to place people from the oil industry in key positions to oversee the 500 million acres of federal land—one-fifth of the country's land mass— and 1.7 billion acres of the outer continental shelf under our management. It would appear that some of our successors were more accommodating. The *New York Times* reported in September 2009 that a previous secretary of the interior was under investigation for granting valuable leases to an oil company at the same time the secretary was in conversation with the company about going to work for them after leaving office.[8] The battle for the soul of natural resource managers is obviously continuing, but change has come to Interior. The 2010 oil leak in the Gulf of Mexico brought public outcries for new regulatory standards and reform. The MMS was formed by Interior Secretary James Watt just months after the departure of Carter administration officials, thereby dismantling our system of dividing the functions of leasing, revenue collection, and regulatory programs into separate offices with appropriate checks and balances. But after learning that MMS regulators were allowing oil industry representatives to write the reports that Interior filed and disseminated as part of their oversight of offshore oil and gas drilling, Secretary of the Interior Ken Salazar reformed MMS. The tide has turned and calls for more effective regulation of the industry will hopefully return us to the principles and practices to which Cecil Andrus and I adhered. But I have no doubt that whenever there is a significant increase in oil prices and the focus is once again on drilling, these principles will be under serious attack.

# CHAPTER 10

# Civil Society

*The Public Use of Private Power*

Jimmy Carter was defeated in the 1980 presidential election. He was badly maligned by the new politics of personal destruction, and it was not until a few years later that many found out what a decent man he was and how much better his performance had been than what was often portrayed.

My final days in the Carter administration were spent first on the campaign trail and later recovering from the stress and strains of national politics. After returning home from a campaign trip in which I traveled long distances to make three speeches in one day—at a breakfast in Miami, a luncheon in Memphis, and a dinner at the mayor's residence in New York City—I failed to negotiate the steps at my home in McLean, Virginia, and ended up in Fairfax Hospital with a badly fractured ankle. I was there long enough to watch from my bed as the doctors and nurses cheered the election of Ronald Reagan.

I was not a politician or a government bureaucrat by nature and had always intended to return to something outside of government, but a few months earlier on my way home from a trip to the Micronesian islands I had picked up a copy of *Jet* magazine in Honolulu and was surprised to read that sources in the White House were reporting that I had been tapped by President Carter to succeed Cecil Andrus as secretary of the interior. Cece had informed the president long before the final days that he was planning to resign early to return to Idaho.

Carter lost the election so I never had a chance to test either the veracity of the article or the strength of my earlier decision to leave government at the end of my four-year term. But it was fitting that at a meeting with Carter and senior administration executives a few days after my release from the hospital, one of his aides looked at the cast on my right leg with my toes dangling out past the wheelchair and said, "I see that the undersecretary of the interior is taking this lame duck business seriously."

The 1980s were more than a time of major political change in the United States. It was in many ways a decade that highlighted the work of civil society around the world, a time when a new burst of citizen activism toppled oppressive governments, opened closed economies, restored human rights, and brought relief to many who were impoverished. It was for me a time of great irony. Born in a low-income community in a largely rural region of southwestern Louisiana, I now found myself a spokesperson for benevolent wealth. Life had been a meandering journey, but the opportunity to promote the values embodied in the idea of civil society seemed like the destination to which I had been traveling.

It was as president of the Council on Foundations that I returned to my earlier interest in the potential of citizen action outside of government. The council was not well known outside the circles of the wealthy and those who dispensed charitable largesse, but without much fanfare and little public notice it became a critical center of civic energy and social capital.

I was standing on the edge of a crowd in the former Soviet Union when an upstart named Boris Yeltsin made his first public challenge to Soviet orthodoxy. I was standing outside of Parliament in Cape Town, South Africa, with a "Free Mandela" sign when F. W. de Klerk announced that Nelson Mandela would be set free and the African National Congress reinstated. On each occasion, I was there with civil society groups determined to shape a new and different future.

Resurrected in the 1970s by the Polish workers' movement and later in debates about perestroika in the former Soviet Union, the idea of civil society has roots in early Christian theology as well as more recent political thought. The attractiveness of the concept lies in its conjoining of private and public good. But in what should be its finest hour, the idea of civil society is in danger of being distorted and hijacked by those who emphasize the potential of private voluntary action in order to bolster arguments for a more limited social role for government.

The efforts to harmonize the conflicting demands of individual interest and social good have brought renewed attention to the moral and ethical visions of public life found in the writings of John Locke, Immanuel Kant,

G. W. F. Hegel, Alexis de Tocqueville, and an array of social thinkers who have been rediscovered. While the idea of civil society has come to mean different things to different people, in its most celebrated form it refers to the contributions of nonstate actors to the public good. It is a term of respect and endearment for the ideas, ideals, individuals, and informal institutions that caused communism to collapse, the Berlin Wall to fall, and adversaries in an apartheid state to beat their swords into plowshares.

When I joined the Council on Foundations in 1982 as president and chief executive officer, there was very little to suggest that the philanthropic sector was destined to be at the heart of the national debate about the social responsibilities of a democracy. A friend even joked that I was joining a no-growth industry. Like many other Americans, he had been seduced by the public attention given to the me generation and its fascination with wealth and power. The high priest of this new cult was a Wall Street speculator named Ivan Boesky. He traveled the country preaching a gospel of self-indulgence and assuring students on college campuses and the young upwardly mobile in the professions that greed was not only acceptable but healthy.

I had just completed four years in the public sector and it was assumed that I would return to the private sector with its many enticing incentives; but I felt the call to something different. I refused to believe that a majority of Americans had become self-centered and uncaring, that there had been an eclipse of goodness. So when representatives of the Council on Foundations approached me in their search for a new president, I initially declined but agreed later to meet with them to determine whether there might be a mutual interest. I had been involved with the council in the early 1970s and felt uncertain about both the vitality of the organization and the vision of some of its members. But I identified very strongly with its basic mission of promoting responsible and effective philanthropy.

As I considered the possibility of leading the council, I could not help but recall how a small group of African Americans had formed the Association of Black Foundation Executives (ABFE) in the early 1970s to open up the council to new ideas and new forms of diversity. As the incorporating chairman of the new group, I became a major critic of the council and the leader of what was viewed by some as an adversarial organization. I was uncertain about the kind of reception I would now receive from council members who might remember me simply as one of the troublemakers who had held up their conference in Montreal until they agreed to elect a more inclusive slate of candidates to the board of directors. I was reassured that much had changed since Montreal and that most council members would enthusiastically welcome me in this new role.

I accepted the council's offer and became president only to discover that the organization was in difficult financial shape and badly in need of resuscitation. I had often joked that blacks were being given the opportunity to lead predominantly white organizations (from cities to civil society) only when they were in danger of collapse, and it looked as if I were to be an example. But I joined the council at the beginning of a major expansion of the philanthropic sector and brought together a very talented staff determined to see the council realize its potential. Within a few years, the council became an international organization with members from five continents and every American state. Hundreds of additional foundations were developed through a council initiative to promote organized philanthropy by wealthy families and within minority communities. Our programs were more diverse, and support for civil society was a major theme of our work.

### Strengthening Civil Society Abroad

I was eager to extend the work of the council beyond American borders, so I responded with enthusiasm to a request from representatives of large international foundations to establish a program within the council to promote international philanthropy. It was against this backdrop that I accepted an invitation to take a delegation of foundation executives to the Soviet Union, in response to invitations from Soviet citizens visiting the United States to learn about the American foundation sector. The 1980s had already seen great triumphs for civil society. Citizen groups in very different societies prevailed in their struggle to alter long-standing relationships between the people and the state. As president of the Council on Foundations, I traveled to Europe, Asia, Latin America, and Africa to help invigorate civil society groups, but nothing at the time suggested the wide sweep of change that would soon follow in many unlikely places.

I had first visited the Soviet Union in the 1970s as part of a delegation of religious leaders, but I was being invited back in a different capacity to meet with those who were launching a civil society sector and demanding increased citizen participation in the public life of their nation. The collapse into independent nations had begun early in 1985, but it was accelerated by the subsequent emergence of glasnost (freedom of speech) and perestroika (rebuilding). Mikhail Gorbachev did not fully realize the extent to which giving people complete freedom of expression was unleashing emotions and civic feeling that had been pent up for years, but once the cracks in government control became evident, many civic activists were eager to learn more about the function of civil society in other parts of the world.

So it was that on March 11, 1989, twenty-five foundation executives and trustees left New York for a two-week visit to the Soviet Union. I asked Sharon Tennison of the Center for US-USSR Initiatives to help arrange and coordinate the trip, often on the spot. She used her connections with Soviet citizens to arrange interviews with whomever we wanted to see and to go wherever we wanted to go.

Some of our colleagues in American philanthropy refused to believe that major changes were taking place in the Soviet Union, and they were convinced that no civil society could emerge in the Soviet state. The timing of the visit was important because it was just before the election of the new Congress of People's Deputies. Yet we could not anticipate how lucky we were to be able to visit in private homes and private offices, to travel to Soviet republics and local communities, and to meet with those who were forming nongovernmental organizations (NGOs) at a time when the struggle to humanize Soviet society through private action was generating worldwide attention. Because we represented neither the press nor government, people spoke openly to us about their hopes and frustrations. We were able to get the story from both the bottom and the middle tiers of society, from activists in the streets as well as from ordinary families in the privacy of their homes.

Some members of our delegation agreed to go with me to the Soviet Union partly out of curiosity, a desire to learn whether a charitable sector was indeed possible in Soviet society. But others went because of a shared commitment, a desire to promote and support the ideals and values of civil society wherever people seemed willing to come together in a nongovernmental context to promote social change and provide civic improvements.

Everywhere we went in the Soviet Union, we found private citizens forming voluntary organizations and developing new alternatives to the governmental process. We found creativity in search of institutional expression, people excited by the possibility of addressing, directly, social needs and social aspirations that had been ignored or stifled for seventy-five years. We found an almost metaphysical liberation of the human spirit, a turning to the church and other spiritual outlets that had been discouraged or denied. We found a renaissance of culture and a new freedom of the mind, a willingness to criticize the past publicly, to think new thoughts and do new things.

In the midst of incredible spiritual, intellectual, and political ferment, we also found a limited knowledge of process and an intense desire to learn from the experience of others how best to translate the many new ideas into effective nongovernmental programs. We found uncertainty about whether the new activism by private citizens could really make a difference. We found anxiety about whether the new openness would last, a lingering fear that the conservative bureaucrats and other agents of the state would not permit this new freedom to continue. Yet we were surprised by the depth of the enthusiasm for change and the many expressions of private discontent. The candidates for political office we met in Lithuania and Ukraine, the returning exiles from Siberia who told us tragic tales of frustration and perseverance, the participants in political rallies we visited in Moscow, and the ordinary citizens who welcomed us into their homes in Leningrad and elsewhere were all eager for change. Some were fighting for change so fundamental that they challenged both the public philosophy and the political structure of the Soviet state. Some wanted political independence for their republics and private ownership of property while others simply wanted more opportunities for citizen engagement and better consumer goods.

But this was only one side of the story. The real story in the Soviet Union at the time of our visit was that of an emerging charitable sector, the flourishing of private initiatives, and the formation of foundations and other forms of organized philanthropy. The newly formed foundations were unique to their cultural and economic context. They differed from private foundations in the United States in that their assets were not gifts in perpetuity, but they tended to share with community foundations the search for funds, large and small, from multiple sources; some designated by the donor for a specific purpose and others contributed simply to meet the needs of specific communities. There was no proposal-writing or grantmaking culture in the Soviet Union, but those who were forming foundations were experimenting with novel forms of fund-raising and fund distribution, while eager to hear from us how we did it in the United States.

There were local foundations like the Lithuanian Women's Charitable Fund in Vilnius, funds for historic preservation in Kiev, and funds for environmental advocacy in Leningrad. There were regional funds, either with roots in local republics or serving as local branches of national foundations headquartered in Moscow. All these were new foundations (many formed within the year of our visit) at a very early stage of development. Many were not yet registered with government authorities, although they had usually opened the much-discussed bank account that appeared to give legitimacy to charitable organizations.

These new foundations operated without a regulatory framework to ensure expenditure responsibility or public accountability. In the absence of statutory or regulatory guidelines, government authorities were in many instances simply tolerating for the moment many informal activities that were formerly underground. Thus, the resources for private philanthropy were available and new information provided on needs that were formerly ignored or deliberately hidden from public view. We heard tragic tales of homelessness in rural areas, of the isolated elderly and handicapped, of orphaned and neglected children, and of environmental abuse, and, even worse, stories of people who were spiritually dead—human lives in which dignity and hope no longer resided.

Even the newspapers and television commentators were beginning to report openly on the activities of civil society institutions to address social needs and solve social problems. They were especially curious about our visit and the messages we were conveying about the potential and limits of civil society. I was interviewed on the popular television program *Good Evening Moscow* and by *Pravda*, the official newspaper of the Communist Party. In addition, I appeared on *Radio Vilnius*, a program that was beamed outside of Lithuania as well as to the local populace. In each instance, we talked about voluntary organizations and alternatives to government as openly as we do in the United States. When I spoke publicly of de Tocqueville's description of voluntary activity in the United States as "habits of the heart," an academic replied, "It was too bad that Marx did not read de Tocqueville's work."

The real question being asked by many in very different ways was whether perestroika and glasnost needed Marx. Some Soviet citizens were even beginning to question the Lenin cult. Many people were showing their frustration with an economy that was getting worse rather than better. And as our visit demonstrated, Soviet citizens were being permitted to rejoin the world.

Yet a Greek journalist offered a caution when he told us, "The Russian soul likes gloom. They argue that the society must be made more plural and more civil, but the totalitarian culture may be inborn, a product of stagnation— making it difficult to push ahead." But the younger generation was clearly interested in private action to create a different kind of society. Many were in the forefront of the effort to set up a charitable sector from the bottom up rather than from the top down as some of their elders were inclined to do.

The members of the Council on Foundations delegation returned home convinced that the charitable sector emerging in the former Soviet Union was being planted on fertile ground and was likely to grow and prosper. While the role of the American philanthropic community was not yet fully clear, many of those who made the trip encouraged their foundation colleagues to find ways to support the development of a civil society, not just in the Soviet Union but in Eastern Europe more broadly. Some found ways to provide grants from their own foundations, while others became civil society ambassadors who validated the authenticity of the changes taking place. My own message to council members was that the worst response would be to ignore this opportunity to reintroduce philanthropy into the minds of a people and the heart of a culture struggling for a moral revival.

### Building a New Movement

My emphasis on expanding the boundaries of philanthropy and the work of the council took another turn. A small group of civil society advocates, including a few from the Soviet trip, met in my conference room in 1991 to consider how best to support this rapidly growing movement that was winning important economic, political, and social victories in so many unlikely places. Out of this small gathering came a call for a larger meeting with representatives from the voluntary sector on each continent.

Brian O'Connell, who was then president of Independent Sector, and I, as president of the Council on Foundations, subsequently hosted a gathering of twenty-seven people from twenty-three countries. They came from a widely diverse political and cultural milieu, and with very different experiences, but they shared a common commitment to what some of us described as civil society. While we were able to speak a common language, we found that the words we used to describe citizen action had different meanings in different cultural and political settings. Philanthropy was in disfavor in some cultures because it implied a form of charitable largesse associated with exploitation by a wealthy class. The word "nonprofit," so easily accepted in North America to refer to voluntary organizations, did not capture the efforts of NGOs that in some parts of the world were both profit making and change oriented. Even the concept of civil society that initially brought us together was rejected by a few who associated it with the "civilizing" influence of those in Western society who were determined to remake others in their own image.

After intense debates about the meaning of our words and the purpose of our meeting, we launched the new organization CIVICUS as a world alliance for encouraging and supporting citizen participation. We selected Miklos Marschall, then deputy mayor of Budapest and a leader of informal organizations in predemocratic Hungary, as executive director. Brian O'Connell and I were elected cochairs, and the report of the organizing committee in 1993 concluded, "We have moved from the condition of unallied doubters to a unified body embracing a shared vision. Despite all our difference and differentness, we are agreed that something very significant may be unfolding in the world and that the moment should be seized."[1] Within a few years, the membership of CIVICUS came to include NGOs and interested individuals from more than eighty countries. It had become an important meeting ground for the leaders of civic groups that had now mushroomed around the world.

As I got more involved with NGOs on other continents, I was invited by Oscar Arias, the president of Costa Rica, to help form a community foundation in that country. I accepted an invitation to lecture in Tokyo and to meet with groups in Japan developing a philanthropic sector. I traveled frequently to Canada, Latin America (especially Mexico), Europe, and Africa. On the African continent, where I helped set up a local Council on Foundations in South Africa and visited with heads of state throughout the region, I was surprised to find that civil society was a multibillion-dollar industry spending more than the World Bank. The ascent and influence of NGOs quickly grew to a point that some were as feared by governments as others were praised by private citizens. The fact that many were funded by Western governments and private Western donors led some political leaders to ask to whom they were responsible. Were they exercising power without responsibility? These NGOs were also having a major economic impact. According to Professor Nicolas van de Walle of the University of Michigan, "in most countries in the African region the aid business is the second biggest employer."[2] There has also been a huge growth of foreign experts who work with local citizen groups. Professor van de Walle estimates that in a typical African country 30 to 40 donors, in addition to 75 to 125 foreign NGOs, fund 1,000 or so distinct projects involving 800 to 1,000 foreign experts. In countries like South Africa, the numbers in the 1990s, when many people in many countries came to help launch and energize the new democracy, were far larger.

Relating the civic and political energies let loose around the world to the American tradition of giving and volunteering was not easy. Americans in the 1980s and 1990s were engaged in a great debate about the social role of government and the public role of independent NGOs. A paradigm shift in the perception of the public function of organized philanthropy was still struggling for public acceptance. At the beginning of the century, the shift from the age of the individual to the age of organization had seen charity, which was basically ad hoc, individual, and affective, give birth to organized philanthropy, which was more systematic, calculating, and cognitive. But there were still many voices and views that sought to reverse the course of history and ask philanthropy to take on the role of charity.

In a 1965 report on private foundations, the U.S. Treasury Department had recognized the special nature of foundations by describing them as "uniquely qualified to initiate thought and action, experiment with new and untried ventures, dissent from prevailing attitudes and act quickly and flexibly."[3] Treasury's perception of foundation philanthropy was analogous to the research and development budget of a business corporation. As long as R&D funds were available in sufficient quantity, the corporation had the resources it needed to remain competitive—developing new products and improving old ones. If, however, research funds were eliminated or greatly reduced in order to put more money into the operating budget, it could lose its competitive edge and soon find itself in serious trouble. The same could be said of the American society if private philanthropy was to become primarily public charity, as some in the 1980s advocated. American society would lose a resource that had enabled it to "experiment with new and untried ventures—to act quickly and flexibly." It would find its unique bank of social capital directed toward ameliorating the consequences, rather than eliminating the causes, of social ills.

## The Redefinition of Compassion

In the 1980s, a new breed of Christian nationalists emerged calling on American society to replace public welfare programs and the liberal approach to private philanthropy (strategic intervention to eliminate the cause of social ills) with private church-based charity. Its leader-thinker was Marvin Olasky, an old nemesis who wrote at least one article a year attacking my views as president of the Council on Foundations as too liberal, a euphemism used often in that period to discredit those rejected on other grounds. Dismissed by reputable scholars as off the wall, his writings were ripped to shreds for their inaccuracies, distortions, and misuse of history. But he continued to attack mainstream philanthropy and the Council on Foundations, writing a forty-page monograph misquoting and using out-of-context excerpts from my speeches going back to university lectures in the 1960s.

Olasky was once a militant communist, but he had "found Jesus" and taken a radical turn to the far right. Finding himself marginalized in private philanthropy, he began a campaign to restore the moral glory of the Gilded Age and to discredit secular civil society. The more he argued for supernatural intervention rather than philanthropy and social service based on empirical research, the more popular he became in the ranks of the rising religious right. As Michelle Goldberg argues in *Kingdom Coming*, Olasky was on the cutting edge of an emergent epistemological revolution that would enable knowledge derived from faith to trump knowledge derived from studying the world. What followed was talk of a different kind of measurement of domestic social policy, one based not on data but on the beliefs drawn from religious faith.

The introduction for Olasky's book *Compassionate Conservatism* was written by George W. Bush, calling this once obscure theorist "compassionate conservatism's leading thinker." The *New York Times Magazine* reported in a 1999 article that one of Olasky's books, *The Tragedy of American Compassion*, was hailed by former secretary of education William Bennett "as the most important book on welfare and social policy in a decade." When Newt Gingrich, the new Republican Speaker of the U.S. House of Representatives, was handed a copy, he reportedly read it from cover to cover and liked it so much he had it distributed to all the incoming freshmen.[4] In his first address to the nation, Gingrich declared, "Our models are Alexis de Tocqueville and Marvin Olasky. We are going to redefine compassion and take it back."[5]

If Marvin Olasky's research and criticism of me had been more objective, he would have found that I have long been a proponent of collaboration with faith-based organizations. He would also have found that the early Christians with whom he was so fascinated were among the first to recognize that virtue alone would not feed the poor. Moral precepts were joined with behavioral injunctions. A vocabulary of duty and obligation developed alongside the language of love and charity. Just as for the Jew, for whom the concept of justice represented a coalescence of love and charity, the idea of compassion was an active rather than passive virtue for the early Christian.

The relationship between faith and philanthropy is both ancient and modern. From the very beginning of the new fascination with civil society, there have been those of us who recognized the contributions of the classic proponents of civil society, from Locke and Rousseau to Hegel and de Tocqueville, but who understood the many ways in which civic culture is also a moral culture that draws upon the ideals of Moses, Mohammed, Jesus, and Buddha.

Religious institutions have always made good partners for philanthropic individuals and institutions. They provide both proximity and trust. In many central city neighborhoods, for example, they are the only institutions left that can both command the respect of their neighbors and serve as vehicles for community development. Religious institutions also provide a good vehicle for donors to broaden their base of information and insight, for example, by including in the planning process those whom they seek to help. It is still true that if strategies to eliminate poverty and advance equity are to be effective, the poor must be included in their own development. Whether one calls this assisted self-reliance or participatory development, as some do, the religious institution in low-wealth communities is still a good place to engage grassroots energies and enthusiasms, not simply in defining problems but in proposing solutions. Experience around the world validated this call for partnership. Many communities came to recognize that when they empower the poor to be active participants in their own development, they have not only broader ownership but good ideas and new strategies as well.

The emphasis on private-public partnerships led the management guru Peter Drucker to coin a new term for this form of collaboration. He called it the "fourth sector," in many ways distinct from the public sector driven by ballots, the private sector driven by markets, and the third sector driven by voluntarism and the institutions of civil society. We now have an opportunity to expand the notion of a fourth sector or, alternatively, introduce a fifth sector where organized philanthropy and organized religion collaborate under a nonsectarian umbrella.

Regrettably, there can be no full-scale endorsement of all faith-based collaborations. There have to be appropriate checks and balances to ensure that the tax-exempt resources of foundations and the public resources of government are used in ways that are transparent and accountable to both private and public donors. The fear that faith-based organizations will intermingle resources for the propagation of the faith with resources for social ministry is a legitimate concern, but there is much that can be learned from the black church in this regard. Because black religious institutions have been under intense scrutiny from the very beginning of their efforts to collaborate with public institutions, many now make it a point to appropriately segregate funds, prudently account for expenditures, and ensure regular audits of their nonsectarian activities.

For most of the twentieth century, government at every level—local, state, and federal—had supported both religious congregations and noncongregation faith-based organizations to deliver needed services. Faith-based groups like Catholic Charities and Lutheran Social Services, for example, have been collaborating with foundations and governments at all levels without incident for a very long time. But they did so with a structure and a process that clearly separated the parochial purposes of their parent bodies from the social services they provided.

### The Limits of Private Action

Private philanthropy and faith-based initiatives are an important part of the American social landscape, but they do not eclipse the need for an active social role by government. When we seek to meet human and social needs primarily through private means, we run into some very serious social limitations. This is the point made by Professor Lester Salamon of Johns Hopkins University in his studies of voluntary action in the United States. He argues that benevolent wealth is limited in its ability to generate an adequate level of resources, is vulnerable to particularism and favoritism, and at times has been associated with amateurism.[6] On the surface, this seems like an unduly negative indictment of a noble enterprise, but Salamon is in fact pointing to the limitation of voluntary action in order to put it in perspective rather than simply to denigrate it. Using Salamon's reasoning, there are at least four classes of limitations on private largesse as a means of meeting social needs.

The central shortcoming of private benevolence is its inability to generate resources on a scale that is both adequate and consistent enough to cope with the social needs of an advanced industrial society. Whenever a large share of the burden of coping with social needs is largely dependent on private action, it is almost certain that the available resources will be less than what a truly benevolent community considers optimal.

The second limitation of private action is individual preference. Those who use private resources for public purposes rarely do so in such a way as to benefit all segments of the community equally. Thus, serious gaps may occur in the coverage of categories of need as well as groups in need. The emphasis is usually on meeting particular needs rather than addressing the general welfare.

The third limitation is democratic process. Exclusive dependence on private benevolence to meet social needs and solve social problems may place the power to define needs and determine which are to be met in the hands of those commanding the greatest resources. The nature and extent of the society's benevolence becomes shaped not by the community but only by its wealthier members.

Does this suggest, then, that private benevolence is of dubious value in maintaining a caring society? Quite the contrary. As I tried to show in two earlier works, *The Charitable Impulse* and *Remaking America*, it emphasizes the importance of developing compassionate values and encouraging private generosity. But it is put in perspective by emphasizing that in a truly benevolent community, the consensus welfare needs of the society are met by the people in common, while philanthropic individuals and institutions—true to their voluntary status—selectively choose which public purpose they will serve. They may choose to provide housing for the homeless. They may choose to feed those who are hungry. They may choose to help heal those who are sick. But when the intention is to promote the general welfare, the well-being of the community cannot be left to the private choices and preferences of those who voluntarily choose to be benevolent.

Fortunately, the idea of neighborhood benevolence—of neighbors looking after one another—is still alive in much of America. But as the boundaries and demographics of community change, so does the sentiment of generosity. As former U.S. secretary of labor Robert Reich reminded us in *Tales of a New America*, even if most Americans had the time or inclination to get to know their neighbors, most would meet people who share the same standard of living as they. If they are poor, their neighborhood is likely to be populated by other poor people; if very rich, by others who enjoy the good things in life; if young and professional, then by others who are young and professional.[7] Thus the idea of community as neighborhood offers a way of enjoying the sentiment of benevolence without the burden of really acting on it. If responsibility ends at the borders of one's neighborhood, and most Americans who are doing well can rest assured that their neighbors are not in dire straits, the apparent civic requirement of helping the neighbor can be satisfied at small cost.

### The Moral Power of Philanthropy

Philanthropy has always been about values. My good friend Paul Ylvisaker, a former dean at Harvard University and a Ford Foundation executive who was for a time the moral voice of philanthropy, not only spoke often of the relationship between philanthropy and ethics but conned many of us into making the trip to Cambridge annually to address his class at Harvard on the subject. One of my first decisions as the new president of the Council on Foundations was to hire Paul as a senior consultant. He liked to describe philanthropy as a salt that cannot be allowed to lose its savor, as a distinctive function that like religion stands essentially on its moral power. In a memorable speech in Atlanta in 1987 at the annual conference of the council, Paul warned against allowing an alien spirit to attach itself to philanthropy. To foundation trustees, he said, "Guard the soul of your organization, even from your own pretensions. . . . Be willing to open up the black box of philanthropy to share with others the mysteries of values and decision making."

To foundation managers, he said, "Guard your own humanity. . . . If you lose your own soul—whether to arrogance, insensitivity, insecurity, or the shield of impersonality, you diminish the spirit of philanthropy." To all associated with philanthropy, he said, "Never lose your sense of outrage. . . . There has to be in all of us a moral thermostat that flips when we are confronted by suffering, injustice, inequity, or callous behavior." He warned that the power of philanthropy could indeed corrupt. But conducted in a human spirit, and with soul, it can also ennoble.

Paul's death in 1990 dealt a serious blow to those of us engaged in the battle for the soul of philanthropy. But he left behind many disciples determined to continue the emphasis on philanthropy as "a distinctive function that like religion stands essentially on its moral power." I felt especially anointed when he offered to write the preface to my book on the charitable impulse, in which he described me as both "a prophet and a defender of the faith" who "speaks constantly and universally of the ideals of philanthropy and of its potential as an ennobling social force."

It was my belief in the moral power of philanthropy that led me to dive head-on into a controversy that some supporters urged me to avoid. In the early 1990s, I shared the indignation of those in Miami and elsewhere who condemned the snub of Nelson Mandela by south Florida mayors when Mandela praised Fidel Castro for coming to the aid of African National Congress exiles under attack by the South African Defense Force. Some local black community leaders called on national organizations to boycott the city of Miami as a conference venue until city leaders offered an apology to Mandela and business leaders took affirmative steps to hire more African Americans in the tourism industry. I had been involved in boycotts before and this was clearly the right response for many organizations, but the council and its members had the kind of clout that could be used to help the committee achieve its objectives if appropriately deployed. The best way of doing this had to be investigated. The answer might be a fuller immersion as an ally of the boycott committee rather than simply a dramatic gesture of avoidance.

The African American leaders who organized the boycott sent letters and a very impressive video indictment of the local mayors and their action to more than a thousand national organizations, calling on them to refuse to hold conferences in Miami. In early 1992, as the boycott was gaining steam, I received a letter from the local boycott committee urging the council to cancel our annual conference scheduled for late April that year. My first instinct was to go to my board and recommend that we either cancel the Florida conference and reschedule it for the next year or begin looking immediately for an alternative location. The annual conference was a big deal for the trustees, officers, and staffs of foundations and corporate giving programs. It had become an important meeting ground for substantive discussions of issues, ranging from threats to the tax exempt status of foundations and the nonprofits they fund to new ideas about how best to tackle serious social problems like those being highlighted in Miami.

The Miami location had been booked at least five years in advance because of the difficulty of finding conference hotels large enough to accommodate a gathering of our size on short notice. This left either the option of going ahead or rescheduling the conference for the next year. Before a report to my board could be completed, we received a letter from the ABFE urging us to cancel the meeting. I had been one of the founders and first chairman of ABFE. Their proposal was in line with the kind of action we had set up the organization to perform. Moreover, when I became president of the Council on Foundations I had urged ABFE leaders to keep the pressure on the council, arguing that I needed allies on the outside pushing for the same changes I was now seeking from within.

As I started to draft a recommendation to the council board, I discussed it with Sanford (Sandy) Cloud, a board member who was a vice president of the Aetna Life and Casualty Company and executive director of the Aetna Foundation. He had previously served in the Connecticut legislature and was a good friend who shared my indignation about the action of the south Florida mayors. I was surprised when he suggested that we look for an option that would not let council members off the hook so easily by joining the boycott and ignoring the many problems that created it. He offered to go to Miami with me to talk to Ruth Shack, the head of the Dade Community Foundation, and local leaders from a broad spectrum of the community, including especially the leaders of black nonprofit organizations who had been eager to have big foundation executives visit them in their neighborhoods.

Sandy and I went to Miami and along with Ruth Shack visited community leaders, public officials, the head of the Chamber of Commerce, local civil rights groups, tourism officials, hotel managers, the editor of the major newspaper, the boycott leaders, and others. Mary Braxton, a senior consultant to the council on communications, went along to staff our visit and coordinate conversations with the Miami press. It soon became clear to me that another option might indeed be possible and certainly worthy of consideration. Suppose we immersed the council directly in the issues involved and used the clout of our members to help solve them. The boycott leaders had added concern about the employment practices of hotels and the treatment of Haitian refugees to their list of grievances. In our meeting with the mayor of Miami Beach where our conference had been planned, there appeared to be an opening that could lead to a new resolution honoring Mandela rather than snubbing him. We held many other smaller conferences in hotels around the country with their executives competing for our business, and we could now demand diversity as a condition of our selection of conference sites. It might also be possible not only to bring foundation executives to local neighborhoods on field trips to see projects, but to hold some of our meetings in neighborhoods so that local nonprofit leaders who could never visit them in New York, Illinois, Michigan, or California could actually meet them in their neighborhoods. And, of course, we could speak to the leaders of the Congressional Black Caucus, already concerned about the treatment of Haitian refugees, about how we could best support their efforts.

I shared this very different option with members of my board and concerned allies who had a long history of seeking to change community practices and decided to flesh it out to ascertain whether it was doable or desirable. Some skeptics felt that this sounded like a cop-out and others did not believe that we could accomplish what the boycott had failed to do in several years. I was now convinced that we might be able to pull it off and decided to examine this option very seriously. My staff began discussions with hotel chains about our intended use of diversity on management staff as part of our consideration of which hotels to use. I spoke again to the mayor of Miami Beach and shared with him a draft of what a resolution honoring Mandela would look like and promised to personally take it to South Africa if the resolution was adopted. We spoke to members of the Congressional Black Caucus and found that they were already planning to speak out on the Haitian issue. I spoke to Maya Angelou, the literary icon who had been an ally of both Malcolm X and Martin Luther King Jr., about the option under consideration and whether she was still willing to be our opening plenary speaker as originally planned. She was enthusiastic about the idea and urged me to give it a try.

The Miami Boycott Committee was still skeptical, so when we arrived in Miami for the conference there were pickets around the hotel. Just before our opening session, I went out to meet with the boycott contingent, shared a copy of the resolution just passed by the Miami Beach Council honoring Nelson Mandela, and informed them that the number two hotel management executive where the conference was being held was now an African American, that the Congressional Black Caucus was taking on their issue regarding Haitian refugees, that the council had developed a model for bringing pressure on hotels under consideration for our conferences to diversify their management, of course, that Dr. Angelou would address their issues as our plenary speaker, and that other sessions were being held in local neighborhoods.

The boycott committee thanked us for our work on their behalf, took their pickets down, and went home. Thanks to the work of Mary Braxton, the lead story on the evening news was about what we had accomplished, and we received the praise of social activists in Miami and elsewhere for daring to take the many risks involved for me and the council. We had successfully demonstrated that while some actions may be bold and dramatic, others may be boring and dull and require far more work, yet have the potential for greater impact. We learned that the best strategy is one influenced by context. My own activism may have gone from the streets to corporate boardrooms and even presidential cabinet meetings, but I retained the same values and pushed just as hard for the same ends. And equally important, I reserved the right to return to the streets if that seemed like the best way I could help bring about needed change.

The period in which I worked almost around the clock in support of the objectives of the boycott was especially painful. My wife, Doris, had become seriously ill, but she insisted that I continue my efforts to support the activists in Miami and even find time to take the resolution of the city of Miami Beach to Nelson Mandela in South Africa as promised. She passed away just as I was about to reschedule the trip, so a few weeks later I went to South Africa where Mandela welcomed me with condolences for Doris and special praise for the Council on Foundations.

I continued to make the case that the tax exemptions private foundations and corporate giving programs enjoy is not a private interest loophole, but a public interest opportunity; that great value is added to democracy when citizens are encouraged to use private resources for a public good; and that a new ethics agenda had emerged that if left unattended could damage their image, diminish their influence, and defer the dreams of those whose vision gave birth to the institutions they represented.

I served as president and CEO of the council during a time of both major growth and major threats to organized philanthropy. But while the political environment changed from time to time, there was always something we had seen before. I was a young program officer at the Irwin-Sweeney-Miller Foundation when the 1969 Tax Reform Act was being debated. It seemed for a time that the explosion of distrust and dissatisfaction might cause Congress to throw out the baby with the bathwater. But organized philanthropy thrived and the council itself was better prepared and more politically adept in 1984 to deal with another round of legislative threats.

I also remember Black Tuesday, that infamous day in October 1987 when the stock market lost its luster and the assets of foundations tumbled. There was talk of raising the required annual payout because so many nonprofits were in crisis. Once again, we spent a lot of time before policymakers and opinion leaders making the case that while perpetuity (a legal term expressing the intent of the donor that the funds of the foundation exist forever) was not a panacea, it was an option that should be preserved. We gave considerable attention to the ethical question of how to balance the obligation to the future with the obligation to the present. I remember my long-term mentor, J. Irwin Miller, saying to me that the great cathedrals would never have been built if the people of that time had focused exclusively on the needs of the moment.

The battle for the soul of philanthropy is not new. What is new is the fact that the environment has changed and the ethical demands have taken on a different character. Paul Ylvisaker was concerned about the tension between the passion of the moral self and the dispassion of the professional self. He urged us not to lose the passion that comes out of the practice of charity nor the search for objectivity that comes out of the tradition of philanthropy. We now face a different kind of tension as private foundations have once again come under congressional scrutiny.

This can thus be a time to retreat into safe little boxes and lower the voices and visibility of private philanthropy, or it can be an opportunity to think outside the box, to refocus the mind and revitalize the soul of philanthropy. Foundations still need to guard against conflicts of interest, learn to value and promote diversity, practice transparency, and ensure that they serve a public purpose. But one of the questions that concerned me as the twentieth century came to a close is still a matter of grave concern. Many foundations and corporate giving programs still do not sufficiently respect the autonomy and integrity of grant seekers. This continues to be one of the most difficult ethical questions. The very act of helping is an expression of power, and it is often difficult to determine when the exercise of that power shifts from reasonable negotiation of a grant to unreasonable manipulation of a grantee. Those who seek grants talk of leveling the playing field where the relationship is one of mutual respect, mutual learning, and a partnership of equals. But how does one resist the temptation to dictate and direct when one may have access to wider knowledge about what works and what fails, and, of course, significant experience in how others have maximized the impact of limited dollars? As president of the council, I often warned new staff that arrogance is both the original sin and the enduring threat to the soul of the professional in philanthropy. I would urge them, therefore, to check their arrogance quotient from time to time, to remind themselves, lest they forget, that great ideas can often come from the most unlikely people in the most unlikely places.

While I remained a strong advocate for civil society throughout the 1980s with its emphasis on voluntarism and philanthropy, I still remain concerned that far too few foundation executives give as much attention to how they give as they do to what and to whom they give. Giving and caring are not only public values that need to be tempered with humility; they should also give rise to an ethic of giving in which how you give matters as much as what you give. Jacob Neusner argued in a 1985 article on Jewish philanthropy in *Foundation News* that responsible philanthropy requires consideration for the humanity of the recipient who remains no different from the donor. Those who receive are not less than those who give. They have not only needs but also feelings. They welcome not only beneficence but also our respect. So when we engage in the act of giving, we must do so in such a way that the equality of the giver and the receiver is acknowledged.

Neusner, who was at the time of his article a professor and distinguished scholar at Brown University, went on to argue that it is not enough to give; responsible giving must be done with thought. It must be marked by reflection, respect for the other party, and enhanced humility on the part of the donor. Neusner was Jewish and he was speaking out of his religious tradition, but one finds much the same moral injunction in Christianity, Islam, and other faiths where private philanthropy in its most widely accepted state is self-giving without being self-serving.

While criticizing foundations is for many nonprofit leaders akin to biting the hand that feeds them, some have been willing to take that risk and ask whether the standards of foundations match the standards of the nonprofits they fund. Many foundations have long tended, for example, to look suspiciously at and define narrowly the administrative overhead of nonprofits. But attacks and obvious misunderstandings of what should be considered the administrative costs of foundations have led them to make clear that philanthropy is far more than simply the giving of money. Some have done a good job in making the case that foundations can often function as effectively through making their staff available to help make a good idea better as through giving money. They may now need to apply the same line of reasoning to their analysis of the administrative overhead of nonprofits, most of whom do not enjoy the benefits of revenue-producing endowments.

Some foundation leaders are beginning to see themselves and the concentrations of wealth they represent as more than simply grantmakers. A prime example is the Heron Foundation, on whose board I have been privileged to serve. A decision was made to put all of the assets of the foundation at the service of its mission while reexamining the organizational model of the private foundation and reimagining it as a social enterprise with widely different opportunities to serve a social good. We have also developed a strategic planning process that considers how best to use not just financial assets but the myriad forms of capital at our disposal: social, intellectual, reputational, moral, and, of course, human capital.

My tenure at the council was characterized by a consistent query to the managers of these private pockets of wealth about diversity: did they fully appreciate the opportunity for a new kind of diversity that does not divide? The 1980s saw the blossoming of members of racial and low-wealth communities formerly associated primarily with the demand side of philanthropy becoming significant contributors to the supply side. They were demonstrating the potential to greatly enrich American civic culture, but they were demanding respect for their primary community of heritage and history before they fully embraced the larger community in which they functioned.

I had spent many years in the field of organized philanthropy, as a foundation executive and trustee, and president of the Council on Foundations, but I still cringed every time I heard some new guru on civil society speak of American generosity as if it was somehow unique to those citizens who traced their ancestry back to Europe. They too easily forgot that the first philanthropists on American soil were not Europeans, but Native Americans whose generosity enabled the new settlers to survive their first winter. Intrigued by this notion and disappointed in what I kept hearing, I began the research for the book I published in 1995 on the benevolent traditions of America's racial minorities. What I found were remarkable manifestations of the charitable impulse and civic feeling that in many instances predated, but were consistent with, the civic habits practiced and the civic values affirmed by the larger society.

As early as 1598 and long before Cesar Chavez started organizing farm workers, Latinos in the Southwest formed *mutualistas* and lay brotherhoods to assist members with their basic needs. Long before de Tocqueville, Benjamin Franklin became so enamored of the political and civic culture of the Native Americans he met in Pennsylvania that he advised delegates to the Albany Congress in 1754 to emulate the civic habits of the Iroquois.

Long before Martin Luther King wrote his "Letter from Birmingham Jail" or gave his "I Have a Dream" speech, African Americans in the nineteenth century formed so many voluntary groups and mutual aid societies that some Southern states enacted laws banning black voluntary activity or charitable organizations. Long before Robert Putnam published his first article on social capital, neo-Confucians in the Chinese community were teaching their children that a community without benevolence invites its own destruction. It should now be clear that it is no longer possible to speak of American civic culture without reference to the varied traditions that are now shaping our civic life.

The role of ethics and public values in the search for the next generation of leaders for private philanthropy remains a matter of great concern. Many new groups have been formed since the establishment of the ABFE in the early 1970s to address issues of diversity and inclusion. We were young and new to the field, but we were eager to help strengthen the leadership of the sector and to make it look more like American society. So one of my colleagues, Harriet Michelle, who was with the New York Foundation, and I called upon the newly appointed leader of one of the larger foundations to offer our help in identifying and selecting a diverse staff. He told us in no uncertain terms, and without embarrassment, that he had his own network from his days as a university president and did not feel the need for any outside advice. He all but implied we must have been smoking something if we believed that there were any blacks prepared to head a foundation like the one he represented. We have come a long way from that kind of talking, but have we come far enough from that kind of thinking? It is true that a decade later Frank Thomas was chosen to lead the Ford Foundation and I was president of the Council on Foundations, but many of the old stereotypes kept the doors closed to others for many years.

Recruiting the next generation of leaders will require that foundation trustees and managers look beyond the boundaries that presently define their comfort zone. The changing demographics of our society and the changing needs of our institutions will require that they include people with very different backgrounds if they are to continue to be effective.

The most fundamental challenge to civil society in the 1980s may have been the romanticizing of civil society as the answer for everything from poverty to marginalization, rather than recognizing it as an important, but by no means an exclusive, part of the answer. I found during my fourteen years as president of the Council on Foundations that some of the advocates for civil society were people who wanted to greatly limit, or even eliminate, the social role of government. Some of us who emphasized the potential of civil society felt an obligation, therefore, to emphasize both the potential and limits of philanthropy and voluntarism.

In 1990, I was invited by President George H. W. Bush to serve as an incorporating director and vice chair of the new Points of Light Foundation to help engage more people and resources in solving social problems through voluntary service. He subsequently invited me to both lunch in the private family quarters at the White House and dinner at the Camp David Presidential Retreat to discuss the idea he had described in his 1989 inaugural address as "a thousand points of light, of all the community organizations that are spread like stars throughout the nation, doing good." While my interest in voluntarism was much broader in scope than much of the talk I was hearing from others around the president, I considered it important to be involved in the conversation in order to make the point wherever I could that while many people saw voluntarism as what people do with their discretionary time, I regarded the civil rights movement as one of the best example of civic engagement and voluntarism in American history. Many of my colleagues on the board agreed, and we spoke often of "other-serving" voluntarism and included the words "serious social problems" in our mission statement.

While I was clearly a Democrat, my support of civic engagement went beyond political labels and partisan party politics. I knew that some of my colleagues were curious about how I could support the Points of Light initiative by a Republican president with whom I disagreed on some major policy issues, so I always made it clear that civic engagement was not a partisan political idea; that while private philanthropy and voluntarism can do considerable good, they can never serve as a substitute for or alternative to government. I shared the belief of many that a good society depends as much on the goodness of individuals as it does on the soundness of government and the fairness of laws, but I rejected the notion of some that private action could meet needs that fell legitimately and necessarily within the domain of government.

I was quite willing to encourage voluntarism, but I had no illusion that voluntary action alone would provide a safety net sufficient to meet the social needs of a complex industrial society. Far too many people associated with the president's political party used this renewed emphasis on the American voluntary spirit as a smoke screen to mask the meanness on display by some of those who led the effort to cut social spending by government.

It was because of my work with the Points of Light Foundation that I met Eli Segal shortly after the election of President William Clinton to succeed George H. W. Bush. Eli was a good friend of the new president's and served as a senior assistant at the White House with responsibility for developing what came to be called AmeriCorps. I called on Eli to urge the administration to support the continuation of the Points of Light Foundation. The president endorsed this program launched by his Republican predecessor, and Eli invited me to conversations at the White House about the development of a commission on national and community service to oversee the work of AmeriCorps when it became operational. It was after one of these meetings that Eli asked if I would be willing to serve as chair of the new commission. I agreed, and the president nominated me for official confirmation by the U.S. Senate. I was unanimously confirmed, and Eli and I worked together to implement what had been a major campaign promise by President Clinton.

The Corporation for National and Community Service is now a federal agency that helps more than five million Americans improve the lives of their fellow citizens through service. Volunteering and service have now become a vital and cost-effective solution to some of the nation's most difficult problems.

As the moral conscience of democracy, civil society organizations in the 1980s gained new attention and credibility as they expanded their activities beyond traditional charity and service to include public advocacy and policy analysis. Not all governments endorsed these new functions of civil society, but many began seeking ways to work together for the common good. In South Africa, for example, the tradition of civil society was deep and enduring. Many NGOs came into being as an alternative to government. With the apartheid state attending primarily to the needs of its small white population, civil society organizations were formed to fill in as much of the gap as possible for the other 90 percent. The primary function of many of these groups was to meet basic human needs and to provide basic social services. Other NGOs were formed to promote social change through policy analysis, advocacy, and protest. It is this latter group that is still struggling to find its place in the new democracy. While there is a role for partnership with government, the memories of an adversarial relationship still cloud and confuse new opportunities for collaboration.

Civil society in many new or reforming democracies faces the same dilemma. How can liberation movements, ecumenical coalitions, and the many informal institutions created to change governments be transformed to serve new purposes and meet new needs when they win their struggles and become the government? Strengthening democracy is rarely as dramatic as promoting liberation. The strategies are less clear and the satisfaction less immediate. There are no easy answers or quick fixes to this problem even in older democracies like the United States, where debates about the roles of government and civil society still stir passions.

What civil society advocates should seek from government is not absolute freedom, but a public space where citizen action is encouraged and the rules of civic engagement clarified. Democracy functions best with a policy framework that defines the parameters in which the three sectors—government, business, and civil society—are expected to operate. While the lines between these three sectors will almost always remain ambiguous, there should be some clearly delineated standards for determining who speaks for the public and what interactions with policymakers are appropriate.

The words "advocacy" and "lobbying" are sometimes confused as interchangeable forms of public action. But as some advocacy nonprofits like to point out, a lot of advocacy is just a matter of seeing a need and finding a way to address it. It means, literally, to plead the cause of another. It is when that pleading by government-endorsed groups (through tax exemptions or other forms of public approval) spills over into the political arena that the public is more likely to seek a measure of proportion in how the power and influence of these groups are used.

While the 1980s were banner years for philanthropy, civic engagement, and my work with the Council on Foundations, they were also a time of great transition in my family life. First, Jeffrey went off to study at Princeton, and a few years later Denise left for Mount Holyoke College. Jeffrey was born in the New Haven hospital as I was completing graduate study at Yale and always wore the Yale T-shirt as a child, but when the time came to make his own choice of a college—something we encouraged—he chose Princeton. Denise was so certain that Mount Holyoke was the college for her that we had difficulty getting her to increase her options by also applying elsewhere. The foundations they received at two of America's best institutions of higher education prepared them for careers of distinction, but, equally important, they reinforced the values and visions that we had worked diligently to cultivate at play and around the dining table as well as through reading and travel. Doris had interrupted a promising career in social work and scaled back her professional ambition in order to be more involved in their lives, but as they went off to college she returned to work—this time in public education. She also found more time to join me in helping to strengthen civil society in the United States and abroad.

The 1980s came to a close with many NGOs very visible in their communities and their activities occasionally dramatic. But while the idea of civil society conjures up visions of mass demonstrations and public protests in some parts of the world, there are many people in many other places working quietly and with much less fanfare, fewer economic resources, and less political power to improve the lives of those who are troubled, marginalized, or discriminated against. For them, civil society has a purposeful result: to change the power relationships in society in ways that allow justice and equality to flourish. I do not have any illusions that civil society, acting alone, is sufficient to meet the needs of a rapidly changing society. I do believe, however, that its encouragement is fundamental to any society that has faith in the essential goodness of the individual.

# IV

# The 1990s

MORAL LESSONS

FROM SOUTH AFRICA

# CHAPTER 11

# From Activist to Diplomat

*Race and Reconciliation in South Africa*

Friday, February 2, 1990, now looms large in South African history. It started out for me as a day of no special promise. I was in South Africa, once again leading a delegation of American foundation executives abroad. The buzz on this trip centered on the wide speculation that President F. W. de Klerk would use the opening of Parliament to make a major announcement. While some hoped that he would lift the state of emergency, others hoped that he would announce new measures to improve life under apartheid for the 90 percent of the population who were left intentionally underdeveloped through the practice of what was euphemistically called separate development.

I had not expected to be a part of the dramatic acts that unfolded, but as I walked outside of my Cape Town hotel a short distance from the regal halls of Parliament, I noticed a large crowd gathering. I saw a stage with microphones and the look of a protest rally, much like the ones I had helped organize in Alabama and Southern California. I soon became surrounded by a large crowd with Free Mandela signs. With a floppy hat and all of the preparation needed for the walk in the hot sun I had originally planned, I listened to the speeches and the call for a march to Parliament to register protest against the conditions of apartheid and the continued exile or imprisonment of their leaders. The protesters seemed to assume that I was a local colored also frustrated and angered by years of white rule, so they handed me a Free

Mandela sign and urged me to join them. Marching and singing, we soon arrived at Parliament.

The rally in front of my hotel and at the Parliament building was led by stalwarts of the United Democratic Front—clergy, union leaders, and educators—some of whom I knew and others I was to meet later. Inside Parliament, after the usual pageantry with women in colorful hats and men in their best suits, de Klerk was introduced for his presidential address. It started out with a long list of greetings, as is the custom on such occasions, but it soon came to the statements that would change life in South Africa forever.

In a few minutes of what was a relatively short speech, it became clear that de Klerk's message was of a very different tone and temperament from that in vogue at previous parliamentary openings. Calling up language from what I later read as page two of his speech, he told his audience, "The season of violence is over. The time for reconstruction and reconciliation has arrived."[1]

By the time de Klerk got to the section "Negotiations," his audience knew that something big was about to happen. It turned out that some antiapartheid leaders had heard rumors that Mandela might be released, but while their first reaction was that this was a trick or some form of trap, there were some high hopes. The suspicion and doubts ended when he said, "There is no time left for advancing all manner of conditions that will delay the negotiating process. The steps that have been decided are the following: The prohibition of the African National Congress, the Pan Africanist Congress, the South African Communist Party and a number of subsidiary organizations is being rescinded. People serving prison sentences merely because they were members of one of these organizations . . . will be identified and released."

The unfolding drama was still somewhat muted until de Klerk said the government noted, "Mr. Nelson Mandela has declared himself to be willing to make a constructive contribution to the peaceful political practices in South Africa. I wish to put it plainly that the government has taken a firm decision to release Mr. Mandela unconditionally." In a 5,160-word speech, de Klerk launched not only the political unraveling of apartheid but an irrevocable change in 338 years of social and political history. It was not just that he announced that Nelson Mandela would be released, but that he had called him "Mr. Nelson Mandela," bringing a new respect and dignity to the public discourse about the man who was an icon to millions but frequently denounced as a terrorist by government leaders, including Ronald Reagan in the United States and Margaret Thatcher in the United Kingdom.

The celebration began across South Africa. The previously banned African National Congress (ANC) flag mysteriously appeared in townships, rural villages, and cities. The lineup on the scaffolding stage outside Parliament was not only exuberant and formidable, but consisted of activists who were to play a major role in the launch and development of the new democracy. The names of the assembled leaders who until February 2 lived with a daily diet of police terror, intimidation, beating, jailing, and often brutal death read like a who's who of those who saved their country from economic and political collapse. Trevor Manuel, who was later to become the internationally respected minister of finance, had chaired the rally. He was joined by then Archbishop Desmond Tutu, who would go on to chair the Truth and Reconciliation Commission (TRC); Terror Lekota, a future defense minister; and Cheryl Carolus, an ANC leader who served later as the high commissioner to the United Kingdom. Others in the audience were to become mayors, members of Parliament, and even business tycoons in the transformation that followed.

In September 1992, I returned to South Africa with another delegation of foundation executives and met with many of the former prisoners who had been released and the exiles who had returned home. The dinner and press conference with Nelson Mandela was the highlight for my delegation. I was especially moved by his usual touch of warmth and humility when he thanked me for coming all the way to South Africa despite the fact that my wife, Doris, had very recently passed away. The next day I went to the new headquarters of the ANC to meet with Thabo Mbeki, who I was told would play a major role in the economic development of the country that had seen a decade of declining gross domestic product. On my previous visit in 1990, we had gone to Cold Comfort Farm in Zimbabwe to meet with ANC leaders in exile to determine whether they would support a call for a reengagement with South Africa by American foundations. We were pleased to see each other again, but this time we talked about more than the role of foundations in the new South Africa. There was talk of negotiating the transfer of power, the role of the larger nongovernmental sector in public life, the need for foreign investors to return, and how to deal with those who had perpetrated gross human rights violations. While difficult negotiations were still ahead, there was already talk of reconciliation as both a public value and a public process.

In January 1996, I was back once again in South Africa—this time as the newly appointed U.S. ambassador. It had been a long journey for Mandela, who went from prison to president, but it was no small step for me either as I went from consummate activist who regularly raised the ire of the apartheid government (and on occasion the sitting American ambassador) to the top U.S. diplomat working with Mandela to build a new democracy.

The 1990s were an incredible time to be in South Africa. But by the end of the decade, it was clear that what was happening was not the miracle some had assumed. The cessation of hostilities, the birth of a new democracy, the public acts of forgiveness, and the dismantling of legal apartheid were indeed extraordinary events, but the hard work that remained to be done was unsettling for some. Many whites and some blacks were trapped in the delusion that in a few years the legacy of apartheid would end. Some whites thought the smooth transfer of political power would be sufficient, but soon found to their dismay that blacks also wanted economic power. Yet, while the 1990s came to a close with a new realism about the task ahead, there was no reason to doubt that the fundamentals of the new democracy were sound and the new leaders determined to avoid the pitfalls of their neighbors in Zimbabwe.

## The Many Dimensions of Reconciliation

It was the spirit and acts of reconciliation that caught my attention as I tried to distill lessons from the South African experience that might have implications for the United States. I very quickly learned that authentic and enduring reconciliation takes place in many forms, but usually begins with the individual. I was able to listen in on private debates at diplomatic receptions, stately dinners, private homes, and even elegantly landscaped golf courses, but my first in-depth conversation about reconciliation in South Africa was with Kader Asmal, one of the architects of the TRC. While Kader was a member of the cabinet in both the Mandela and Mbeki administrations, he may be remembered best for what he had to say about reconciliation. He described individual reconciliation as "an existential rebalancing of the self, the undoing of historical illusions, deceptions and misteachings." To make this point, he liked to quote William Wordsworth, who wrote, "To be mistaught is worse than to be untaught. No errors are so difficult to root out as those which the understanding has pledged to uphold." Kader was an erudite academic and independent thinker who spent thirty years in exile in Ireland before returning to South Africa to help build the new democracy. For many years, he was the driving force behind the Irish antiapartheid movement while serving in senior faculty positions at Trinity College Dublin. The son of a small-town shopkeeper from Natal on the west coast of South Africa, he left home for London at an early age. I found him to be witty, combative, articulate, and urbane, but fiercely dedicated to the work of the ANC.

At a get-acquainted luncheon in one of his favorite restaurants near Parliament shortly after my arrival as the U.S. ambassador, Kader spoke of dignity as the human condition at the heart of reconciliation. "Apartheid," he said, "stripped our dignity away every bit as brutally and systematically as it curtailed our human rights. Voting in our first open and inclusive election has been a major step in giving it back." As a great legal mind and at that time one of the most popular ministers in the Mandela cabinet, it might have been expected that he would begin our first conversation with his thoughts about constitutional development or U.S.–South Africa relations, but here he was asking me whether there could be a more important human condition than dignity.

Forgiveness research in the field of clinical psychology provides clinical evidence to support Kader Asmal and his colleagues' emphasis on forgiveness as a necessary part of not just dignity but individual and communal health as well. Forgiveness works in two ways: (1) it reduces the stress that comes from anger, hostility, bitterness, hatred, and resentment, all of which lead to high blood pressure and impaired neurological function; and (2) people with strong networks of friends are often healthier than loners. Everett Worthington, executive director of the Campaign for Forgiveness Research, has identified two kinds of forgiveness.[2] The first is decisional forgiveness, a behavioral intention statement in which we say, in essence, "I'm going to control my behavior. I am not going to try to get even." The commitment is to moving on, just letting go of whatever has caused the alienation, a willful decision to no longer seek revenge or to extract anything from the offender (like apology or remuneration).

The second is emotional forgiveness, a process rather than a point-in-time decision. It is a process of replacing negative, unforgiving emotions with positive other-oriented emotions like empathy, sympathy, compassion, and love. While this can take a long time, these positive emotions are able to neutralize the negative emotions until the latter dissolve, thereby causing an internal state of ease and relief from one's own suffering. Long before forgiveness researchers, Confucius seems to have anticipated their scientific work when he warned, "If you devote your life to seeking revenge, first dig two graves."

The second dimension of reconciliation emphasized with great care and feeling by Nelson Mandela and Desmond Tutu was communal. It was based on the natural urge toward bonding and community, but the South Africans had a special word for this form of community. They called it *ubuntu*, an understanding of the human connection that was often expressed by the Xhosa proverb, "People are people through other people." It followed that to deny the dignity or damage the humanity of another person was to damage or destroy one's own. Ubuntu provided an alternative to revenge, an opportunity for forgiveness. It did not mean that the victim forgot, but it did mean recognizing that without forgiveness sustainable reconciliation is very unlikely.

This will to include everyone in the circle is the deeper motive for reconciliation. It creates a context for learning to live together, to deal with disputes, opposing ideas, and even violent conflicts. The notion of embracing others has deep roots in the South African experience. Some of the early warring tribes had "war healers," individuals on each side who sought after combat to engage the other side in the construction of a relationship that recognized the dignity and humanity of the former adversary.

Desmond Tutu frequently emphasized that communal reconciliation is also about creating a caring space for communication, providing opportunities for careful listening and deep conversations that enable people with profound differences to hear each other, respect each other, and begin the difficult work of building new relationships. The agreement to talk to the adversary is often the first step in finding solutions to what once seemed to be an intractable alienation. At a gathering of fellows in the leadership program I launched at the University of Cape Town, Charles Villa-Vicencio, director of the Institute for Justice and Reconciliation, who served previously on the staff of the TRC, called this "negotiating with one's memory and deciding which is to have the last word."

The third form or dimension of reconciliation pursued in South Africa was cosmic or spiritual, the claim common to all religions that we are not here alone, that each of us is a part of something bigger and more mysterious than the self. It is to say that the search for a higher level of being, the urge toward a universal connectedness, is a reflection of the human condition. It is thus in our common search rather than our different answers that we find common ground.

The many religions of South Africa may define and address holiness from different perspectives, but they are one in their recognition that because of our spiritual kinship with the larger universe, prejudice and discrimination should have no place among people of faith. That was the message of Muslims, Jews, Hindus, Buddhists, indigenous religious groups, Protestants, Catholics, Orthodox Christians, and others who came together at the Anglican Cathedral in Cape Town for the inaugural ceremony of the TRC. Sitting right up front with my new wife, Mary (Doris had passed away four years earlier), we listened intently to the prayers of the many religious leaders participating as they suggested one after the other that we diminish the preciousness and sacredness of life when we denigrate, disrespect, or oppress people based on the color of their skin, their ethnicity, or culture. To deny the dignity or humanity of another, they said, is to dishonor the sacred in the world, in one's self, and in others.

For all of our oneness in spirit, the touchstone of human interaction for Dullah Omar, South Africa's first minister of justice, began with the human community. And that is why the fourth dimension of reconciliation pursued in South Africa was political. Dullah, another great legal mind, had founded the Community Law Center at the University of the Western Cape and he understood that different kinds of conflict require different forms and ways of reconciliation. Political reconciliation is not dependent on the kind of intimacy that other forms of reconciliation may require. Rather, statecraft and politics require peaceful coexistence. Forgiveness may come later, after the creation of confidence and the building of trust. Charles Villa-Vicencio liked to tell the story of a Dinka elder who, in reflecting on the Sudanese conflict, said, "Reconciliation begins by agreeing to sit under the same tree with your enemy, to find a way of addressing the conflict." At one level, this may mean simply to stop killing one another. On another level, it involves a willingness to work together with one's enemies and adversaries in pursuit of a solution that is not yet at hand. Although this sense of reconciliation is incomplete, it does interrupt cycles of conflict and lay the groundwork for something deeper and different. It is, in Nelson Mandela's words, an attempt to resolve conflicts by the use of our brains rather than our blood.

Much was made in these early days of the so-called South African miracle. Yet the word "miracle" may not have been the best way to describe the transformations taking place. I had no theological problem with the use of the word, but I agreed with those who suggested that it may have been misleading. The word implies an act that is both extraordinary and complete. What happened in South Africa with the launch of the new democracy in 1994 was, indeed, extraordinary, but it was part of a process that will continue long into the future.

I was optimistic from the outset about the future of the economy and the next phase of political leadership and transformation, but what was really unique about South Africa was the way in which the country was tackling some of the most profound moral and ethical questions facing the world then and now; questions about truth, forgiveness, justice, and community. After a period of romanticizing the new beginning, South Africans settled down to the hard issues of the day. As the then deputy president Thabo Mbeki told a local audience at the height of the euphoria, "When we begin to grapple with real issues, when you pass beyond the hallelujah, what a lovely thing we have done, then problems begin. In reality, you cannot have real national reconciliation of a lasting kind, if you don't have a fundamental transformation of society."

It was Mbeki who most frequently reminded South Africans that a critical, but still very much unfinished, form of reconciliation in the South African lexicon was economic, removing the old barriers and developing new opportunities for black South Africans to earn an income, acquire assets, and accumulate wealth. In South Africa, as in the United States, race is so closely associated with class that it is not possible to speak of enduring reconciliation without recognition of the many ways in which economic policy under apartheid increased the wealth of the 10 percent of the population who were white and restricted the accumulation of wealth by the other 90 percent who were people of color.

Archbishop Tutu, the chair of the TRC and spiritual leader of those urging forgiveness, joined Mbeki in urging caution about a reconciliation process that was at best incomplete. He warned that the whole process of reconciliation had been placed in considerable jeopardy by the enormous disparities that remained between the rich and the poor. And it is this gap between the haves and the have-nots that posed the greatest threat to authentic reconciliation and enduring stability. The question here was not whether there should be some additional national effort to empower those who had been rendered powerless by years of intentional underdevelopment, but how it should take place. I heard the archbishop, affectionately referred to as "the Arch," warn on numerous occasions that unless houses replace the hovels and shacks in which most blacks continue to live, unless blacks gain access to clean water, electricity, affordable health care, decent education, good jobs, and a safe environment—things that a vast majority of whites and a small black elite have—South Africans, despite the painstaking work of the TRC, "can just as well kiss reconciliation good-bye."

These are not the words we tend to hear about South Africa from those seeking reconciliation in the United States. The emphasis is on forgiveness from those who have been the victims while very little is said about the responsibility of those who have benefited, and what measures of redress are morally necessary and politically feasible. Much the same can be said about the way we have sanitized the meaning and carefully selected the messages from Martin Luther King Jr. We gather annually in solemn assemblies across the United States to honor his memory and celebrate his life as an authentic American hero, but we focus on only a very limited aspect of what he had to say about reconciliation. Bill Chafe, a former dean at Duke University, argues that latter-day King celebrants focus on his support for reconciliation without acknowledging his prophetic anger.[3] King told his followers that standing beside love is always justice; not only are we using the tools of persuasion, we've got to use the tools of coercion. He went on to say, "The Negro's great stumbling block in his stride toward freedom is not the Ku Klux Klanner, but the white moderate who is more devoted to order than to justice; who prefers the negative peace which is the absence of tension to a positive peace which is the presence of justice."

When Desmond Tutu used a visit to Atlanta to propose a truth and reconciliation commission for the United Sates, the response of many African

American leaders was that what we need is a justice and reconciliation commission; that even those who wrote the American Constitution understood that if they were to finally form a more perfect union, they would have to first establish justice.

The South Africans also debated whether they should form simply an amnesty commission, a truth commission, or a justice and reconciliation commission. They chose truth and reconciliation because they recognized that they also had to reconcile conflicting images of the past. The United States has a different problem. We need to recognize conflicting images of not just the past but the present as well. When Ralph Ellison wrote *Invisible Man*, he pointed out how we had made the poor invisible, but today many white families know, or know about, at least one black family that is doing well, so they tend to live in psychological exile. They refuse to accept the reality that so many other blacks are doing badly. And where they accept it, they tend to reject any claim that this is somehow attributable to the legacy of slavery or segregation.

Truth and reconciliation commissions that simply allow people to tell their story may have some short-term therapeutic value, but if they are to contribute to long-term healing and reconciliation that can endure, they must seek not only forgiveness but restitution as well. The wealth profile of the United States is far more unequal than that of any other advanced country. And what was widely dismissed as a temporary blip or even a misreading of economic data is now an undisputed trend.[4] Most economists believe that the distribution of wealth as well as income is more unequal now than it has been since before the onset of the Great Depression.[5] Yet those who make that point in public discourse are likely to be accused of engaging in class warfare. But it is these differences in wealth and income that have such a devastating impact on the sphere of life ruled by money.

Wealth and whiteness have long been very comfortable bedfellows, but when Martin Luther King Jr. set out to launch a poor people's movement, he became more dangerous to the status quo precisely because he sought to join the civil rights struggle with a larger coalition of the American poor. What should concern Americans is that in the years since the Poor People's Campaign marched on Washington, economic inequality has risen rather than declined.

### The Utility of the South African Model

Those who wonder whether a truth and reconciliation commission might work in the United States should examine the South African model more closely. Before establishing the commission, South African leaders looked at more than twenty variations on this process from around the world. Most of the others were called truth commissions and did not share the wide ambitions of the South Africans to restore dignity, establish a true picture of what actually happened, and provide a mechanism for granting amnesty. The South Africans understood the benefit of learning from other nations, but most of the lessons seemed to come from the mistakes of others rather than successes.

The South Africans also understood the importance of the choice of who should lead the commission, not simply in managing the process but in what the selection symbolized about the integrity of the process. Nelson Mandela's appointment of Desmond Tutu as chair, although some had expected someone with a judicial background, was not altogether surprising. In 1976, the year of the Soweto rebellion that saw Hector Peterson and many of his youthful cohorts gunned down simply for demanding that English be the primary means of classroom instruction, Tutu was appointed Anglican dean of Johannesburg. Shortly thereafter, he wrote a letter to Prime Minister John Vorster in which he called attention to the need for "real reconciliation with justice for all." Twenty years later, he was asked to take a formal leadership role in healing the country's division. With an emphasis on truth rather than justice, members of the new commission were frequently told by both critics and supporters that it is not truth but justice that leads to reconciliation. A family member of one of the victims of apartheid-era violence said, "Tutu is a man of the cloth, a man who believes in miracles. But I cannot see him being able overnight to cause people who are hurt and bleeding simply to forget about their wounds and forget about justice." Tutu was not asking South Africans to forget. He was asking them to forgive, to be reconciled. Yet even Tutu acknowledged that it was mostly blacks who were doing the forgiving and whites who seemed to be asking everyone to forget. In the final report, Archbishop Tutu wrote:

> I want to make a heartfelt plea to my white fellow South Africans. On the whole we have been exhilarated by the magnanimity of those who should by right be consumed by bitterness and a lust for revenge; who instead have time after time shown an astonishing magnanimity and willingness to forgive, but we have seen it happen. And some of those who have done so are white victims. Nevertheless, the bulk of victims have been black and I have been saddened by what has appeared to be mean-spiritedness in some of the leadership of the white community. They should be saying: "How fortunate we are that these people do not want to treat us as we treated them."

While there are those who argue in South Africa and elsewhere that truth does not necessarily lead to reconciliation, for some in South Africa it already has. None of us who watched the proceedings of the TRC can forget the expressions of generosity and forgiveness by those who had been victims. One woman who had experienced the worst of apartheid's horror said, "I want to know who did what in order to know whom and what to forgive." After hearing a policeman confess in amnesty hearings before the TRC, another woman commented, "If I understand correctly this thing called reconciliation—if it means this perpetrator, this man who has killed my son, if it means he becomes human again, this man, so that I, so that all of us, get our humanity back—then I agree, then I support it all."

The victims who testified before the commission generally asked for very limited reparation, medical treatment, a tombstone, the restitution of land, and so on. I was reminded of this in seeing a woman at one of the hearings cry out, "Please can't you bring back even just a bone of my child so that I can bury him?" The commission was able to do so for some families, enabling them to finally experience a form of closure.

It was not only South Africans who demonstrated a remarkable capacity to forgive. The spirit let loose in South Africa was contagious. The Biehls from California, whose daughter Amy was killed in a township near Cape Town, faced her killers at a commission hearing and said that in the spirit of reconciliation they forgave them. This was a white American family who upon learning the truth about how their daughter died decided not to seek retribution, but to start a foundation in South Africa to continue her work. I asked Peter Biehl whether he could have ever imagined that he had within him the capacity to urge forgiveness for someone who had killed his daughter. He replied that he was influenced by the spirit of forgiveness and reconciliation in South Africa, plus he was certain this was what his daughter Amy would have wanted. Upon getting to know the young men involved, the Biehls were moved to help them and hired two of them to work for the Amy Biehl Foundation the Biehl family established.

The focus on reconciliation in South Africa in the 1990s was made more remarkable by the wide differences in tradition and theology that produced the architects of apartheid and those who paid so dearly for this heinous crime against humanity. As Allister Sparks reminds us in his superb book *The Mind of South Africa*, the early Afrikaners developed, in their way, perhaps the most boundless individualism that has existed anywhere. They built few villages and felt cramped if they lived within sight of a neighbor's chimney smoke. Here was the ultimate loner who needed to take no one else into account. The Afrikaners would come together briefly in times of danger, but otherwise each would be on his own, doing his own thing. So he became inward looking, concerned only with himself and his immediate family, unaccustomed to relating to others or to considering the views and feelings of outsiders.

This strong, almost fierce sense of individualism on the part of the Afrikaner was repressed somewhat during the later stages of Afrikaner nationalism, but it still remains a central part of the Afrikaner character. As such, it is the exact opposite of the communal tradition of the early Africans, who emphasized the group and the larger setting in which its members struggled to survive. It is when one understands this clash of concepts of community that the process of reconciliation led by Mandela and Tutu becomes truly remarkable. Apartheid literally meant the irreconcilability of people, while ubuntu emphasized a common humanity. Thus, many are led to ask, "What was the genesis of the early spirit of reconciliation?" There is no doubt that for an older generation of Africans like Nelson Mandela and Desmond Tutu, it came from the inner core of their being. Whether it was a form of African humanism or a fusion of Christianity and ubuntu, it was for them a moral imperative. For a younger generation of Africans, however, it may turn out to have been simply the practical reality of a negotiated settlement that required a process for providing amnesty and ending apartheid. As Tutu has acknowledged, South Africa's security forces would not have agreed to a peaceful settlement and transition from repression to democracy if they had thought there would be Nuremburg trials.

From the beginning, some whites voiced misgivings to me about the work of the TRC. While it was a product of an agreement by those who negotiated the new democracy, there was an attempt to equate the brutality of the apartheid state with the resistance activities of those who opposed it. Some whites still argue that the country's history is a clash of two legitimate patriotisms that are morally the same and should be treated similarly. Never mind that the TRC introduced us to some of the worst monstrosities that the mind could imagine. We listened with horror to tales of the bestiality of apartheid armies, sat in disbelief as we watched the stonewalling of F. W. de Klerk and the defiance of a recalcitrant P. W. Botha. Policemen told stories of festive celebrations and barbecues as they tore the bodies of prisoners apart limb from limb. Yet through twenty thousand statements of human rights abuses and more than seven thousand applications for amnesty, we experienced the surreality of the almost complete absence of vengeance. Of course, there was Winnie Mandela admitting that she lived through terrible times in which things went horribly wrong, and other blacks acknowledging that they sometimes struck back, although almost always to their detriment. But to call this a clash of patriotisms is like equating the resistance of an occasional Jew with the horrors of Hitler.

When the TRC finally presented its report to President Mandela in October 1998, there was consternation on all sides. While the report identified apartheid as the original sin, describing it as a crime against humanity, it also painted a broad brush of human rights violations that included those battling against apartheid. Many ANC members were confused, some even angry, that the abuses they had personally reported to the commission might now be seen as morally equivalent to the atrocities of the apartheid state. When we gathered at the Sammy Marks Conference Center in Pretoria for the presentation of the report, the atmosphere was tense. Joe Modise, the minister of defense and former head of the ANC's military wing, sat in the second row with ministers and diplomats, but he was visibly upset. Even the normally jovial Tutu wore a frown on his face for much of the ceremony. Mary and I sat with his wife, Leah, during the lunch after the proceedings, and while she was her usually warm and welcoming self, it was clear that she shared the archbishop's dismay.

The report made it clear that it did not hold all parties equally responsible, but it grouped the ANC and the apartheid state together in the section on "Gross Human Rights Violations." That, in the eyes of some, was unacceptable. The ANC went to court to seek a delay of the report until its leaders had time for further consultation with the commission. The court ruled against the ANC and the report was released as scheduled. President Mandela had insisted on transparency in the process and immediate release to the public once it was submitted. He stuck to his guns, acknowledging imperfections in the report as he accepted it, but commending the commission for its important and outstanding work. The ceremony ended with Mandela and Tutu toyi-toying to the music of the choir. When I saw Tutu later, he was calmer and more relaxed, but the scars of the preceding twenty-four-hour court battle were still visible. He continued to argue that while the liberation struggle was a just cause, a just cause does not exempt an organization from pursuing its goals through just means.

When the two houses of Parliament convened in a joint sitting in Cape Town on February 25, 1999, to consider the report of the TRC, sparks continued to fly. While saluting the TRC for its work in various areas, Thabo Mbeki, speaking for the ANC, again voiced serious reservations about the definition of the concept of gross violations of human rights. Mbeki argued that grouping the ANC with the apartheid state under the heading "Gross Human Rights Violations" served to "delegitimize or criminalize a significant part of the struggle of our people for liberation." He went on to say that "the logic followed by the TRC, which was contrary to even the Geneva Conventions and Protocols governing the conduct of warfare, would result in the characterization of all irregular wars of liberation as tantamount to a gross violation of human rights."

From the diplomats' gallery in the National Assembly chamber, I could feel the tension and anger of the debate; but when all was said and done, with appropriate references to the report's imperfections, there was wide agreement that the commission had made an extraordinary contribution to reconciliation.

### The Apartheid Era's Dirty Tricks

The testimony of scientists who headed the apartheid government's secret poison program should have laid to rest any notion of moral equivalency between the activities of the apartheid state and those who struggled against it. Tutu's response to the information they shared and the review of documents from meetings of the Security Council was, "I'm horrified. I am trying to retain faith in humanity." The commission thought it had seen and heard the worst of apartheid-era horrors until it learned of the work of the Roodeplaat Research Laboratories, which produced chemical and biological weapons for apartheid security forces. The revelations began with minutes of a meeting in 1986 where it was argued that if Mandela was to be released from prison he should first be given small doses of thallium poison, which would cause brain damage similar to meningitis, making him a frail and sick man who would pose no political threat.

This was just the tip of the iceberg of subsequent revelations about the hideous chemical and biological weapons used against those who opposed the policies and practices of the state. The men at Roodeplaat had spearheaded efforts by the government to develop chemicals and antifertility drugs that would work only against "pigmented people." They were responsible for the development of James Bond–type screwdrivers and umbrellas to kill and assassinate; the spiking with toxic substances of cans and bottles of beer intended for distribution to ANC activists in neighboring states and former homelands; T-shirts laced with carefully selected drugs that were to be handed out at rallies and meetings of the opposition; large quantities of deadly cholera and anthrax cultures that could kill tens of thousands of people; and tons of ecstasy and mandrax drugs to spray into the air and pacify angry young blacks.

When questions were raised about how many of these were actually used, the scientists claimed they were asked only to produce these biological weapons, not to make moral decisions about how they were to be applied. Some witnesses did tell hair-raising stories, however, of how a snakebite serum was used to kill a serviceman "with leftist leanings" and how Russian technicians were killed with anthrax bacteria. Another indicated that the poison that nearly killed the Reverend Frank Chicane, the former head of the South African Council of Churches, came from his lab. Dullah Omar, the former Cape Town activist who served as justice minister in the Mandela government, had also been a target of the "doctors of death" who tried unsuccessfully to doctor his heart medicine.

Other plots uncovered included one by the Intelligence Agency to spread HIV/AIDS by passing the disease to prostitutes. The TRC commissioners also found evidence that the apartheid state had fueled rebel movements against the governments in Angola and Mozambique, and conducted raids into Botswana, Lesotho, and Swaziland as well as military involvement in hit squads across other national boundaries. Undercover operations were also discovered in Europe that extended to Sweden and Norway by the 1980s. There were claims also of cooperation between South African agents and their counterparts in many other countries. One of the most blatant examples of South African aggression against neighboring states was the massacre in Angola in 1978, when about six hundred people died. Yet no South Africans were ever brought before the International Criminal Court.

As these stories about assassinations and near misses came out, one was forced to ask how many activists and supporters who appeared to have died of diseases and natural causes were actually killed by these evil substances. Some of the merchants of death who testified at TRC hearings showed no remorse. Many were prominent doctors, who worked for the personal physician to the apartheid head of state, P. W. Botha. One said, "I did it for God and fatherland." Others may have done it for money. They were the ones who chartered Lear jets to watch rugby matches in Scotland and traveled the world staying in the finest hotels.

Despite these horror stories told to the commission by some of the apartheid state's most notorious assassins, I frequently encountered white South Africans who insisted that these stories were fabricated by a biased ANC-dominated TRC. Never mind that these were the confessions of white former government agents, not representatives of the ANC. Never mind that television audiences were treated to a daily diet of bloodcurdling stories of human rights abuses by apartheid-era officials whose faces and mannerisms could have just as easily been those of Hitler's ss troops in Germany or the Ku Klux Klan in the United States. Well-dressed women at dinner parties and well-heeled men on the golf course continued to reject these confessions as the honest truth about the past. They preferred to speak of the wonderful days when crime was confined to the townships and their children did not have to go to school with kids who were "unwashed and undereducated."

While the debate about the value and utility of the TRC continues, what is not debatable is the reconciling spirit of the many victims who seem to harbor no bitterness. Paramount among these was Nelson Mandela, who said, "I am often asked how it is that I emerged without bitterness from so long a time in prison. This question is intended as a compliment, and I can appreciate the motives of those who ask it. Nevertheless, it must be said that millions of South Africa's people spent an even longer time in the prison of apartheid. Some were imprisoned by the apartheid laws in a condition of homelessness and near despair. Others were imprisoned in the racism of the mind. These are places where some still languish."

One final thing stands out in my experience of reconciliation in South Africa. It could have been easy to simply focus on the perpetrators of violence and not the victims, but the TRC, under the leadership of Archbishop Tutu, was a form of ministry to the victims. It reminded South Africans of the horrors of the past, but the real story is not yesterday's inhumanity. It is the compassion and respect for humanity that shocked the world and won new supporters for the work of the commission. It is the story of the paradigm of ubuntu setting free both the perpetrators and the victims to build a new national community, where, in the words of the Xhosa proverb, "people are people through other people."

What happened in South Africa, what remains with me as a prevailing insight, is that the healing of a nation requires an active process, not just some dramatic event, and that the TRC contributed magnificently to that process. Some fear that the gains made under the leadership of Nelson Mandela, Desmond Tutu, and others of their generation are unraveling. There is no doubt that reconciliation is under the strains of new realities, but the course has been set and the majority of South Africans, white and black, are committed to building a democracy that serves all those who live within the national boundaries.

# CHAPTER 12

# Dismantling Apartheid

*The Unfinished Agenda*

The Parliament was buzzing with excitement on May 8, 1996, as I took my seat in the gallery with my colleagues in the diplomatic corps. With a late-night agreement between the African National Congress and the National Party the night before, all that was left to adopt the eagerly anticipated constitution was the drama of debate, the final voting, and the celebration of what Cyril Ramaphosa, the ANC cochair of the Constitutional Assembly, described as the "birth certificate" of the new South Africa. The Greeks and Romans may have set the early standards for political oratory, but the South Africans, who have their own gift for political theater, seemed determined to set new standards of their own.

Leading off for the ANC, Deputy President Mbeki gave a poetic and moving speech that brought many in the audience to tears. It was not the expected political speech, but an elegant literary statement of what it means to say, "I am an African." Mbeki's emphasis on his personal connection to the land, the people, and the wide diversity of South Africa's heritage set a tone that all subsequent speakers sought to emulate. F. W. de Klerk, the leader of the National Party and the second deputy president in the Mandela government, reminded the assembly that he too was an African. But the most important part of his message was the formal announcement that the National Party would join the ANC in voting for the constitution. This assured cheering delegates that the votes needed for adoption were now publicly committed.

Tony Leon, the leader of the very small but influential Democratic Party that Helen Suzman had once nurtured, was next. The major suspense was not about the party's vote but about how Leon would be greeted after several days of bashing both the ANC and the National Party. To the surprise of many, he assumed the mantle of a statesman, looked beyond his European heritage, and spoke about his African roots that went back four generations. At the end of his rhetorical flourish, he announced that despite some lingering concerns, the Democratic Party felt compelled to support the new constitution.

The drama mounted as General Vilhoen, the former defense minister in the old government and leader of the Freedom Front, came to the podium to speak in both Afrikaans and English. His colleagues in Parliament cheered with increasing enthusiasm as he announced that there were too many good things in the constitution for his party to vote against it, but the cheering came to an abrupt end when he told his attentive audience that the Freedom Front would abstain. The spokesman for the Pan Africanist Congress followed. After expressing his delight as a nationalist that all of the preceding speakers had espoused the African consciousness of his party, he voiced reservations about whether the constitution was as much an African document as he had hoped, but endorsed it as a major step forward.

The final speaker was the leader of the Christian Democratic Party. He argued that the Bible had primacy over the constitution and the preamble was deficient in not making this clear. The assembly was not surprised to learn that his party would cast its two votes against the constitution. The final vote was 421 yes, two no, and ten abstentions. The Inkatha Freedom Party did not participate in the Constitutional Assembly, and its representatives were not present for the final debate, but even if their votes were recorded as no, the constitution would still have been approved by 85 percent of the members of the assembly.

After the official vote, President Mandela closed the proceedings with an appeal to all South Africans to continue the efforts at reconciliation under way and to adopt a new patriotism that moved away from the sectional interests of the past to embrace the commonweal.

### Sharpeville Revisited

Later that year, South Africans from across the country gathered in Sharpeville for the final signing of the constitution. The sun was hot, the crowd was jubilant, and both the old guard and the new leaders of South Africa toyi-toyed to the music of Hugh Masekela. They had come to Sharpeville to sign and celebrate the new constitution. Twenty-two survivors of the 1960 Sharpeville massacre were also present to witness this final consignment of apartheid to the dustbin of history. The signing ceremony took place in front of the thousands of local residents, South African dignitaries, and foreign diplomats who had come to help usher in this new period of constitutional democracy.

The security was tight and highly visible from the city limits to the George Thabe Stadium. There seemed to be as many soldiers and police as spectators. The Venezuelan ambassador commented to me in a whisper that the armored vehicles looked exactly like the ones used to control demonstrations in the dark days of apartheid. They probably were, but this time they were protecting the people they had once assaulted.

I arrived at the stadium early with a bottle of water and wearing a Cape Town 2004 Olympics cap. For the next three hours, I was thankful that I had been urged to take these precautions. The heat was fierce and my mouth, which always seemed to be dry in South Africa, was parched again. My colorful Cape Town cap did not go well with my dark blue suit, but I knew that the guests at the reception immediately following the ceremony would be decked out in what were euphemistically called lounge suits. I was right, and I was able to uphold the standards of the diplomatic corps that dressed up even for the omnipresent South African *braai* (barbecue). I had once been stunned when one of my ambassadorial colleagues showed up in a suit and tie for a group walk up Table Mountain.

The constitution President Mandela signed entrenched the values that had driven the long struggle for liberation, whose final triumph we had come to celebrate. De Klerk was there along with both the architects of apartheid and the authors of the new document guaranteeing a new democracy. I sat for most of the three hours behind Walter Sisulu and de Klerk. I am not sure what went on in their minds as they shared this moment side by side, but I could not help but think that the day and the moment meant different things for each of them. For Sisulu and many in the audience, sad memories undoubtedly came flooding back as they recalled how thirty-six years before, on the twenty-first of March, sixty-nine of their relatives and friends were silenced forever by some of the same tanks now parked outside the stadium to protect the aging revolutionaries. The day was as much for the dead as it was for the living. The music of Hugh Masekela made this point as he implored all the ancestors to join the celebration.

De Klerk was probably focused on the future, as he was when I had spoken to him a few days earlier. At that time, he had predicted an eventual party realignment that would bring his party and its leadership back to the center of South African life. I remember thinking how tragic he looked and sounded, like a man who was saying what he thought he had to say but really did not believe. He looked somewhat out of place, but there he was in Sharpeville with a group of people who were celebrating the accomplishments of the ANC as much as the signing of a constitution.

## The Wild Card in the South African Future

President Mandela called on the audience to work together and to put the public good ahead of partisan clashes. Even on the grounds where in 1960 bodies lay prostrate, crying in anguish, awash in blood and bullets, Mandela could call for national reconciliation. Such was the measure of the man and the moment. Yet the wild card in the South African future is not simply race and reconciliation, but equity and inclusion. Having ended legal apartheid, the South Africans were committed to nation building that goes beyond racial to national claims. Leaders of the large African majority acknowledge, however, that the deracialization of South African society will require race-specific remedies that take race into account. Some white South Africans argue that this is inconsistent with the ideal of a nonracial society. They call instead for race-neutral approaches. But as the highly respected former speaker of the South African Parliament, Frene Ginwala, reminded me in Cape Town, "This is manifestly not possible. To deracialize," she argued, "we have to focus on race. Together with the racially based inequalities we inherited, we find that the very instruments we must use to manage society and to overcome the legacy are themselves shaped by racism and designed to perpetuate unequal relations." Black South African leaders argue that they cannot go beyond race until they have removed the barriers created because of race. The government's approach is increasingly called corrective action.

The full flowering of democracy in South Africa may require a new language of nonracialism and corrective action, but for the immediate future it will sound very much like multiculturalism and affirmative action in the United States. It is as true in South Africa as it is in the United States that no well-intentioned equal opportunity policy can be successful without recognition of differences. If it was group identity that created a problem, group identity must be considered in resolving it. To make this point more clearly, some in the United States use the analogy of a man whose leg has been broken intentionally before he is allowed to compete in a hundred-yard dash. There is no equal opportunity until there has been corrective action to mend the broken leg.

The question about the role of race in guaranteeing equality of opportunity and the elimination of apartheid's nasty legacy is part and parcel of the larger question regarding the building of a new South Africa. In the book *Conflict and Peacemaking in Multiethnic Societies*, Uri Ra'anan argues that because of the rise of the nation-state as a fairly recent phenomenon, it has over the last fifty years become fashionable to "clean up" the ethnic map. This has included genocidal measures against "Jews and Gypsies under Hitler, Ibos in Nigeria, Southern blacks in the Sudan; both Tutsis and Hutus in Rwanda and Burundi; Kurds in Iraq and overseas Chinese in certain parts of Southeast Asia."[1] The list goes on of people who have been expelled and populations that have had to take flight from their homelands because of fear. Almost everywhere we look, there is testimony to the difficulties of forging a nation-state from multicultural, ethnic, or multiracial societies.

When I first visited South Africa in 1974, I got into trouble for describing apartheid in a widely published press interview as a "pigmentocracy" where rights and resources were apportioned in accordance with the pigmentation of the skin. The old pigmentocracy is gone, but a new form of "pigmentology" has emerged. It can be seen most conspicuously in the search of some of the mixed-race members of the colored community for an identity separate and apart from white or black. During my first visit, I noticed that most members of this community referred to themselves as "so-called" coloreds. The term "so-called" was rarely in use when I returned some years later, as many colored South Africans now identified with the European part of their heritage and supported white-dominated political parties. It has usually been assumed that a sense of difference leads to discrimination, but this is a case where discrimination has led to a stronger sense of difference.

While the emphasis has been on reconciling whites and blacks, many of the coloreds in the Cape are increasingly restless about their own identity and status. Some even prefer to be seen as brown Afrikaners rather than be identified with black Africans. They claim that they were not white enough under apartheid and are not black enough now to ensure an equitable sharing of the economic benefits of the new democracy. While many coloreds occupy high positions in the ANC, the ruling party, and the government, the legacy of separate development still perpetuates the divisions the apartheid state fostered and practiced.

Under apartheid, the South African population was divided into four major racial categories: Africans (usually blacks), Europeans (whites), coloreds, and Asians. While the separate development laws have been abolished, these categories are still in use when groups describe themselves or each other. Coloreds are primarily mixed-race people, but the category is used to describe some of the indigenous population groups as well. They compose about 9 percent of the population. Whites or Europeans, who compose about 10 percent of the population, are primarily descendants of settlers who came from the Netherlands, England, Germany, and France. Many arrived in the eighteenth century and now regard themselves as Africans. Black Africans compose about 80 percent of the population, including the still-influential Zulu and Xhosa tribes. The Asians are a much smaller group who are primarily the descendants of Indian workers who were brought to South Africa to work on the sugar estates, located primarily in the province now called KwaZulu-Natal.

The legacy of identifying people by color continues to cast a long shadow on the South African landscape, where many whites are still living in denial about the past. It is difficult to find anyone in South Africa who will admit to having supported apartheid. Many whites claim to have had no knowledge of the brutal means used by the state to support the quality of life they enjoyed. It is not surprising that the debate about how to eliminate racial inequalities is beginning to echo the debate in the United States.

### Color Blindness and Honorary Whites

Some South Africans are beginning to recognize that before addressing the limits posed by the legacy of separate development, they will need to come to grips with the fallacies of the notion of a color-blind society; how, for example, it perpetuates white privilege gained through apartheid rather than increasing racial equality. The American society provides a good example of what South Africans must avoid. In the United States, many well-meaning people believe that they are now living in a postracial society. But the ideas of color blindness and even racial reform have had a complicated and uneasy history in American society. For much of the twentieth century, the United States pursued a policy of separate but equal in which a paradigm of segregation based on race prevailed. Those of us who studied in segregated schools witnessed firsthand the fallacy of the separate but equal doctrine. Neither the society nor the courts embraced color blindness and race neutrality where doing so might have led to the demise of white privilege. In the second half of the twentieth century, beginning with the *Brown* decision in 1954 outlawing segregation in public schools, advocates of color blindness surfaced in larger numbers. With whites firmly entrenched in privileges provided by a rigid segregation in which they were subsidized across virtually every social, political, and economic domain, the paradigm of nonracialism helped to preserve rather than challenge the status quo.

In apartheid South Africa, the architects of separate development invented a novel category called "honorary white" for those foreign nonwhites they wished to temporarily exempt from the rigid restriction imposed by the state. The Japanese were the most prominent group in this category, but non-whites representing business interests from other countries were also given that designation when it was necessary to permit them to travel, reside, or conduct business in South Africa. Some observers of the role of color and race in the United States argue that we are seeing the emergence of an honorary white status in American society as well. It is more of a cultural and psychological shift than a formal policy, but it is part of a larger transition from a biologically based definition of race toward one that is culturally and socially based. And while there is a continuing evolution in who counts as white, particularly as it relates to the new immigrants from Latin America, the stain of African ancestry ensures a continuing stigma for black people, whose skin and other features have traditionally identified them as nonwhite. For the most exceptional and especially those who by feature or acculturation no longer remind whites of the enduring negative traits associated with blackness, an honorary white status is permitted—much like the Brazilian notion that money "whitens."

Many who study the evolution and impact of color blindness, moreover, suggest that even under a redefined white category, racial hierarchy will continue as the links are strengthened between nonwhite identity and social disadvantage on the one hand, and whiteness and privilege on the other. To claim that color blindness is the way forward, then, is to protect a new racial politics that clothes itself in the language of civil rights while maintaining white privilege acquired by restricting the opportunities of those who were identified as black.

Nonracial or postracial politics may be in our future, but for the moment both Americans and South Africans will need to learn to value differences. The British rabbi Jonathan Sacks, who wrote *The Home We Build Together*, argues that the more diverse we are, the richer our culture becomes, and the more expansive our horizon of possibilities. He went on to say, "If we were all the same, we would have nothing unique to contribute, nor any thing to learn from others. We need to see our differences as gifts to the common good. Without a compelling sense of the common good, difference spells discord and creates not music, but noise."[2]

When some South African analysts look to the future, they worry about the impact of race on politics, arguing that the ANC is too strong and too black for the ultimate good of public life. Developments within the ANC since the Mandela years may demonstrate just the opposite, that what is to be feared is not the ANC's strength but its weakness. The white authors of the book *Comrades in Business* point out that a strong ANC is a large tent. It represents many races and many views, ranging from conservative to liberal, thus ensuring that its policies are moderated by the need for consensus. What all of us should want and support in South Africa is the kind of political pluralism in which its people are free to choose their own leaders, shape their own politics, and govern with the needs of all the people in mind. It is up to them, not outsiders, to determine which parties are strong and which parties are weak.

The seeds of division that led to a split within the ruling party were highlighted in the struggle for party leadership between Thabo Mbeki, Mandela's successor, and Jacob Zuma, whose brand of populism struck a chord with many who remained trapped by the legacy of apartheid. The rise of a black middle class and the small, but high-profile, black elite are developing interests that are increasingly different from those of their alliance partners in the Congress of South African Trade Unions. Moreover, nearly one-third of South African voters are too young to have any direct memory of apartheid and the struggle against it. But while the Mandela magic and the memories of the ANC as a liberation movement have started to fade, I am convinced that both will continue to influence South Africa's politics far into the future. Mbeki was deposed from his leadership role in the ANC by an alliance of those alienated by his personality, policies, and politics. But while many in this new alliance differ on priorities and strategies, a large majority are still wedded to the ideals and goals of the ANC.

White South Africans seem to scare themselves in cycles. When I first visited the country in the 1970s, there was a fear of *swart gevaar*, the black threat. The fear is no longer simply about race. Yet one cannot forget the hysteria in the white suburbs just before the 1994 election of Nelson Mandela. The advice heard most frequently was, "You better stock up on canned foods, water, guns, and ammunition because there is going to be chaos." Of course the sky did not fall, and most came to regard Mandela as almost a saint as he counseled blacks to forgive and to move on.

When Mandela's term neared its end and it was clear that Thabo Mbeki would succeed him, many whites feared either that socialism was around the corner or that Mbeki was a closet racist intent on depriving them of their wealth and their apartheid-era benefits. In fact, Mbeki turned out to be a strong apostle of a market economy. The whites who owned the economy got wealthier, and the masses they feared Mbeki would favor saw little economic advancement. This cycle of fear of the black "other" reached its crescendo in the appointment of a finance minister and the governor of the Reserve Bank. Many have forgotten their own rage about the appointment of Trevor Manuel and Tito Mboweni. Manuel, the former Cape Town activist who was a founder of the Democratic Front, became so good at his job that both the World Bank and the International Monetary Fund now regularly seek his advice and assign him leadership roles in economic forums. At home he is revered by whites as the premier example of an efficient and effective government official. At the same time, Mboweni steered the course at the Reserve Bank for years with skills that both the local and international financial communities regularly celebrate.

In 2009, Jacob Zuma was elected president, with the ANC receiving almost 70 percent of the vote. In a campaign where whites in the opposition Democratic Alliance had predicted the end of the ANC, some reverted to the old cycle of periodic anxiety and fear. The old fear of "the blacks" reemerged. Some who were convinced in 1994 that the reins of government had been taken over by their maids and gardeners suddenly relived those earlier fears. Apartheid had robbed them of a relationship with blacks of different standing, so their image of the new leaders mirrored that of the blacks they knew. Meanwhile, the poor who had become frustrated by the failure to bring them into the mainstream economy could have burned down buildings and created havoc for those enjoying the fruits of a growing economy. Instead, they did a strange thing. They used the democratic process to change leadership.

While the Mandela presidency focused on individual and communal reconciliation and the Mbeki presidency continued the emphasis on economic reconciliation that began while he was Mandela's deputy, Jacob Zuma was more of a reconciler by instinct. He had no grand design for uniting a still badly divided society, but he demonstrated the kind of personality that brings people together and the wherewithal for sage political judgment. Even before the election, he reopened conversation with right-wing Afrikaners and later appointed one a deputy minister in his cabinet. As a cultural traditionalist himself, he understood and respected the aspirations of the Afrikaners to maintain their culture. It was for this reason that he had been asked, in the years of negotiating a new democracy, to play a leadership role in bringing Afrikaner dissenters in the National Party and Zulu traditionalists in the Inkatha Freedom Party to the negotiating table.

Zuma's traditionalism dogged him from the beginning of his presidency. For some in the rising black middle class, he was too African. They feared he would reinforce old stereotypes. For some in the white English community, he, like the Afrikaners before him, disturbed their comfort zone with displays of a culture they regarded as not only different but inferior to the Anglo-Saxon identity they touted. They were open and accepting of those black South Africans who were willing to become black Saxons with an acculturation to Western values and social etiquette. But the sight of their president dressed in animal skins at traditional Zulu celebrations was only slightly less offensive to the English sensibility than his practice of polygamy.

Zuma answered his cultural critics in a 2010 interview at the World Economic Forum in Davos. He said that polygamy and his personal practice of multiple wives were part of his culture, and those who thought their culture was superior had a problem. He went on to say that in South Africa, "We follow a policy that says you must respect the culture of others. It does not take anything from me, from my political beliefs, including the belief in the equality of women. The problem arises," he added, "when people think their culture is the only right one . . . the only one accepted by God"[3] The clash between traditionalism and modernity continues in South Africa, but Zuma's election reinvigorated the masses who voted overwhelmingly for him because of his commitment to social justice as the preeminent public value of the patriot. Many who had lost faith in the ability of the government to deliver on its original commitment to reconstruction and reconciliation were led by Zuma's election to a renewed sense of ownership of their democracy.

Yet it would be a mistake to overlook the less than favorable images of Zuma held by many other South Africans, some of which were exposed by the boos that greeted his arrival at the Johannesburg memorial services for Nelson Mandela. Although the ANC, with Zuma at the top of the national ballot, garnered more than two-thirds of the vote in the 2008 elections, there were still others who quickly reminded everyone in hearing distance of the allegations of corruption and the charge that he had engaged in sex with a friend's daughter with HIV. Zuma was never convicted of any of these charges, but there are still South Africans who speak with great disdain for the president others revere. Frequent articles in the press alleging corruption in the Zuma administration have added to growing disquiet, although recent rankings by Transparency International of the most corrupt nations have found South Africa to be far down the list of the 182 nations studied and ranked annually.

An October 2012 article in the *Economist* argued that South Africa is sliding downhill while the rest of the continent is clawing its way up.[4] Touting the predominantly white Democratic Alliance as the party with the right ideas, the article had to acknowledge that since black majority rule began and South Africa became a full democracy, its people have made real progress. Many more now have access to clean water and electricity. The proportion living on less than $2.00 a day has fallen from 12 percent to 5 percent. Millions of blacks now have housing. The racist legislation of apartheid (more than two hundred laws) has been abolished. The new constitution is progressive and even inspiring, and white business executives who criticize Zuma for allegedly mismanaging the economy are seeing record profits.

I was back in Cape Town for the opening of the 2012 Parliament, as I had been for sixteen years, and observed with some amazement the very positive reaction to Zuma's state of the nation speech by some who had been his harshest critics. Zuma was poised and well prepared as he reported on the state of the nation and articulated his government's plans for the future. Many commented in the press and at social gatherings how much more comfortable and presidential he looked. With the successful management of the World Cup soccer tournament behind him, the unemployment rate falling, and new infrastructure projects successfully completed, he had more than a well-delivered speech going for him. It seemed for a moment that the old South African cycle of fear followed by a new optimism might be on the upside again, at least among those who now argued that while Zuma had not done much good for the country, neither had he done much harm to the economy.

It did not take long, however, for the old fears to return. The wave of in-dustrial action that saw the killing of thirty-four striking miners in Septem-ber 2012 brought back reminders of life under apartheid. The incident once again tarnished South Africa's image and raised fears that investors might choose to take their capital elsewhere. It also took a toll on Zuma's image as young radicals in the ANC Youth League alienated some important support-ers. They claimed first to speak for him, but later sought to defeat him for maintaining what they described as white privilege. Zuma sometimes seems almost oblivious to the growing negative image of his presidency.

But if populism still means respect for the rights, beliefs, and virtues of common people, Zuma is a populist president who came into office with deep and wide support from the masses who had come to feel left out of the new democracy. He restored the feeling among many that it was still their democ-racy, but as some of his former supporters now remind me, it is the prob-lems of this group that remain to be addressed. Many are still prisoners of apartheid, the nameless, faceless victims who wake up every day to apartheid's legacy, still suffering from the impact of forced removals, job reservations, pass laws, and institutionalized racism. There are also many whites who are beneficiaries of apartheid but still living in psychological exile, refusing to ac-cept the reality that the quality of life that a large number enjoy is the result of the exploitation of those they now malign as unqualified or inept.

When all is said and done, the ultimate question is not whether truth leads to reconciliation, but whether there can be reconciliation without eco-nomic justice. As early as 1997, Thabo Mbeki reminded South Africans that reconciliation must mean more than the mere possibility that a black and a white will have tea together. He emphasized the importance of a national reconciliation process that provides access to wealth as well as equality in sacrifices.

There had been some talk of a one-time wealth tax on those who profited under the apartheid system, but it would have been used to pay reparations for only the victims of gross human rights violations. The present leaders, like their predecessors in 1994, seem to be focusing on expanding opportunity and improving the quality of life for those outside the mainstream economy through economic growth and affordable social programs rather than a massive intervention in the private economy. As a result, economic reconciliation lags far behind political reconciliation in both pace and prospect. While much is made of the new black elite and a growing middle class, whites still dominate the economy and hold most of the wealth.

But there is also some good news that rarely makes the headlines. No banks or other major financial institutions in South Africa failed during the Great Recession. With growing evidence of a commitment to the new development plan, a successful public works program providing increased employment, tourism at almost 10 million arrivals in 2013, and the construction boom that preceded the World Cup in 2010, the fundamentals are still sound and still provide a foundation for the economic empowerment of the majority population. But while some in South Africa are getting restless about the pace of progress, it would be a mistake to assume that the masses have lost faith in the future or that a major leadership alternative has emerged.

I found when I arrived in South Africa as the new ambassador that many South African businessmen most critical of the ANC government, even under Mandela, were sitting at the top of companies with record profits. The same is still true almost twenty years later. Even some of the old struggle leaders who malign Zuma with regularity are now beginning to acknowledge the contribution he made in limiting the influence and power of those on his left whose policies would have nationalized much of the economy and returned race relations to apartheid-era levels.

New criticisms of Zuma emerged in the run-up to the 2014 national elections over the use of public resources to build a presidential residence that seems to many more like a presidential village. His supporters counter that it is needed for security and adequate housing for an unusually large family. His practice of polygamy, which is permitted under the South African constitution, has led to multiple wives with multiple families and scores of children to be housed, fed, and educated.

It is not altogether clear whether Zuma was directly involved in the decisions about how luxurious the Nkandla house would be. The response of several Zulus interviewed on the issue after the 2014 elections was that they always expect their leaders to live well and did not share the concerns of some of the critics. This may be largely a cultural difference of the kind I experienced in the black church in the United States. People who were poor gave generously to ensure that their minister had a Cadillac to ride in and a superb home in which to live. While I was often critical, I came to understand that there was a psychological transference in which people identified with what they provided for their leader as though it were their own. This may partly explain why Nkandla was a nonissue for many of the voters who reelected Zuma overwhelmingly.

### The Remaining Barriers to Reconciliation

The talk of reconciliation has not faded away, but with the high-profile public process a distant memory and the voice of one of its most vocal proponents now silenced, some who remember the euphoria of the early days looked back to see how the truth and reconciliation process has fared. This was certainly on the minds of many of my colleagues in the antiapartheid movement and the diplomatic corps when we gathered at the National Cathedral in Washington, DC, to celebrate Mandela's life and legacy. For those of us who had spent much of our adult lives in the movement to free Mandela, the moment in DC was like a family reunion. Any objective assessments now must conclude that while there have been many individual acts of forgiveness on the part of victims, there has been far too little in tangible deeds by those who benefited from apartheid. Even Tutu has lamented the absence of concrete signs that whites recognize the generosity of blacks in not seeking retribution.

Twenty years after the launch of the new democracy and the emphasis on reconciliation, most perpetrators have not acknowledged guilt or sought amnesty. But they are still walking the streets and, in many instances, living in luxury. Very few prosecutions of human rights violations have occurred.

The Truth and Reconciliation Commission has been highly praised in many nations, with ten similar commissions set up in other countries. Yet some in South Africa believe its legacy is still in jeopardy. Part of the unfinished business, according to Tutu, is the need to hear white people say how lucky they are that black people who were oppressed for their benefit have not sought revenge.

Tutu also has words for the growing black middle class and the new black elite, suggesting that original sin has no color bar. His voice is part of a new chorus of critics who question whether the altruistic spirit of the movement has evaporated, whether some of the former revolutionaries are more interested in self-aggrandizement than reconciliation and community benefit.

More truth is still needed to bring closure for both the nation and the victims of apartheid. That is the conclusion of Charles Villa-Vicencio, the commission's former director of research. "We did a survey shortly after the TRC and asked people what they thought was the most important thing to come out of the TRC and they said, information, truth. Even now, ten years later, they want to know more about what happened."[5]

While Mandela is fondly remembered, and justifiably so, there seems to be a reconciliation fatigue among some black South Africans. They are the ones who question whether their leaders went too far in letting perpetrators off the hook. They were particularly stunned and disapproving of President Mbeki's gestures of reconciliation in response to the death of P. W. Botha, a former apartheid-era president who presided over some of the worst state-initiated and state-sanctioned atrocities. He passed away in 2006 but remained unrepentant. Despite the protest of both blacks and whites who once felt the brunt of his cruelty, the state flag was flown at half-mast and Mbeki attended his funeral. It was the kind of gesture that would have been expected of Mandela, but many wanted Mbeki to be less conciliatory and say that there has been enough forgiveness.

The fear of the other—which continues, or gives rise to, racism—has re-emerged in some parts of the white community. The South African focus on reconciliation led early on to a belief by some that a radical utopia might indeed be in sight. Visions of a nation without racism danced in their heads. But the deeply embedded fear of the blacks in the psyche of whites during the apartheid years has been rekindled by the media's obsession with and often exaggeration of high-profile crimes. In the suburbs, where many whites live behind security gates and high walls, some are absolutely certain that the nation is unraveling. Many of the old stereotypes have reappeared, sometimes overtly and other times unconsciously. Whites thought they could give up political power while retaining all of the benefits of economic power. But they were surprised to find that the formerly disempowered wanted not just the income that would allow them to get along, but the assets needed for them to get ahead.

I lived full-time in South Africa for much of Nelson Mandela's presidency and part-time for all the years since, but it is only recently that I have heard so many disparaging comments about the early commitment to movement values and Mandela's emphasis on what is right rather than simply what is in the national interest. Many of the younger generation want more pragmatism in both foreign and domestic policy. They see no reason why South Africa should be the conscience of the world as it was under Mandela. Their model of foreign engagement is what they describe as a new pragmatism.

What is unique, then, about South Africa that argues for learning from its experience at a time when the early optimism is beginning to fade? First of all, South Africans began their new democracy under the tutelage of Nelson Mandela and Desmond Tutu. Rarely has a nation been blessed with the presence of two cultural icons of their stature in the same generation, and with such a strong commitment to reconciliation and community. They seemed to instinctually understand the tensions between not only white and black, but traditionalism and modernity as well. Leaders who follow them are automatically diminished in stature because icons like Mandela, Tutu, Tambo, and others in their generation are both rare and extraordinary. But while it is right and appropriate that we give due credit to Nelson Mandela, almost every time I heard him speak, he emphasized that very little could have been accomplished without a cadre of competent and committed colleagues from all sides of the political spectrum. Some of those colleagues are still exercising influence and helping shape policy in the Zuma government. Others are deployed in key positions in the economy and civil society. And as I discuss in chapter 14, there is also an extraordinary group of younger leaders who have demonstrated great potential for assuming greater leadership responsibilities in the near future.

At a time when many South Africans continue to look for the next Mandela, there are excellent people in the present generation who are poised to play an effective role in public life. Many South Africans are hoping that Cyril Ramaphosa, the new deputy president as of 2014, will help Zuma bring into government a group of younger leaders prepared to take South Africa into the future. Cyril cut his teeth as the leader of the National Union of Mineworkers, which at its founding congress had 14,000 members with him as the only full-time employee. In less than four years following its first congress, the union had enrolled 344,000 members. It is no secret that Mandela had wanted Cyril to be the first deputy president in his administration and his presumptive heir when Mandela would retire five years later. After losing out to Thabo Mbeki, with Mandela yielding to the desires of the returning exiles, Cyril entered business. During this period he and I discussed how many in the United States go from government to business and back again, and it was clear to me that if the ANC ever came calling, he would be open to one of the top positions.

Many South Africans had long fantasized about Cyril someday returning, so when he was elected deputy president of the ANC at the 2012 conference hopes skyrocketed. It is not altogether clear whether Ramaphosa can succeed Zuma as president of the country because some influential Zulus, having seen one of their own in power, are already speaking privately about keeping the position in Zulu hands. But Ramaphosa's reappearance in the potential line of succession has fueled expectation that he will have a positive influence on ANC policy and South Africa's image abroad.

There are many other South Africans in the ANC and elsewhere poised and well prepared to take the country into the next stage of its development.

It has become fashionable, however, for the opposition parties and their allies in the press in South Africa and elsewhere to point to the failings and high-profile corruption of some South African leaders to the exclusion of many in government, business, and civil society who are capable and committed, efficient and ethical. The latter group needs to be encouraged and even celebrated in order to enhance the image of the country outside its borders as well as improve the morale of those on the inside who are dedicated to doing what is right.

Another South African who seemed destined for a time to play a significant role in the future of South Africa is Mamphela Ramphele. While her first trial in the rough-and-tumble world of politics in the run-up to the 2014 national election exposed some of her weaknesses, she should not be dismissed prematurely in regard to her potential for major contributions in other ways. I first met Dr. Ramphele on a 1990 visit to South Africa when I was told that this young academic was someone to watch. She advanced rapidly to become the first black African to head the University of Cape Town and later an executive director at the World Bank. After years of refusing to enter government, she entered politics in 2013 with the formation of her own political party (Agang). Bringing with her an impeccable reputation for integrity and competence, she formed the party amid much pomp and fanfare. Shortly thereafter, the Democratic Alliance, the second largest political party after the ANC, invited Mamphela and her party to join forces with them to contest the national election with her as their candidate for president of the republic. Five days later, Mamphela withdrew from the grand bargain and announced that she was not interested in a merger with the Democratic Alliance.

The breakup was not only political. It placed great strain on a personal relationship that went back to the years when Mamphela was Steve Biko's partner and Helen Zille, now the head of the Democratic Alliance, was the antiapartheid journalist who revealed the circumstances of Biko's murder in police custody. Zille admitted that her long personal friendship with Mamphela had "taken a bad knock." Mamphela had assumed that she could be the candidate of both the Democratic Alliance and her own party. The Democratic Alliance insisted that she become a member of their party. Mamphela's reply was, "There are millions of South Africans who would never vote the DA, but they want a home which Agang can offer."[6] Mamphela called her choice to stand as the Democratic Alliance's candidate a rush decision, but I had heard rumors of the party's wooing of Mamphela for several years before the announcement of a partnership.

Agang's performance in the 2014 election was dismal, winning only two seats in Parliament and 0.28 percent of the vote. Commenting on Agang's poor performance, Helen Zille, whose Democratic Alliance won 22 percent, said, "I offered Mamphela Ramphele the world, she wanted the universe . . . and now she has ended up with a shack in Pfadder (a small town in Northern Cape province)."[7] Her new political party may have done poorly in the 2014 elections, but Mamphela still has much to offer as a public intellectual willing to introduce ideas and provide useful criticism where it is warranted. In a letter published on Agang's website after the election results were formally announced, Mamphela said that she would not be going to Parliament but rather taking a break from politics. She added, however, "I will remain available to provide counsel and advice to the Parliamentary team and help them enrich the national debate."[8]

There is now an attempt to recruit other black Africans for leadership roles in the Democratic Alliance, which has shown great racial tension in its ranks since the elections. Its leader in Parliament, who was for a time the most high-profile black member, announced shortly after the final results of the 2014 national election were in that she would take a leave of absence to study at Harvard's Kennedy School. The discussion about why she decided to leave led to considerable acrimony.

The rise of support for the Democratic Alliance from 16 percent of the national vote in 2009 to 22 percent in 2014 may have created a false confidence about the future. Many in the black majority still consider Zille's party to be serving the interests of white and wealthy South Africans. Moreover, the ANC's fall from 65 percent of the vote to 62 percent must be seen against the backdrop of the formation of the Economic Freedom Fighters from within ANC ranks. This new party won 6 percent of the national vote while the gains of the Democratic Alliance came primarily from its obliteration of some of the smaller parties rather than from taking away former ANC voters.

While the ANC is not likely to be threatened nationally within the near future, I agree with analysts like Steve Friedman, who writes for *Business Day*, that the decline in its share of the urban vote should be a matter of concern. No meltdown appears imminent, but as the brand of the ANC as a liberation party continues to dissipate with the passing of time, new opposition may rise from within its own ranks. The first threat was from its urban middle class and the Mbeki diehards who rebelled against how he was treated when Zuma was selected by the political party to replace him. The second, as demonstrated in the 2014 election, is from the followers of Julius Malema and his supporters, who wanted a more activist state in the response to poverty and the ownership of wealth. A third threat from within ANC ranks will likely come from those union members who are now considering the development of a socialist party. But while the ANC may be destined for a decline, I agree with those analysts who say that this is likely to occur rather slowly over the next twenty years.

The idea of a leadership deficit is more widely discussed than race, but it is clear that race continues to be a problem in South Africa. What is positive about race relations, however, is that it remains under the lens of a public microscope. People are talking about it and some are doing something about it. Many of those who have seen the worst of apartheid are determined to write a new history in which South Africans in all their diversity can say to each other, in the words of the old charter of the ANC, "South Africa belongs to all who live in it."

Having been a pariah in the world for so long, South Africans like being engaged with the rest of the world and seen as a nation serious about addressing the issues of its past. As one white South African said to me, "When I traveled abroad in the past I was reluctant to admit that I was a South African. Now I can do so with pride. Whereas people once vilified us, they now praise us for what we have done." Even the Afrikaner winemaker who was very skeptical about the wisdom of the changes made in 1994 is now grateful that he can sell his wines throughout the world. It makes it easier to move beyond race when it is profitable to do so.

But South Africans continue to vigorously debate the present course of their democracy. Some even argue that the quality of life was better under apartheid. And if you were a part of the less than 10 percent of the population who benefited from the exploitation of the other 90 percent, it was. It is easy to overlook the many advances that have brought water closer, made electricity more widespread, and made housing more readily available to the masses. If one always enjoyed the right to vote, the access to good health care and quality education, it is easy to say that nothing has changed. The fact is that in only twenty years of democracy major changes have occurred, but after three hundred years of social engineering designed to underdevelop the black population, there is still much to be done.

The focus in South Africa on writing a new constitution and the emphasis on forgiveness and reconciliation may have overshadowed the national debate about how to dismantle the economic infrastructure of apartheid, and how to promote equity and inclusion as originally envisioned by the liberation movements. It is only fitting that serious questions are now being raised about the unfinished agenda of economic reconciliation. In my conversation with policy analysts in the ANC, some call it the second transition, in which the political empowerment of the majority is complete but the hard work of economic empowerment remains a grave challenge.

The Congress of South African Trade Unions has been unhappy since the onset of the new democracy with the macroeconomic model, and while its alliance partner in governing has kept the coalition together by making concessions from time to time, the basic fundamentals remain the same. The Democratic Alliance, the major political opposition, is now touting its own economic model, but it represents a constituency that is in general doing quite well under the present model.

As the ANC celebrated its one hundredth anniversary in 2012, party stalwarts were also engaged in internal policy debates about how best to fulfill the goals of the predecessor liberation movement. It was not just poverty, unemployment, and education that were under scrutiny, but the compromises negotiated in establishing a new democracy, including land distribution, the preservation of wealth, the social role of private business, and the role of the courts in contributing to transformation. Questions about the role of the courts have made a disproportionate contribution to the rise of the anxiety level of those accustomed to periods of free-floating anxiety. There is widespread concern that tinkering with the courts, even examining their role in transformation, would violate the values enshrined so carefully and with much struggle in the constitution.

Those who benefit from peddling fear—newspapers that sell more papers, opposition parties that attract more members, television commentators who increase their ratings, and those who remain uncomfortable with a black-led government—give little attention to the reality that many judges are products of the old order that was devoted to the subjugation of black people. It would be as much a mistake, however, to cast all white members of the judiciary as opponents of transformation as it would be to assume that all of them had a Damascus conversion akin to that of the Apostle Paul. The story of the role of the courts in the United States in enforcing segregation, and even selecting a president along party lines, reminds us of how difficult it is for members of the judiciary to rise above their own social conditioning.

Critical questions are also being raised about the public values introduced and affirmed by the architects of the new democracy. The Mandela contribution, with its emphasis on reconciliation, a new patriotism, and a new kind of global citizenship, deserves to be placed on the same level as the contributions of James Madison and Thomas Jefferson in the United States and Jawaharlal Nehru in India in framing a memorable public philosophy for their respective countries.

And yet there was talk even before Mandela's death in December 2013 of a need "to move past Nelson Mandela and the Rainbow Nation thing" toward a more muscular national identity abroad and more intervention in the economy to promote equity at home. In the 1990s, it was easy to conclude from my interaction with then President Mandela and his executives in the ministry handling foreign affairs that South Africa was developing a foreign policy to fit its past, setting itself up as a moral beacon domestically and a global conscience in international relations. While not all South Africans have given up on the idea that their country should act as the social conscience of a dangerous and divided world, the track record since Mandela retired from public life seems to suggest some vacillation about what kind of country they want to be both domestically and internationally. Very important voices in the debate about the way forward are now pointing to the pragmatism of China as a potential model for South Africa as the new democracy grows beyond its teenage years. But the South Africans are also pragmatic and while they will borrow from other nations they will more likely continue to shape their democracy to fit their own needs and circumstances.

The early emphasis on public values has in some ways given rise to a debate about public philosophy. This debate was sparked initially by Thabo Mbeki, who was not only Mandela's political heir and soul mate but a prime contributor to the intellectual content of the Mandela mystique. Mandela touched and moved people by who he was, what he suffered, the magnitude of his capacity to forgive, and the magnetism of his personality. Mbeki's introduction of the concept of an African renaissance, the rebirth and renewal of the African continent, is what first brought him to the attention of those looking for new insights out of the new Africa. While he is no longer president, some of his ideas are reemerging.

What defines a South African, according to Mbeki, is not merely color or race. It is the product that comes out of this mix of people, different colors, different cultures, and different histories. He spoke often of a South African personality forged out of its pluralist diversity. He embraced Afrikaans as a South African language and the Afrikaner people as fully South African. He was proud of his Xhosa heritage, but he understood that building a new future required respect for the heritage of others. This notion of a South African personality forged out of its pluralist diversity may be as important to understanding the new South Africa as the idea of an African renaissance was at that time to understanding the new Africa. The language of renaissance is no longer used as frequently, but there are clear examples of where Mbeki had it right as the scramble for Africa begins anew.

The new public values on display in South Africa had first to be enshrined in a constitution and placed beyond the reach of what former justice minister Dullah Omar described as "temporary majorities." In both the preamble and the epilogue of the 1996 constitution, the former adversaries committed themselves to creating a nonracial society; healing the divisions of the past; achieving the peaceful coexistence of all South Africans; creating development opportunities for all, irrespective of color, race, class, belief, or sex; and improving the quality of life for all citizens.

One of the clearest indications of the uniqueness of the early years of the new democracy is to be found in this statement in the preamble: "We, the people of South Africa, recognize the injustices of our past . . . [and] believe that South Africa belongs to all who live in it, united in our diversity." The idea of a South Africa that belongs to all who live in it was taken directly from the ANC's Freedom Charter, which even in the darkest days of separate development expressed the capacity of an oppressed people for embracing even the oppressor.

It is still early in the South African experiment with democracy, but all evidence points to a South Africa that has its feet firmly planted in both the first and third worlds. It is those first-world elements that are being put to work in the development of a national economy that works for all South Africans. In the end, South Africa may be able to become a nonracial society, but it will have to recognize, respect, and help to sustain cultural differences. It is their culture that Afrikaner traditionalists want to retain. It is their culture that Zulu chiefs and their followers in rural areas want to retain. The old hierarchical pluralism is going the way of the dinosaur, but a new egalitarian pluralism may be absolutely necessary if national harmony is to be maintained and national community achieved. This new form of multiculturalism seeks equal respect for both the Anglo-Saxon tradition of the Europeans and the African culture of those whose heritage and color made them the butt of stereotypes that denied their dignity and depicted their humanity as not simply different but deficient.

# CHAPTER 13

## Ethics and Statecraft

*What I Learned from Nelson Mandela*

I first met Nelson Mandela in Washington, DC, in June 1990 when I shared the dais with him on his first visit to the United States. A few months earlier, in February of that year, I had been standing outside of Parliament in Cape Town with a Free Mandela sign when then president F. W. de Klerk announced that Nelson Mandela would be set free and the liberation groups unbanned. Now I was helping host his visit to the nation's capital and, like thousands of others, I was struck by his great dignity, the warmth of his personality, and the way he charmed everyone he met.

In 1992, I was back in South Africa leading a delegation of foundation executives eager to find out how American philanthropy could support the transition taking place in that country. It was in Johannesburg at a small dinner we hosted in Mandela's honor that we first caught a glimpse of his humility and common touch. With men and women representing great wealth waiting to greet him, he entered the hotel and went first to shake the hands of hotel staff before joining us. At dinner, he made everyone in the delegation feel like longtime friends. No one felt like a stranger, even those meeting him for the first time. Earlier that evening at a joint press conference, we had also seen the special sensitivity for which he was known when he thanked me profusely for coming all the way to South Africa to meet him and other representatives of the South African people, although my wife, Doris, had recently passed away.

It was as a diplomat, however, that I got to know Mandela best. He is widely praised for his commitment to reconciliation, but I learned very quickly that he was also an astute politician who had an uncanny instinct for moving and motivating people, changing attitudes, and appealing to the best in human nature. He was an international icon who was revered and honored by heads of state, royal families, and social elites around the world, but it was clear that he never lost sight of the fact that he had been put in power by the poorest of the poor. He was an African with strong attachments to the continent and its people, but his appeal and his embrace were universal.

The question future generations may well ask is how an elderly African leader in a small country with a small gross domestic product and an efficient but small military attracted such unique affection and influence—not just in Africa, but in Europe, Asia, the Americas, and the rest of the world— at a time when politicians were widely distrusted and global influence was measured largely by military might and economic muscle. Mandela emerged from incarceration when the projection of state power beyond its borders had become the domain largely of the warrior caste. But he influenced events and shaped opinions far beyond South Africa's borders because of who he was rather than because of the power and influence of his country. His capacity to win over his adversaries was so complete that he not only made friends of the wardens in the Robben Island prison in which he was incarcerated, but invited several of them to his inauguration as his special guests. When others doubted it was still possible for old enemies to beat their swords into plowshares, he showed us how.

### Principled Diplomacy

I am often asked what it was like to work with Mandela. Was he as principled in the exercise of his responsibilities as president as he was as a person? Did his well-known commitment to forgiveness and reconciliation in his private life influence the way in which he conducted the foreign affairs of the Republic of South Africa? I was present in settings where he embraced and shook hands with heads of state and others that some in high places in the United States considered adversaries, but to know the man was to understand that as a diplomat he had no permanent friends or enemies, only friends and those with the potential for becoming friends. At home he warned against the politics of vengeance and abroad he pointed to the moral pitfalls of selective national memory that focuses on the barriers that once limited relationships rather than the potential for beginning anew.

Principled diplomacy for Mandela was not a theory. It was a way of being. Scholars in the realist tradition of international politics would undoubtedly raise a skeptical eyebrow at the notion of placing ethical boundaries around diplomacy. Such an effort might even be dismissed as an attempt by an idealist to attribute good to an area of activity where one must be prepared to do and say anything to promote the interest of the nation. It is true that heads of state, and the diplomats who represent them, in any transaction are expected to ask what is in the national interest; but Nelson Mandela often baffled his own diplomats, not to mention those from other countries, by asking what is right. It made him unpredictable, but it was precisely this independent streak that caused him to be so widely admired and respected.

In getting to know him, I was struck by the fact that his extraordinary capacity to do the right thing had more to do with his natural disposition than it had to do with public relations techniques or good spin doctors. I once congratulated a member of his communications staff on the way in which he and his colleagues always seemed to put Mandela in the right setting at the right time and with the right message. He looked at me in amazement and said, "It is not us. It is the old man himself."

I refer in chapter 7 to Carl Jung's notion of synchronicity to describe those moments when things come together in an almost unbelievable way, when events that could never have been predicted seem remarkably to guide us along a path. The early 1990s were without doubt a time of synchronicity in South Africa.

In Mandela's book and the 2013 movie *Long Walk to Freedom*, we are provided with a personal, reflective account of his journey of self-discovery, struggle, setback, renewed hope, and ultimate triumph. Through the telling of his life story, he provided a glimpse of how the stage was set for the South African transition that occurred not only without violence and retribution, but with a remarkable spirit of healing and forgiveness. He never allowed himself to be seduced by the trappings of power, because like Robert Greenleaf's notion of the servant leader, his first choice was the choice to serve. Leadership is what followed.

### An Astute Politician

What about Mandela the political animal? As a politician, he made the profession seem noble. But while some are inclined to portray him as a saint, I heard him say on several occasions, "I am no angel." Those who knew him best are the first to remind us that when one considers that he survived in the rough-and-tumble politics of the African National Congress for years, it would be naive to assume that he did not master the pragmatic art of politics as well as he mastered the ability to channel his frustration into constructive public action. He loved to quote from W. E. Henley's Victorian poem

"Invictus"—"I am the master of my fate and the captain of my soul"—but he also understood what it means to be the captain of the fate of others.

Mandela's reference to "Invictus" was used later as the title of a film in which we see him presenting a copy of Henley's poem to François Pienaar, captain of the South African rugby team. In real life, however, Mandela gave Pienaar a passage from a speech by former U.S. president Theodore Roosevelt. Referred to as "The Man in the Arena," the speech was given at the Sorbonne in Paris, France, in 1910, where Roosevelt said,

> It is not the critic who counts, not the man who points out how the strong man stumbles, or where the doer of deeds could have done them better. The credit belongs to the man who is actually in the arena, whose face is marred by dust and sweat and blood; who strives valiantly . . . who at the best knows in the end the triumph of high achievement, and who at the worst, if he fails, at least fails while daring greatly, so that his place shall never be with those cold and timid souls who neither know victory or defeat.[1]

Mandela was both the captain of his own soul and the man in the arena who knew in the end the triumph of high achievement because he dared greatly. The political scientist James MacGregor Burns wrote a classic text on leadership in which he made a distinction between transforming and transactional leaders. It is thus natural to describe Mandela as a transforming leader, but in truth he was both. He could have satisfied his conscience and accomplished nothing for his constituents if he had not been willing to get his hands dirty, to negotiate, make deals, and engage in compromise in order to achieve a larger public good. At a time when South Africa was in danger of being pulled apart by the tension between traditionalism and modernity, Mandela was able to bring these into balance in his public life as both a moral leader and a politician.

He was very much a product of the older tribal tradition he describes in *Long Walk to Freedom*, of a chief accountable to his people, settling their disputes with careful courtesy, making them all feel important and representing them with a dignity and bearing that was as regal as anything we have seen in the history of the most admired royals. Yet I was surprised by how modern he was in his very effective use of the tools of the modern politician. He had a brilliant sense of texture and timing and was a master of imagery who knew instinctively how to work the room or flatter an adversary. I marveled at his mastery of the photo op—asking my wife and me once whether we would do him the honor of taking a picture with him. He also benefited from his natural mastery of the sound bite, the seductive smile, the intimate handshake, and disarming charm. The difference from so many other politicians I have known is that all this came naturally. It was not Nelson Mandela playing a role. It was simply Nelson Mandela being himself.

## A Transactional Political Culture

The political culture in South Africa is grounded in negotiation. I learned very early by personal experience that everything had to be negotiated—not just bilateral trade incentives, multilateral political agreements, or even the agenda and schedule for a visit by a head of state or a senior cabinet member, but how many cars could be in a motorcade and how many Secret Service agents could accompany the president of the United States when he addressed Parliament. This culture of negotiation may have had its trivial side, but it was grounded in the belief that most of the matters that divide individuals and communities are potentially negotiable. While old-line diplomats and foreign policy experts are often jaded by the hard lines they have encountered over the years, Nelson Mandela brought a fresh optimism to old issues. He often repeated his belief that disputes should be settled by "brains, not blood."

Nelson Mandela's moral standing and his commitment to transcendent values drove him to continue his efforts to transform not only South Africa but also the region and the continent. He increasingly found others, both on the continent and in other parts of the world, looking to him to help resolve regional conflicts, ranging from his efforts to promote a nonviolent end to the Mobutu regime in what is now the Democratic Republic of the Congo to his work for democratic evolution in Nigeria. In the international arena, he was an especially important voice in efforts to maintain the nuclear nonproliferation edifice. He had special credibility in this regard because one of his first acts as president of South Africa was to dismantle South Africa's nuclear capacity. He was also a strong supporter of a ban on chemical and biological weapons, the banning of small weapons, and the elimination of land mines.

Mandela's belief in the potential of negotiating with those considered pariahs by others was never more evident than in his involvement in persuading the Libyan leader Muammar Gaddafi to turn over to the Scottish court the Libyan suspects in the 1988 bombing of Pan Am Flight 103 over Lockerbie. While there was mixed reaction to his involvement in this issue, the one thing about which there is no doubt is the tenacity with which Mandela and his chief of staff, Jakes Gerwel, negotiated independently on this issue. The many contacts with Tripoli by Gerwel, and especially Mandela's visit in March 1999—against the wishes of Western powers—came out of the belief that Gaddafi could be persuaded that it was in his own interest to turn the suspects over for trial. Some State Department and White House officials were outraged when during President Clinton's visit Mandela insisted on a private discussion of the Lockerbie bombing; and then, after keeping both of their aides, including the usual note takers, out of the bilateral discussion, his friend Prince Bandar of Saudi Arabia miraculously entered the room from a side door for a closed conversation on the matter. But President Clinton took it in stride, demonstrating instead the great respect and warm affection that he and Mandela shared for each other.

The second chapter of the story that finally saw Libya reestablishing normal diplomatic relations with Western nations was written much later, as was the third chapter that saw Gaddafi's downfall from a fleeting moment of grace, but the first chapter was certainly dominated by the diplomacy of Nelson Mandela. The final chapter was, of course, Gaddafi's demise, but South African leaders like Mandela's successor Thabo Mbeki still believe that if NATO and the Western powers had listened to their advice and given the African Union more credibility, much of the bloodbath could have been avoided. They remain especially piqued that the West considered Gaddafi more of an Arab than an African and gave more credence to the views of the leaders of Arab states than the organization of African heads of state he once chaired.

### Mandela as Multilateralist

Nelson Mandela's leadership style was honed in the political culture of the African National Congress with its emphasis on cooperative and consultative leadership, so it should be no surprise to learn that in the international arena he sought, first and wherever feasible, to work through multilateral organizations. These usually included the United Nations, the Non-Aligned Movement, the Organization of African Unity, and the Southern African Development Community. I was present in New York in 1998 for his speech to the General Assembly of the United Nations in which he argued on behalf of the poorer nations, "The very right to be human is denied every day to hundreds of millions of people as a result of poverty, the unavailability of basic necessities such as food, jobs, water and shelter, education, health care and a healthy environment."[2]

While he became for a time the most important spokesperson for the developing world, Mandela sought also to be a bridge builder between rich and poor nations. He was an especially strong moral voice in two areas. First, he sought development aid rather than charity. He preferred participatory development and assisted self-reliance that could help eliminate the causes of poverty rather than charity that seeks only to ameliorate the consequences. Second, he urged donor countries to abandon the notion that the strategies used in the development of their own particular countries were the best for all other countries. He pointed to the importance of context and culture and was a vigorous cheerleader for President Clinton's statement to the South African Parliament that the developed world had been asking the wrong question. "We have been asking what can we do for Africa, what can we do about Africa," President Clinton said. "We must now ask what can we do with Africa."

Mandela's approach to multilateralism differed greatly from that of the United States and other nations, who at the time of his ascension to the presidency derived their notion of what was best for the world almost exclusively from what seemed best in the short run for them. The underlying premise of some was that Mandela was a good man, but he was naive in matters having to do with the relationship between nation-states. They took the position that international relations are relations of power, not principles; power prevails and principles legitimize what prevails. The practitioners of this form of multilateralism are not without principles. They simply derive their principles from the perception of national self-interest. They are convinced that the values from which the world benefits are their values. For many Americans who think this way, American power must, thus, be used to impose not only its interest but also its views and values on the world.

I found in my interaction with American policy elites, business executives, and religious leaders that support for this particular belief in American exceptionalism came from three primary sources: (1) a marriage between two unlikely bedfellows, religious fundamentalism and market fundamentalism; (2) the advocates of geopolitical realism, who have long maintained that the primary role of the state in international relations is to pursue its national interests; and (3) the alliance between the state and big business that former U.S. president Dwight Eisenhower called "the military-industrial complex."

Mandela's approach to multilateralism ran counter to the prevailing trend of the nation-states whose influence came primarily from military and economic power. His emphasis on cooperation was more humbling and seductive than Big Brother dominance. Yet while his standing and stature around the world had no rival, it was at the regional level, especially his efforts to work through the Southern African Development Community, that I first saw the difficulty of transforming leadership from an elected head of state when he or she moves outside national boundaries. Mandela discovered very early that South Africa's dominance in the region, and on the continent, caused it to face the same problem with its African neighbors that the United States faces in the world. There is a natural suspicion of the intentions of the dominant power in any relationship, even when those intentions seek to serve a larger public good. The dilemma for Nelson Mandela was that if he spoke out, he ran the risk of being accused of throwing his weight around; but if he did not, he ran the risk of being accused of inaction and indifference.

This fear of South African dominance actually robbed the region of the full potential of his leadership, but one has only to look at the extent of South African dominance to understand the caution with which Nelson Mandela had to act and the sensitivity other nations felt. At the time in the late 1990s when I served as U.S. ambassador, South Africa had only 21 percent of the population, but 76 percent of the GDP (excluding Angola) of the eleven-nation group that made up the Southern African Development Community. It accounted for 75 percent of the region's trade, received 84 percent of foreign direct investment, handled 89 percent of the tonnage in the region's ports, had 61 percent of the rail network, and generated half the electricity of the entire continent.

The dominance of South Africa in the region had three major consequences for multilateral diplomacy. I have already mentioned the natural suspicion of the intentions of the dominant party in a relationship. The second consequence was the imbalance in the institutional capacity of other governments, nongovernmental organizations, and other leaders to participate fully in regional development. The Southern African Development Community could have been an important vehicle for regional cooperation, but the other countries in the region simply did not have sufficient staff, professionalism, or resources to share equal responsibility for the functioning of committees or the development and management of programs. A third by-product of South Africa's dominance in the region was that while Nelson Mandela was a larger-than-life international hero and cultural icon in most of the world, his stature and standing generated envy and jealousy among some regional leaders, especially Robert Mugabe, who had once been the most revered and respected leader in southern Africa.

Despite these limitations, Mandela could not ignore his African neighbors. It was not only that their problems were spilling over into South Africa. Mandela himself had become a symbol of a continent seeking to escape its colonial past. Like his deputy Thabo Mbeki, he believed in the potential for African renewal and insisted that the time had come for a new generation of African leaders to make the idea of an African renaissance real.

### Both African and Universal

Much is made of the universality of Nelson Mandela's embrace, but he was an African who took pride in his African identity as well. In a 1994 speech in

Tunis, he spoke of the responsibility to restore to the African continent its dignity. He said the great giants of Africa, such as "Gamal Abdel Nasser of Egypt, Kwame Nkrumah of Ghana, ... Patrice Lumumba of Zaire, ... Agostinho Neto of Angola, ... Samora Machel of Mozambique, ... W. E. B. Du Bois and Martin Luther King of America, Marcus Garvey of Jamaica, Albert Luthuli and Oliver Tambo of South Africa," had given him reason for hope. He also celebrated African contributions to the condition of civilization, "like the pyramids of Egypt, the sculptures of the ancient kingdoms of Ghana, Mali and Benin, like the temples of Ethiopia, the Zimbabwe ruins and the rock paintings of the Namib deserts."[3]

One could not get to know Mandela either up close or through his description of his early life in *Long Walk to Freedom* without getting a keen sense of his Africanness, without recognizing that even his regal bearing reflected the tradition of tribal chieftancy. He was one of the first to leap to his feet in appreciation for Thabo Mbeki's "I Am an African" speech at the parliamentary assembly that adopted the South African constitution. It was his ability to identify with and celebrate the uniqueness of his heritage and identity, while respecting the uniqueness of others, that enabled him to make friends of enemies at home and gain such wide respect and acceptance abroad.

In my conversations with Mandela, he warned on several occasions that the West should be more circumspect in the advice our leaders provide. He was especially mindful of what he considered draconian budget policies by which the International Monetary Fund and the World Bank practically ran the economies of a debt-ridden continent during the last two decades of the twentieth century. He felt the same way about the charges of bad governance that seemed to fall so naturally from the lips of those who claimed to be experts on African development. While the Western press portrayed the continent as a region in crisis, he saw it instead as a continent in renaissance from the burdens of cruelty and depredation imposed by the West.

It is easy to forget the many impediments to African development that came directly from Western intervention. As Jeffrey Sachs reminds us in *The End of Poverty*, these include: (1) three centuries of slave trade, from around 1500 to the early 1800s; (2) another century of brutal colonial rule that kept Africa bereft of basic infrastructure, properly educated citizens, public health systems for all the people rather than just a small white elite, and economies to serve their own needs rather than simply the home country of the colonizers; (3) a period of postcolonialism that saw new governments struggling to create viable states out of arbitrary colonial lines that divided ethnic groups, ecosystems, watersheds, and natural resources; and (4) the use of African states as pawns in the Cold War, where the West opposed African leaders who preached nationalism or demanded better terms for Western appropriation of African minerals and energy deposits.[4]

Especially worth remembering is how the approach taken by the West to independence often frustrated the will of the people in selecting their own leaders. I remember being in Ghana in 1966, when everywhere I went I heard rumors that the United States had manipulated the price of cocoa on world markets to punish Nkrumah for his neutrality between the Soviets and the West. Many still believe that the CIA had a hand in his violent overthrow. Whether accurate or not, it is undeniable that the West had a hand in (1) the assassination of Patrice Lumumba in the Congo and the installation of the tyrant Mobutu Sese Seko; and (2) providing strong support for Jonas Savimbi in Angola on the grounds that he was an anticommunist, when he was in fact a violent thug.[5] The litany of rejection of certain African leaders by the West in favor of others goes on. Indeed, almost every African political crisis—Sudan, Somalia, and a host of others—has a long history of Western meddling among the many causes.[6]

The pat answers to Africa's economic development problems were also frustrating to Mandela and a new generation of African leaders. Particularly incredible and insulting to Mandela were the claims that African corruption was the basic source of the problem. How do these critics explain, for example, that the countries in Asia perceived to have extensive corruption (such as Pakistan, Bangladesh, Indonesia, and even India) were doing better at the time than relatively well governed countries in Africa (such as Ghana, Mali, Malawi, and Senegal)? Using formal statistical tests from the Global Corruption Report by Transparency International, it turns out that Africa's per capita economic growth was significantly better than that in developing countries with comparable levels of corruption.[7]

There may be many explanations for the West's blind spot about Africa, especially the misperceptions and prejudices that give Africa such a bad rap, but Mandela was correct when he identified not just drought, disease, and Western meddling as major factors, but racism also. He understood that even when negative sentiments are not racist in intent, they survive in our societies as conventional wisdom because of the widespread existence of racism.

Despite all the factors that have contributed to slow economic development in Africa, Mandela believed that while the problems were difficult, they were solvable. He agreed with Jeffrey Sachs that diseases could be controlled, crop yields could be sharply increased, and basic infrastructure such as paved roads and electricity could be extended to the villages. In fact—despite the impediments of geography with few rivers or navigable inlets for trade, the restraints of history, and the impact of geopolitics—Mandela argued that underdevelopment was not an inevitable destiny. Moreover, he saw it as increasingly in the self-interest of the West, especially the United States, to join in partnership with Africa to develop the economies of a continent with more than a billion consumers and natural resources that could help maintain the quality of life Americans enjoy.

While it is correct to emphasize Mandela's Africanness, it would be a mistake to overlook how his notion of who he was, and where his moral obligations were, included his connection with all of humanity, especially the poor and the marginalized. Members of royal families, heads of state, legislative leaders, and power brokers from every corner of the globe made their way to South Africa during his presidency in hopes of getting a photo opportunity for their family albums, political campaigns, company brochures, or the national press; but Nelson Mandela is surely best remembered as the champion of the underdog—the people's president who brought the races together in a country where most of the world expected a bloodbath rather than a new democracy.

The adulation he received from the world's elite was in stark contrast to British prime minister Margaret Thatcher's assertion that Nelson Mandela was a terrorist, and anyone who thought the African National Congress would someday form a government was living in cloud-cuckoo-land. I was never clear about the meaning of that phrase, but I did understand that it was not intended as a compliment.

Mandela's authorized biographer wrote later about Mandela's first state visit to England, when the British monarchy was so under siege that even the royals were hoping to benefit from the mystique of their regal visitor. Lady Thatcher was up front, basking in Mandela's glow and beaming about the magnanimous qualities of this great leader, but it was the queen who seemed so much at home and at ease in his company. One observer wryly commented that she had a lot in common with Mandela because they had both spent a lot of time in prison.

It is not easy for an objective observer to get beyond the icon. The myth is usually so powerful that it blurs the reality, but I often found the reality to be even more appealing than the myth. Consider what Mandela had to say during his state visit to Britain, when he was surrounded by hundreds of years of pomp and circumstance: "The history of liberation heroes shows that when they come into office they interact with powerful groups; they can easily forget that they have been put in power by the poorest of the poor. They often lose their touch and turn against their own people."

Mandela never lost either the common touch or his sense of connectedness with all of humanity. He was African, with great respect for his tribal tradition, but he was driven by the idea that the individual comes into full humanity only as there is acceptance of the full humanity of others. He believed strongly in the tribal tradition of ubuntu—described more fully in chapter 11—that all of humanity is bound together in a relationship that is larger than any one individual or group. As the Xhosas put it, "People are people through other people." It follows then that to damage the humanity of another person is to diminish one's own. Writing about ubuntu in *No Future without Forgiveness*, Archbishop Emeritus Desmond Tutu reminds us that it is not "I think, therefore, I am. It is I am human because I belong. I participate. I share because I am made for community. The highest praise that can be offered anyone is to say he or she has ubuntu, which means that they are generous, hospitable, friendly, caring and, of course, forgiving."[8]

The hallmark of the modern age is alienation; a sense that diversity divides rather than enriches; a disenchantment with politics and politicians; a continuing quest for a better quality of life, but a sense of emptiness and disappointment with what each advance brings; and even a sense of betrayal by our latest gadgets and newest technology—what Amitai Etzioni calls the "insurrection of the instruments."[9]

It is difficult to contemplate Mandela's world, where "people are people through other people." It is much easier to fill the void with political ideology or religious fundamentalism, but all evidence seems to point to our connectedness and the need for new paradigms and community-building strategies that borrow from the best of all of our traditions rather than any one taken alone.

### Economic Diplomacy

Economic diplomacy was at the core of Mandela's foreign policy, but while he believed that markets were good for democracy and democracy good for markets, his government sought to ensure that economic growth contributed to the empowerment of the economically marginalized, and not simply the small minority who continued to control most of the nation's wealth. Operating out of a paradigm of corrective action, Mandela's South Africa required potential investors to show what value, what social good, would be added by their presence. While the capitalism that took root looked remarkably like its Western counterpart, it had to undergo a vetting, market reforms, and empowerment strategies that reflected South Africa's unique situation. No South African could simply say we are going to do it the American way. It had to look South African and be South African before there could be South African endorsement or South African ownership.

Mandela's South Africa embodied the new reality of the world of foreign policy. Many of my conversations with other ambassadors most desirous of economic engagement with the United States found them balking at any effort to induce or require them to do things the American way. The groups that have been demonstrating at meetings of multilateral trade organizations to protest the globalization agenda of the rich nations are speaking for a much larger group when they seek to make the point that their issues are being ignored. In South Africa, there was clearly a suspicion that globalization favored the developed nations by allowing nations like the United States to ship their goods, open their factories, and move capital anywhere they wanted. There was a feeling that whether it was deliberate or not, poorer nations were being kept uncompetitive through tariffs and quotas.

For Mandela, globalization had its limits. His reservations were not about the reality of economic interdependence, but about the way the game seemed to be rigged to favor the most competitive nations. As the leader of the nonaligned nations, he felt it important to point out that even when governments wanted to do the right thing, to open markets and expand the architecture of democracy, AIDS, foreign debt, and other impediments forced on them by globalization made it hard to reach the lift-off stage that all parties desired. Kofi Annan, secretary general of the United Nations, echoed these concerns when he told a group of business executives at the January 2001 World Economic Forum that "the unequal distribution of benefits and the imbalances in global rule-making, which characterizes globalization today, inevitably will produce backlash and protectionism."[10]

Mandela understood that development would require both aid and trade, but he strongly disagreed with those economists who suggested that developing countries must adopt Western economic institutions to achieve Western levels of development. He was especially perturbed by the inability of development specialists to see or understand the limits to development that come from unequal economic structures inherited from colonial regimes, malarial climates, distances to major markets, unchecked population growth, and, for many countries, access to navigable waters. He urged multilateral organizations and developed countries to create a more pragmatic country-by-country approach to development rather than the self-serving consensus on universality that seemed, for a time, to prevail.

### Bilateral Diplomacy

In international diplomacy, interaction takes place not so much between persons as between organized communities, but Mandela demonstrated that the persona, the public and moral consciousness of the individuals who represent their communities, can also play a critical role.

In a world of technicians and intermediaries, Mandela reveled in personal diplomacy, relating directly to other heads of state—often calling them up as if bureaucracies and embassies did not exist. I was fortunate that he kept me in the loop; usually on a weekend I would get a call informing me that he wanted to speak to his friend Bill. The staff in the White House Situation Room grew accustomed to my calls, often at irregular hours. Mandela greatly admired Bill Clinton, and the feeling was mutual. I remember a White House reception where President Clinton said, "Every time Nelson Mandela walks into a room, we all feel a little bit bigger, we all want to stand up, we all want to cheer, because we would like to be him on our best day."

While Mandela had a warm personal relationship with Bill Clinton, he also understood and respected the role of the American ambassador and the U.S. embassy in coordinating bilateral relations. His respect and appreciation for my long involvement in the antiapartheid movement—raising funds for filming the liberation classic *Last Grave at Dimbaza* and serving as a founder of TransAfrica, for example—often helped to smooth out difficult and potentially damaging issues. The ambassador is the chief of the diplomatic mission and the personal representative of the president of the United States, but that fact alone does not always lead to the kind of access to the host country president I enjoyed. Our relationship was seriously threatened on one occasion, however, when a deliberate leak of a confidential cable to the State Department was distorted by a press critic with a bold front-page headline: "American Ambassador Calls Mandela a Marxist." When Mandela read the morning paper, his very controlled temperament nearly went off course, but he was calmed by a reminder from his advisors that I was a friend and supporter of long standing and would not have made such a statement. I offered to meet with Mandela and to bring a declassified copy of the cable to show him what I actually wrote, but while he was willing to meet with me, he wanted me to know that he had dismissed the headline as deliberate mischief. The next time we were together in public, he made a special effort to warmly embrace me in full view of the press to make the point he had made in private.

When the American embassies were bombed in Kenya and Tanzania, I was in Washington for meetings, but the first person I heard from was Mandela. His office called to inform me that he had dispatched extra security around my embassy and my home and wanted to know whether my government had taken necessary precautions to ensure my personal safety. Embassy Pretoria was at that time one of the largest American missions, representing more than twenty government agencies, including most American intelligence and law enforcement agencies. But for the rest of my tenure, someone from the South African VIP Protection Unit was always close by, whether I was going to the bathroom, addressing a public gathering, or visiting a township.

As the U.S. ambassador I was a very public figure, frequently serving as a spokesperson articulating and interpreting U.S. policy to business groups, the press, opinion leaders, local policymakers, and my diplomatic colleagues from more than one hundred countries. I was also an advocate for American business. President Clinton instructed all his ambassadors to support trade and investment, but while this is usually the work of the Foreign Commercial Service and the economic team, we went much further in South Africa. We understood the importance of foreign investment to creating jobs for the many black South Africans still victims of apartheid's legacy, so we set up a country commercial team to identify how each agency might contribute. We also conducted a series of "fireside chats" with managers of American businesses and worked closely with the American Chamber of Commerce and others to carry out our mandate in this area. The results were truly exceptional. By the time I left my post at the end of 1999, more than eight hundred American companies were involved in the South African economy. They had invested more than $10 billion of assets and provided almost 100,000 South African jobs. We also made contributions to South Africa's macroeconomic policy, signed trade agreements, and developed a framework for expanding trade, opening markets, and resolving trade disputes.

South Africa was an especially important country to the United States. We were committed to helping Nelson Mandela and the new democracy succeed, so we welcomed and supported many high-level visits. The most important was that of President Bill Clinton (see chapter 14), but other important visitors included Vice President Al Gore (three times), the First Lady, Secretaries of State Christopher and Albright, Secretary of Defense Bill Cohen, Secretary of the Treasury Robert Rubin, and nine other presidential cabinet secretaries at least once. Highly ranked visitors also included governors, congressional delegations, subcabinet officials, agency heads, and business delegations. To coordinate and increase the assistance provided to South Africa, President Clinton appointed a binational commission of cabinet members to work in partnership with ministers from the Mandela government. The commission was cochaired by U.S. vice president Al Gore and South Africa's deputy president Thabo Mbeki. It was indeed possible for me to say to South Africans, as I often did, "Identify a problem in your country and you are likely to find a representative of the U.S. government or an American nongovernmental organization working with a South African counterpart to resolve it." In addition to the enormous investment by American business, the United States

Agency for International Development provided hundreds of millions of dollars, and American foundations that I had previously cultivated provided at least $50 million a year.

Providing aid and supporting trade included bringing in the Peace Corps and providing support for conflict and dispute resolution. We signed a special memorandum of agreement through the binational commission authorizing the use of Peace Corps volunteers to help deal with the deficit in mathematics and science education created by the apartheid state. We supported the training of more than seven thousand South Africans in conflict resolution, and we provided assistance for the development of community radio stations, including the training of community radio managers, editors, and on-air talent. Aaron Williams, the head of USAID in South Africa, played a key role in the creative use of American aid in the development of the new democracy. He later became director of the U.S. Peace Corps in the Obama administration.

My oversight of the bilateral relations also included serving as the chief executive officer of a large organization with a multitude of programs. During my tenure, we grew from 182 Americans representing seven agencies to more than 300 representing twenty-three agencies and offices. At the same time, our staff of Foreign Service Nationals (local employees) increased to more than 400 employees. The responsibilities of the ambassador also extended to the many Americans living in South Africa, often playing a role similar to the mayor of a small city, where people bring their personal problems as well as those of their families and visiting friends.

The relationship with President Mandela and his government also included handling very sensitive issues, from resolving the Armscor case, in which the apartheid government had transferred high-level military technology to a third party, to handling politically sensitive visas for South Africans with apartheid-era convictions for their antiapartheid activities. In the latter case, U.S. laws and regulations restricting the entry of visitors with a prison record made it necessary to handle each problem individually, often causing embarrassing delays for policymakers and opinion leaders whom we needed as local supporters.

Of course, the image of bilateral diplomacy as something that takes place at elegant dinners and receptions with exquisite wines—the idea of eating and drinking for one's country—is not totally misleading. But while many important contacts and much useful information came from these social interactions, the hard work and long hours during the day were motivated as much by a desire to help President Mandela succeed as to meet my obligations as a diplomat. At the end of my tenure as U.S. ambassador, the South

African government presented me the Order of Good Hope, the highest honor presented at that time to citizens of another country.

## Mandela as Moral Leader

The key ethical norms and personal traits that provided the grounding for Nelson Mandela's transforming role in international affairs began with his appeal to people's better nature. He believed very strongly in the potential of individuals and even nation-states to change. This was not the naiveté of an idle dreamer, but the conviction of a man who had been involved in causing major change, both publicly and behind the scenes. It is this belief that people can be lifted to their better selves that was the secret to his ability to connect with other people, even his adversaries.

Mandela also believed that it is important to know your enemy much better than he knows you. The Afrikaners whose forebears had been the architect of the brutally repressive apartheid state were surprised at how well Mandela spoke Afrikaans and how much he knew about their culture and history. Even members of the right wing were often neutralized by his ability to develop a quick rapport, to see a problem through the eyes of the adversary as well as his own.

People throughout the world marveled at Mandela's ability to forgive, his lack of bitterness after twenty-seven years of imprisonment. They wondered whether this was a characteristic unique to his tribal community or culture, but his spirit also had a contagious effect on others. I have already written about Peter and Linda Biehl, the American parents of Amy Biehl, who was killed as the new democracy was about to be launched. They never imagined that they too had the capacity to forgive. But one day they found themselves before the Truth and Reconciliation Commission publicly forgiving and recommending amnesty for the young men who had murdered their daughter. Nelson Mandela sought to remind us that this same potential is in each of us.

Mandela was always open to the possibility of human error by himself and human wisdom in others. It would have been easy for him to believe that all those who preceded him in government were rascals who should be thrown out. In fact, it was his job to throw out the perpetrators of gross human rights violations, but he also believed that in every group of people there are some who share the same values. The supreme challenge was to identify them and to make them allies rather than adversaries.

Mandela loved to reminisce about his boyhood days and lazy afternoons herding cattle and imagining a different future. He lived in the moment and soaked in the wisdom of his elders, but he had his eyes fixed on a larger prize, not so much for himself as for his people. While some South Africans preferred a Nuremburg trial option for dealing with the injustices of the apartheid state, Nelson Mandela and his colleagues chose a public process that would facilitate healing and forgiveness. The genius of Nelson Mandela was not only his honesty in admitting that he was still seeking answers, but his ability to persuade others that it would be a mistake to follow those who claimed to have all of the answers.

Nelson Mandela certainly had his own failings in diplomacy and as a person. His official biographer, Anthony Sampson, referred to his stubbornness, fixed loyalties, and princely detachment. I occasionally saw those traits in my interactions with him on American foreign policy; but in the arena where history and legend merge with reality, he stood for millions of people around the world—as few others ever have—for the triumph of dignity and hope over despair and hatred, of self-discipline and love over persecution and evil, and for principled diplomacy over the idea that anything goes. In international affairs, as in domestic leadership, he always sought to appeal to a higher purpose, satisfy higher needs, and engage the full person, but he was also a practical man who understood the imperfections of our humanity as well as its potential. He remained an influential statesman even when he no longer had formal authority because his appeal was based on something deeper and more enduring than position or power.

# CHAPTER 14

# Presidential Diplomacy

*The Clinton Visit to South Africa*

Like Nelson Mandela, Bill Clinton was a master of presidential diplomacy. Shortly after I accepted his invitation to become the U.S. ambassador to South Africa and his personal representative to the Mandela government, he promised that he would come and visit. While I was preparing for the Senate hearing and looking forward to relocating to Pretoria, I learned that Jesse Helms, the powerful chair of the Senate Foreign Affairs Committee, had other ideas. Helms assured me that he rather liked the idea of someone with my experience in government, business, and civil society serving as the U.S. ambassador to this new democracy, but the North Carolina senator was locked in a series of policy battles with President Clinton regarding the future of the Agency for International Development and had pledged that no ambassadors would be confirmed until the president made major concessions. Helms had justifiably earned the nickname "Senator No," so this standoff lasted for several months.

I was eventually confirmed by the U.S. Senate and sworn in a few days later on January 4, 1996, by Supreme Court justice Sandra Day O'Connor, who as a colleague on the board of the Colonial Williamsburg Foundation had volunteered to do the honors. My confirmation hearing had gone smoothly, and my new wife, Mary, and I were preparing for the long-delayed trip to Pretoria when the Washington, DC, area was hit with a powerful snowstorm that also blanketed much of the East Coast. We had survived the Helms delay and even the shutdown of government that caused us to hurriedly plan a makeshift swearing in, but we were now stuck in a downtown DC hotel and unable to get home to complete our packing. The infamous blizzard of 1996 started at 10:00 p.m. on January 6 and lasted until the afternoon of January 8, paralyzing the city for a week. With the help of friends, especially Bill and Betty Norman, we made it through the ice and snow to gather our clothing and finally head to South Africa.

My arrival in Johannesburg was very different from previous trips. This time I was greeted at the airport by government officials and escorted to a VIP room to meet senior members of my country team from the embassy. We arrived later at the ambassador's residence to meet house staff, also standing in line to greet us although it was late in the evening and we were exhausted from the long trip. Looking at the butler, cook, maid, and others, it seemed for a fleeting moment that even our delayed honeymoon was worth it. But while the residence was beautiful and the support staff plentiful, the challenges waiting for both of us the next morning reminded us that this would be a seven-day-a-week job, starting immediately.

After a series of comprehensive briefings by the members of the country team, I went to work on the many issues that had been awaiting my arrival and made protocol visits to members of the Mandela cabinet and leaders in Parliament, business, and civil society. I also had to immediately allay the concerns and raise the morale of embassy staff who had not been paid because of the U.S. government shutdown. Some of the South African staff were even more alarmed because they thought the U.S. government was broke and might not be able to meet its obligations. Shortly thereafter, the standoff in Washington ended, morale improved, and within a few weeks I presented my credentials to President Mandela. Mary and I rejoiced that the long wait was finally over and I was now officially the U.S. ambassador to the Republic of South Africa.

I was already looking forward to visits by First Lady Hillary Clinton, whom I had once succeeded as chair of the board of directors of the Children's Defense Fund, and of course her husband the president. But I could not have anticipated how much of my time would be spent hosting other officials in the Clinton administration, congressional delegations, and many other highly placed Americans eager to support the transformations taking place in South Africa. Vice President Al Gore cochaired the United States–South Africa Binational Commission that brought him and many cabinet members to South Africa regularly, but it was the promised visit by the president that Mandela frequently inquired about. Not only is a visit by the president of the

United States the ultimate form of diplomacy, but the accompanying press helps showcase the host country to the world.

### The President Arrives

Bill and Hillary Clinton arrived in South Africa on a clear March evening in 1998 with the full beauty of Cape Town illuminated by the bright lights that brought the distance closer and made the Mediterranean-like charm clearer. The sight of the president of the United States and the First Lady disembarking from Air Force One with the presidential seal on its fuselage, a U.S. flag embossed on its tail, and the winds the locals call a Southeaster howling in the background will remain forever etched in memory. The warmth of a Cape Town welcome was everywhere evident, but on the way to the airport Mary and I passed Death to America signs. The large Lincoln Town Car easily identified me as the American ambassador, but as we stopped at a robot, what Americans call a stoplight, the demonstrators moved closer.

My driver remained calm and slowly pulled away. The beauty and size of the car concealed the sophisticated armor underneath, but we breathed a sigh of relief, nevertheless, when we made it through the tightly guarded airport entrance. We were joined on the tarmac by Foreign Minister Alfred Nzo, Cape Town mayor Theresa Solomon, and Franklin Sonn, the South African ambassador to the United States, who had become a close personal friend. As Mary and I drew closer to the red carpet to extend a welcome and introduce the greeting party, we could also see two stretch limousines, security and communications vehicles, and the rest of the motorcade that was to become our constant companion for the next three days. While I could not see them, I knew that snipers were on the roofs and sniffer dogs and bomb disposal units were close by. This, after all, had been part of the protracted negotiations with the South Africans.

It was an early hour of the morning, so greetings were brief and the journalists and other spectators were kept under wraps as the motorcade sped to the waterfront hotel that had been carefully selected to house the president and some of his entourage. Most Capetonians were asleep, but the city was braced for what was undoubtedly one of the biggest events in its history. In the afternoon newspaper, President Mandela had described President Clinton as one of South Africa's best friends. Her Worship the Mayor of Cape Town (a title that seemed more ecclesiastical than political) had hailed the historic visit as a great opportunity to showcase this vibrant and dynamic African city she called home.

The main presidential party stayed at the Cape Grace Hotel, where the First Lady had resided on her first visit. This time, however, three navy diving teams and an underwater demolition crew monitored the surrounding waters around the clock. The security net included patrol vessels and a minesweeper as well as members of the South African police and army. On the grounds and in the hotel could also be found members of the well-publicized Secret Service. The mayor had made claims that she was shoved around like a sack of potatoes on Hillary Clinton's previous visit.

Frene Ginwala, the Speaker of the Parliament, was quoted as saying that she had ordered security in Parliament to be handled by South African, not American, personnel. I promised the mayor in jest that I would protect her from what she had described as the CIA, the FBI, the VIP Protection Unit, the army, and the navy. And of course I negotiated with the Speaker on how many security agents would be in Parliament and how many and what kind of weapons would be allowed.

President Clinton awoke to a bold headline in *Business Day*, a leading South African daily. It screamed in bold print, "Mbeki Attacks US Trade Bill as Clinton Flies in." It so happened that the president's first appointment was a visit by the deputy president, who was as mystified as I was since there was nothing in the article to support the headline. I had been a victim of the same practice on other occasions, so I commiserated with Mbeki as we sat together waiting for President Clinton to join us in the library at the Cape Grace. The trade bill—which provided debt relief, greater access to U.S. markets for African exports, and the creation of an infrastructure fund—was an important initiative not only supported by President Clinton, but introduced by several members of the president's traveling party from the U.S. Congress. The South Africans had previously voiced concern about the market reforms required for an African country to be eligible for some of the provisions of the bill, but they had not indicated anything like the opposition the headline implied.

In the private meeting with President Clinton, Thabo Mbeki made his government's position on the trade bill clear. He was not opposing it. He was simply seeking consultation on the conditions it imposed.

### Promoting a New Partnership

On her 1997 visit to Cape Town, First Lady Hillary Clinton had been greatly impressed by the work of the Homeless People's Federation in the Victoria Mxenge housing project and promised that she would someday return. The women in the Guguletu project saved their own money through the federation and built their own homes brick by brick. When the First Lady first visited, the project was just beginning. Now there were more than a hundred homes. The love affair between these women and Hillary had been obvious, but they did not believe she would return. They were overjoyed when I notified them that Mrs. Clinton was coming back and wanted to see how they had progressed.

What we did not tell the Homeless People's Federation was that Hillary was bringing her husband. The First Lady had pledged us all to secrecy. She wanted this to be her surprise. When the motorcade arrived at the Victoria Mxenge project, women screeched with delight and children ran through the streets telling all in the township that the president of the United States was in their neighborhood. The president and the First Lady had not come simply to demonstrate support for the women but went immediately to work, adding bricks to the structure on which a group of women were working. After laying a few bricks, the president said, "Some thirty years ago, I spent time building houses. When I learned what hard work it was I went into politics."

The crowd cheered for the president, but it was Hillary who had stolen the hearts of the local women. The head of the group, a former domestic worker, announced that the project had acquired more land to build a second phase of housing, and one of the streets would be named after Hillary. The group also presented her with a membership certificate and a T-shirt, informing her that now that she was a member, they would expect two hundred rands for the membership fee and thirty rands for the T-shirt. They were obviously entrepreneurs at heart. Before leaving, the president and First Lady dropped by the home of Velisma Mbeki (no relation to the then deputy president), whose house-in-progress Hillary had visited on her previous trip. She was delighted to find two newly painted bedrooms, a kitchen, a lounge, and a flush toilet. As she shook hands with well-wishers, President Clinton commented, "All over the world people will see what you are doing in this neighborhood and will say, 'I want to do that.'" This was a good final touch since a major purpose of the Clinton trip was to highlight success stories in the new Africa.

A twenty-one-gun salute signaled the arrival of the president of the United States at the second stop. The public highlight of the three-day visit was undoubtedly the welcoming ceremony in front of the stately parliamentary buildings and the address to Parliament. Standing tall with Mandela by his side, Clinton followed the red carpet to a specially constructed red podium before inspecting an elite naval guard with Hillary and Graça Machel, Mandela's new partner, looking on. Standing at the head of the line that included members of the U.S. cabinet and U.S. Congress, Mary and I were once again the beneficiaries of official protocol that placed the American ambassador next to the president.

At the end of the ceremony, Mary and I were escorted to our seats in the gallery alongside Hillary. This was a far cry from the day I had stood outside those same parliamentary gates with my Free Mandela sign. This time I was inside listening to the president of the United States pay tribute to "South Africa's heroic sacrifice" and "breathtaking walk out of darkness." Not only was Mandela free, he was sitting in the chamber as president of the Republic of South Africa, and applauding his friend "Beel" with a Xhosa accent.

This was a great day for South Africa, but in many ways it was also a great day for the United States. We were finally acknowledging the coming of age of Africa, not just the renaissance Thabo Mbeki liked to talk about, but the fact that this was a country with brains, resources, and a future. The long odyssey of the 12 percent of Americans with African roots was finally reaching an overdue epiphany. "Although terrible conflicts still tear at the heart of the continent, democracy is growing and the boundaries of peace expanding," Clinton told a warm and enthusiastic audience. It was clear that this was a new day when he said, "Africa still needs the world, but it is equally true that the world needs Africa." Representative Charlie Rangel and Jesse Jackson, with whom I had worked on South African issues for decades, were in the audience. Maxine Waters, the chair of the Congressional Black Caucus, and former congressman Ronald Dellums were also a part of this historic moment. All of our work over the years now seemed vindicated when President Clinton said, "In the past, Americans use to ask what can we do for Africa or about Africa. That was the wrong question. The right question is what can we do with Africa? What can we do together?"

Working with Africa was the theme of the new partnership President Clinton had come to Africa to announce. But his motive was also in part to "help the American people to see Africa with new eyes, and to focus on new politics suited for the new millennium." It was at the same podium that I had heard Thabo Mbeki introduce the notion of an African renaissance, and here was President Clinton not only using the language of renewal to describe the new African reality, but saying, "Let us build together."

While not referring directly to former archbishop Desmond Tutu's notion of a rainbow nation, the president concluded with the reminder, "There is every conceivable difference on the surface between the Americans and the South Africans in this great hall of freedom. Different races, different religions, different native tongues, but underneath the same hopes, the same dreams and the same values."

Frene Ginwala, who was of Indian descent, was determined to showcase the rainbow nation, selecting Democratic Alliance MP Dene Smuts to respond to Clinton's address. A white woman of extraordinary eloquence, she referred to Clinton's words when he accepted the nomination as president of the United States: "I still believe in a place called hope. Not just your birthplace, Hope, Arkansas, but that metaphorical place from which and towards which we all travel." She concluded, "Here in the Cape of Good Hope, at the tip of our continent, the tide of history has turned toward hope, and in favor of open societies and free markets." The tide of history had indeed turned. The president of the United States and I soon headed upstairs to meet with opposition leaders, including some who had been present when past presidents of South Africa had declared that such a day would never come.

### Sitting Down to Talk

The carefully planned bilateral meeting between the two presidents and their senior advisors the next day turned out to be a one-on-one meeting instead. Needless to say, it caused considerable consternation. Only Mandela could get away with ignoring both the wishes of the White House staff and the recommendations of his own staff. Rumors had been rife that Mandela wanted a private meeting with Clinton, but a private meeting usually included senior aides and a note taker. But after assurances that the ambassador and two senior aides would be included, Mandela chose to simply ignore what had been carefully negotiated, diverting Clinton into his private office while we waited in the presidential conference room. After more than an hour's wait, it became clear that Mandela did not intend to include staff, no matter how senior, so we shifted venues and waited outside with South African Foreign Minister Nzo and Ambassador Sonn, who were also cooling their heels.

The press conference that followed was notable for Mandela's demonstration of great respect and admiration for his distinguished visitor. He warmly welcomed the state visit as a "high water mark" of his four years as president. As the two presidents stood side by side, Mandela reached out and grasped Clinton's hand as he said, "This is one of our proudest moments. . . . You helped us before you became president and continue to help us as president of the greatest country in the world." He praised Clinton for his impeccable "political instincts," noting that while the two countries had differed on certain issues, in the end the mutual respect had been enhanced because of respect for each other's sovereignty and good faith.

It was when Mandela started to dish out some fatherly advice to his younger colleague that the differences with the United States that the press had come to hear about surfaced. Referring to the United Nations charter, which calls on all member states to try to settle their differences by peaceful methods, Mandela said, "That is the position that has influenced our own approach toward problems." The ANC had sat down with "repugnant" people to negotiate a settlement; thus, "the United States as leader of the world should set an example to help eliminate tensions throughout the world. And one of the best ways of doing so is to call upon its enemies to say, 'Let's all sit down and talk peace.'"

This was an obvious reference to U.S. relations with Iraq, which the United States had not only come close to bombing a few weeks before, but which had caused a cancellation of the trip to South Africa by Vice President Al Gore for the meeting of the United States–South Africa Binational Commission he cochaired with Deputy President Mbeki.

The press finally had their headline when Mandela declared that South Africa's moral authority dictated, "We should not abandon those who helped us in the darkest hours in the history of this country." He went on to say that he had invited Cuban president Fidel Castro, Iran's former president Hashemi Rafsanjani, and Libya's president Moammar Gaddafi to South Africa. To the amusement of many in the audience, Mandela went on to say that those who criticized him for maintaining ties with old friends should "go and throw themselves into a pool." The heartiest chuckle came from Clinton, who time after time demonstrated a maturity and sensitivity that endeared him to his South African hosts.

Local newspaper headlines the next day described the statement as a Mandela lecture to the U.S. president. But as one bemused member of Congress said to me, "Only Mandela could have done this." Probing a little more widely with some of his colleagues, I found an overwhelming recognition that it was foolhardy to expect Mandela to change his tune of loyalty to friends. He was merely being consistent, but as I had said to him on several occasions in the past, South Africans should also remember how many friends in the United States had fought long and hard for a new South Africa, a representative government, a free people in a free country. It was true that Reagan and Thatcher had considered the ANC terrorists when Castro and others were helping its freedom fighters fend off brutal attacks by the South African Defense Force, but the relationship between our two people had always been on two tracks, government to government and people to people. The latter had consistently seen groups of Americans around the country fighting for Mandela's release from prison and often taking great risks in support of the dissolution of apartheid.

President Clinton demonstrated the same respect and admiration for his host that the world's most respected statesman had showed to him. He could have been referring to the strong winds that plagued Cape Town during part of his visit or Harold Macmillan's famed "Winds of Change" speech in the 1960s when he said, "I am pleased that we are committed to harnessing the winds of change together." Calling them "winds of good fortune," he went on to say that the United States was South Africa's biggest investor and intended to do more. Responding to the misinformation spread by the media, he reminded his audience that at the same time "increasing trade did not mean decreasing aid." He promised to work with the U.S. Congress to restore levels of aid to Africa to their historic high.

If his reception at Parliament was a triumph for Bill Clinton the president, his warm and sensitive dealing with Mandela at the press conference was a triumph for Bill Clinton the man. Even his critics had to admit that Clinton was hard to dislike. His humanity leaped out to embrace all those he encountered, whether they were critics or supporters. All those with whom he engaged, even if only for a few seconds, felt that he had taken a personal interest in them and their story.

### A Triumph of the Human Spirit

Clinton's adoring respect for Mandela was nowhere more evident than on the visit to the Robben Island prison cell where South Africa's most revered political prisoner had spent eighteen of his twenty-seven years of confinement. The trip to Robben Island was another of those experiences that will remain etched in memory forever. Mary and I had been to Robben Island many times—with Al Gore, Hillary Clinton, and on our own as the new ambassadorial couple—but this was different. It was our first ride in the Marine helicopter that often transported dignitaries from the White House to Camp David. After a wait in Cape Town for President Mandela's helicopter to take off, we set out for the island, where we ended up circling for a while in order not to violate protocol by landing early.

On the island, the two presidents walked arm in arm from the prison courtyard to the bleak corridors of the B section where Mandela had trained so many of his future colleagues in government. Jailed in 1964, he had transformed the prison into what became known later as Robben Island University, as he persuaded many of his fellow political prisoners to read, study, and prepare for the future leadership of their country. The grilled door to Mandela's old cell was open to reveal the small space that had been his home. Pointing to the size of the cell, he said, "You know, it was so big at the time; I don't know why it is so small now." Clinton was clearly moved as Mandela told him about some of the hardships of prison life. He described, as he had done the year before for Hillary, how he would stack the little cupboard with tiny portions of sugar, peanuts, and honey and try to make them last for a month. Still spartan in appearance, the cell retains the blanket and metal cup that was used by the most famous prisoner ever to occupy a space in the prison.

When Clinton pressed his head against the cell window to peer into the courtyard, a Clinton advisor could be heard saying, "That's the picture I didn't want." But this was not Michael Dukakis, a former candidate for president, on a tank with an oversized hat. The picture made the front page of many newspapers as expected, but it portrayed a pensive president looking out of the window with a stoic Mandela. The expression in Clinton's eyes was one of empathy and compassion as his hands gripped a cell bar and his eyes followed the path of Mandela's pointing finger.

The two presidents were driven around the island to see the limestone quarry where Mandela toiled daily, leaving a legacy of chronic eye problems from the blinding sun and dust, and badly damaged knees from the exhausting work. But the Robben Island Clinton saw was not just about hard labor, long hours, and abuse. It was a monument to the triumph of the human spirit. The former prisoners did not want pity for their suffering. They wanted visitors to recognize the potential in each of us to rise above hardships and to transcend the worst forms of inhumanity.

Later that day, we traveled again by Marine helicopter to the Vergelegen wine estate, where the ANC had held its first meeting after being unbanned. Mandela, who had a warm place in his heart for the beautiful spot with its three-hundred-year-old camphor trees, had carefully selected it for the state dinner he hosted. Under a giant marquee, the 750 guests were treated to an elegant evening with Clinton and Mandela. While the order of events had been carefully planned and, of course, negotiated, we arrived to a light drizzle that must have caused a little apprehension for those who had to wait in line to get through security. But nothing could damage the spirit of the evening. Bishop Tutu offered a mood-setting invocation, and Clinton was presented the Order of Good Hope by his host. It had taken an embarrassing amount of time to get approval from the White House for this award to be presented, since it had only recently been presented to Gaddafi. But this too was behind us. Clinton was gracious and eloquent in accepting. As he referred in his statement to Mandela's unbroken spirit, the winds began to shake the large tent disturbingly. As if part of his planned statement, Clinton, after saying "unbroken," interjected, "a condition I hope the tent will maintain." Mary and I sat next to President Mandela and Graça Machel. It was a delightful evening that dulled all the memories of the tough negotiations that preceded it.

### Embracing the African Renaissance

The next morning found us headed to Johannesburg. Mary and I were excited about accompanying the president and the First Lady on Air Force One. We went directly to the airport instead of traveling with the motorcade.

This time there were no demonstrators, only a rope line of consulate employees, both American and South African, and their families. Jesse Jackson, the president's special envoy, also arrived early, pausing to take pictures with us in the shadow of Air Force One before walking the rope line as if it had been arranged especially for him. Mary was taken onto Air Force One early, where she was given a guided tour by a steward. I waited for the presidential motorcade and walked the rope line with the president and the First Lady.

When it came time to board the plane, I started toward the side door where the VIPs traveling with the president had entered, only to be told by the White House's chief of protocol that as ambassador I should enter through the same door as the Clintons. I was instructed to wait until they got to the top of the stairs for the customary wave to the crowd and then to follow after they disappeared into the plane. I was uncertain whether it was appropriate to wave to the staff when I got to the top, but decided I was supposed to sneak in unobtrusively.

We enjoyed the comfort of Air Force One, which from the outside looked very much like any other 747-200. But with its leather seats, wood-grain furniture, and paneling in beige and blue, we were quickly reminded that this was no ordinary plane. I had traveled with the vice president, the First Lady, and the secretary of state on their own planes, but this was the top of the line. The president's private quarters contained an executive stateroom with dressing room, bathroom, a private office, and a separate conference and dining room. There was also an office area for senior staff members and a small medical facility. We were seated around a table in the separate accommodation area provided for special guests with representatives Charlie Rangel, Maxine Waters, and Donald Payne, all strong supporters of the president's Africa policy in Congress. It was a good opportunity to check the pulse of the visit and to find out how they felt about the rest of the trip. They had obviously been excited when we saw them at the reception Mary and I hosted at our residence for them and the Clintons, but I wanted to know about their reaction to the press conference, the Robben Island visit, the state dinner, and the like. To a person, they were full of enthusiasm and praise. This had been a historic return to the continent of their ancestors, and the opportunity to take their place in a Parliament full of "former terrorists" led by the legendary Mandela was the highlight of the trip.

We landed in Johannesburg to another motorcade and a substitute car and driver for the ambassador. Much to my dismay, the new driver got a little excited and could not start the car as the motorcade started to drive off. With customary speed that waits for no one except the president, the cars behind us started to pull around. But before complete embarrassment, our car started and we found a new place in the motorcade. Our first stop was the hotel where we checked in and got ready for the next appointment.

After visiting a school in the nearby township of Thokoza, we made our way to the Hector Pieterson Memorial in Soweto, the site where the twelve-year-old Pieterson was shot dead by South African police in the 1976 student uprising. After escorting the president and First Lady to the memorial, we planted a tree as a symbol of the hope of the new South Africa. Soweto residents were out in full force, but we were a bit embarrassed by the heavy security blanket thrown around the event. The advance team had been very anxious about a demonstration scheduled for Johannesburg to protest local matters, so the South African police had overreacted with barbed wire and police vehicles of all types. From whatever vantage point they could find, Sowetans cheered the president and welcomed him to the city that had been the heart and soul of the liberation struggle. As we had done when Hillary visited, we again toured the photographic display of pictures taken during the uprising. Our guides included world-renowned photographer Peter Magubane and others whose works were on display.

President Clinton concluded this emotional day with a celebration of the life of Ron Brown, the former secretary of commerce who had earlier in the year lost his life in an airplane crash shortly after my dinner with him in Botswana. Naming the U.S. commercial service center in Johannesburg in Brown's honor, he called for new investments in Africa. In a speech aimed primarily at the U.S. audience watching via television, Clinton sounded the themes of the African renaissance. He reminded American business that the return on investment in Africa was 30 percent, compared with 11 percent worldwide. According to figures released by the U.S. Commerce Department, this compared to 12 percent in Latin America, 13 percent in the Asia Pacific region, and 17 percent in the Middle East. Ron Brown, who as secretary of commerce had frequently urged American business to invest in Africa, would have been proud of these new indicators of American economic engagement with the continent. Trade with Africa was now 20 percent greater than with the republics of the former Soviet Union and supported more than 100,000 U.S. jobs. To the applause of a crowd of five hundred, mostly businessmen, the president said, "I hope they are listening back in America. This is a good deal, folks." Clinton challenged other industrialized countries to offer more debt relief so that resources could be freed up for health, education, and sustainable growth.

After a quiet night on his own, the president, and the VIP delegation, arose early to worship at the local Catholic church in Regina Mundi Township. The president and I arrived separately, but we met together in the courtyard and moved quietly toward the entrance where the local priest and his bishop greeted the president with great enthusiasm. The church had once sheltered antiapartheid activists from tear gas and police bullets. Some of the bullet holes were still visible from the 1976 uprising in which more than one hundred students died and thousands protested.

As a symbol of the reconciliation between once-warring factions, the church leaders had welcomed many visitors from around the world, but this was different. The president of the United States had come to worship with them. Sharing a pew with the president, the First Lady, and the Reverend Jackson, Mary and I accompanied them to the altar for Holy Communion. It was a solemn occasion in a greatly revered setting. Regina Mundi had been the scene of turbulent unrest that had almost torn the community apart in the fading days of apartheid. But the church leaders had brought the community together to stand united in the demand for change. It was the perfect place to end the president's trip.

We left the church with a great sendoff from the crowd outside and headed for the airport. As he boarded the plane and said good-bye, the president thanked me for what he described as a truly great visit. The longest leg of his Africa trip was now over, and the pundits were left to analyze the meaning of his historic three-and-a-half-day visit to South Africa. Local press coverage had been extensive, but it was the 150 members of the traveling press corps we were depending on to tell the story of South Africa back home. We were not disappointed. My wife and I had hosted, along with the Freedom Forum, a press luncheon on the waterfront in Cape Town. Many of the big names in the American media were present. They had traveled the world and seen almost everything there is to see. But we could tell that they shared our belief that Cape Town was special. The allure of the mountains, the magnificent ocean vistas, the charm of immaculately landscaped wine estates, and the dramatic attractions of the waterfront were all in full view. Through both print and visual images, they introduced the world to the beauty of South Africa, its democratic reforms and economic potential, its emphasis on healing the wounds of the past and building a truly nonracial community. The emphasis on the African renaissance also benefited from the presence of an international press corps. People around the world were reminded that Africa was a vast continent, now more than a billion people, a continent whose new leaders were convinced that the twenty-first century might well be the African century. They effectively conveyed the diversity of Africa: that what seems self-evident in one area may not be the reality in another.

This emphasis on the other Africa was badly needed. Far too many people who would not dare speak of a homogeneous Europe or Asia speak of the more than fifty independent nations of Africa as if the continent were a single political entity. It has been indeed difficult for many to grasp either the extraordinary range of cultural, economic, and political diversity or the immense size of a continent so large that the whole of China, the continental United States, Europe, Argentina, India, and New Zealand can fit within its boundaries.

It is a great pity that the press for much of the 1990s focused more on Mobutu and the former Zaire than men like Museveni in Uganda and Rawlings in Ghana, for it was clear that they represented the future and Mobutu the past. There was a new breed of African leaders, embodied not so much by Mandela, who, like Gandhi and Churchill, transcends history, but by mere mortals who are, nevertheless, pragmatic—aggressively opening their societies to outside markets and strongly committed to the rule of law.

Speaking both as a son of Africa and secretary general of the United Nations, Kofi Annan on an earlier visit had described the momentous changes in Africa as part of three waves. First came decolonization and the struggle against apartheid. Then came a second wave, too often marked by civil wars, the tyranny of military rule, and economic stagnation. He argued that a new era was in progress, Africa's third wave. Whether you call it an African renaissance as Thabo Mbeki did, or a third wave as Kofi Annan did, there was no question that something new and different was happening on the continent.

Both concepts are important to the political discourse about the awakening and reawakening of Africa. As they gain credence as new paradigms for showcasing the other Africa—separate and apart from the one portrayed as rife with greed, corruption, and tribal conflicts—pundits debate whether these are simply new slogans destined to be cast aside like the old ideas of pan-Africanism, African socialism, black consciousness, ubuntu, and negritude. Or could it be that Mbeki and Annan were describing a real and sustainable attempt to recapture the public space, reconstruct economics, and reinvent the philosophy and practice of governance?

The African idea of renaissance was a revival or renewal of Africa after waves of colonial domination by the French, Portuguese, British, Belgians, Germans, and others who contributed to the factional rivalries, corruption, distorted economies, and exploitation by elites that they now deplore as somehow unique to Africa. Even the United States used the failed states as a tool in its Cold War adventures. But what was most promising about Africa's reawakening was that while its new leaders recognized the persistence of the old legacies and the problems they continued to create, they also recognized that the continent had to look beyond its colonial past to find the vision and resolve for solving its problems.

The Clinton visit is at best a distant memory for many, but the potential of the continent that Clinton emphasized is now being realized. While the image of many American investors is still clouded by the old stereotypes of Africa as primarily a place of war, disease, and poverty, China has come to the continent with a new vigor, optimism, and winning embrace—building universities, investing in infrastructure development, and providing significantly increased aid—while at the same time drawing closer to the vast natural resources that can fuel its booming economy.

The potential Clinton saw is now being validated by analysts with a new story to tell. A 2010 report by McKinsey and Company, for example, offered a very optimistic view of the African continent, arguing that global business cannot afford to ignore its potential.[1] According to the report, Africa's billion people spent $860 billion in 2008, more than India's population of 1.2 billion. Whereas other economies were devastated by the recession of 2009, twenty-seven of the thirty largest African economies experienced accelerated growth, while throughout the continent budget deficits declined and inflation rates fell. In South Africa, not a single financial institution failed during the Great Recession that almost caused the collapse of the economies in the richer nations.

Many who sought to discredit the idea of an African renaissance are now forced to acknowledge that despite some continuing problems, signs of progress and growth abound, not just in the economy, but in education, housing, and most other indicators of economic and social well-being. Americans can now be thankful that at a critical moment when respect for the United States was on the decline, the presidential diplomacy of Bill Clinton countered the faltering views of the United States on the continent and kept the doors open for both investments and political partnerships that would help resolve some of the great issues of the twentieth century.

# V

# The Twenty-First Century

. . . . . . . . . . . . . . . . . . . . . . . . . . . . . . . . . . . . . . . . . . . . . . . . . . . . . . . . . . . . . . . .

LEADERSHIP AND

PUBLIC VALUES

# CHAPTER 15

# Leaders Learning from Leaders

My appointment as an American ambassador officially ended in January 2000, four years from the date Supreme Court Justice O'Connor swore me in. Still undecided about my next step, I traveled across South Africa and the United States asking many whom I had grown to respect what needed to be done to sustain the gains of the liberation struggle.

Some, like Thabo Mbeki, at that time the new president of South Africa, spoke of the need for a new kind of civil servant who recognized that bureaucracies could be both efficient and humane. Others, like Bill Gray, a former congressman from Pennsylvania then president of the United Negro College Fund, spoke of a need for political leaders who sought power in order to redistribute it rather than simply hold it. My good friend Eli Segal, the head of AmeriCorps and senior advisor to President Bill Clinton, emphasized the importance of leaders who understand the value of service and see nonprofit organizations as custodians of values as well as resources. My old mentor J. Irwin Miller, the former head of Cummins Engine Company, spoke of a need for corporate statesmen who see ethics as contributing to the bottom line.

As I continued my conversation with other veteran leaders, it became clear that I was being urged to help prepare emerging leaders to cope with the moral challenges of an increasingly complex world. I had failed in my attempts to persuade the United States–South Africa

Binational Commission to establish a subcommittee on civil society along-side the one on trade and industry, so I also felt an urge to pursue this idea in some form.

My wife, Mary, who had first visited South Africa in 1992, shared my enthusiasm. She was the first person to whom I spoke when the idea of using my experience and networks to help develop a new generation of value-driven public leaders surfaced. A former award-winning television journalist, she had some ideas of her own about how she could also make a contribution. She had already interviewed Nelson Mandela for the Discovery television channel in the United States and contributed to a documentary shown on South African television and PBS in the United States featuring Archbishop Desmond Tutu and John Hope Franklin, a widely read African American historian. Filmed in Senegal at the slave castle on Gorée Island, the documentary included twenty-one young students from South Africa, the United States, and Senegal who spent a week together examining issues of race and reconciliation. The two wise men joined them from time to time to help them work out the more complex issues that impeded their ability to find common ground.

Persuaded that there was a role for both of us in the new South Africa, I decided to develop a nongovernmental organization on leadership and public values that would include a binational forum on civil society. Two close friends, Jakes Gerwel, Nelson Mandela's former chief of staff, and Wilmot James, the dean of the newly established Graduate School of Humanities at the University of Cape Town, joined me in incorporating a new nongovernmental organization in South Africa. Lance Buhl, another friend and former academic at Harvard and executive at British Petroleum, joined me in incorporating a similar group in the United States.

At the same time, I was being recruited by a variety of institutions in business, academia, government, and civil society looking for an executive with my experience. I decided that the commitment to supporting the transformations in South Africa was far too deep for me to consider anything that would not allow me to continue a direct involvement with the challenges now facing this young democracy. I had first fallen in love with South Africa during my visit in 1974, but I could not consummate that love affair until the launch of the democracy twenty years later. This was not a time to end the relationship.

What started out as the establishment of a binational nonprofit organization with offices in South Africa and the United States took another turn. I had served on the advisory board of the predecessor institution at Duke University that is now the Sanford School of Public Policy, and I was being strongly urged and recruited by Susan King, a friend and Duke trustee, to consider this highly regarded institution as a potential home for both teaching and a continuing engagement with South Africa. Susan was persistent, even sending Duke T-shirts to my two immediate assistants in Pretoria to ensure that they accepted her calls. Meanwhile, Mamphela Ramphele, at that time the head of the University of Cape Town, invited me to serve as an honorary professor at her institution.

This led to my proposing a center for leadership and public values as a partnership between the two institutions. The idea was accepted with enthusiasm and I became a full-time professor of the practice of public policy at Duke and an honorary professor at the University of Cape Town. Having jettisoned the idea of an independent nongovernmental organization, I went back to some of the people I had consulted earlier and invited them to serve on an advisory board for the new center.

Kenneth Kaunda, the former president of Zambia, joined me at Duke to announce the formation of the new United States–Southern Africa Center for Leadership and Public Values. The South African ambassador, Sheila Sisulu, hosted a reception at the embassy in Washington, DC, to introduce the center to the vast network of South Africa supporters in the metropolitan region. Former congressman Bill Gray, who was one of the first to commit to serving on the board of the new center, was asked to offer a toast, but while he reminded me that he was a Baptist minister, he did it with his usual grace and charm.

With the birth certificate of the new center now signed and sealed, it was time to raise the funds and hire staff. I had not embarked on this venture without some early assurance of support, and Lance Buhl, who was to become my deputy, was already serving as a consultant. Malusi Mpumlwana, a former associate of Steve Biko's and at that time a local bishop and the southern Africa representative for the W. K. Kellogg Foundation, was enthusiastic about the idea and took the lead in convening a meeting with his colleagues from the Ford and C. S. Mott foundations. After a discussion of the concept and mission of the center, Christa Kuljian of Mott and Gerry Salole of Ford met again with Malusi and worked out among themselves how they would support the first three years of the center, while challenging me to bring in other funding sources for the second three-year cycle.

With a center now established at Duke, I worked with the director and faculty at the Graduate School of Business at the University of Cape Town to do the same at their institution. Ceri Oliver-Evans, who had been working in the office of the vice chancellor, was hired as director, and Kurt April, a rising star on the business school faculty, was recruited to be academic director.

What was novel in the decade that followed was not so much the success of the partnership, the committed people who served on the staff, or the quality of the participants we attracted as fellows. It was the innovative pedagogy and practices of a program of leaders learning from leaders. With the program centered at the heart of two great universities, it might have been expected that the center would focus on teaching, research, and the dissemination of knowledge in its classical forms to traditional constituencies. But this was a program that integrated the experiential and the theoretical, putting knowledge at the service of the larger society rather than simply the students and graduates of the two universities. We also decided from the outset that our focus would be on leadership as a way of being rather than simply knowing and doing. The emphasis from the outset has been on how a leader needs to be rather than simply what the leader needs to know or do.

With the proliferation of leadership programs and publications now constituting a virtual leadership industry, we were concerned that while leadership gurus and studies have much to offer that is useful, many of those who write and teach about leadership have never been a leader and many have never even known a leader. So we tilted our program heavily in favor of the experiential while also making a clear distinction between managing and leading. I have been a manager and I have been a leader, but I found that as a manager I needed order to be effective, while being a leader often required a willingness to risk chaos. Moreover, this was a program about leadership values and the capacity to deal with not just moral absolutes but moral ambiguities as well; not just with the microethics of individual behavior but the macroethics of our aggregate existence, whether as institutions, communities, or cultures.

We defined leadership as a way of being with four elements: emotional, social, moral, and spiritual intelligence. And we set out to cultivate these qualities among the best midcareer leaders we could identify and attract. Of course, Daniel Goleman had given us much with which to work from his research and writings on emotional intelligence,[1] but we needed a living prototype. We wanted to examine the qualities of a high-profile leader who embodied not just emotional intelligence but the other forms as well. It became clear to me that in using these categories I was describing not only some of the best leaders with whom I had worked in the past, but the most revered leader of our time, Nelson Mandela.

The journey that began with my first visit to South Africa as an anti-apartheid activist in 1974 was now taking me in a different direction, but to the same destination I had been traveling to for more than a quarter century. Apartheid had ended, Nelson Mandela had been released from prison and elected president, and a new democracy had been launched, but there was still much work to be done. I decided to become a part of that work and to identify and train the younger Mandelas already emerging in southern Africa and communities of color in the United States. I had initially thought of the program as exclusively for southern Africans, but when I shared the idea with Susan Berresford, president of the Ford Foundation, she suggested that it might be good to add leaders from communities in the United States with similar histories of struggle.

Looking back as we move further into the second decade of the twenty-first century, it is rewarding to see graduates of the program now serving as mayors, members of Parliament, CEOs in business, foundation executives, and leaders in education and religion. Yet leadership remains an elusive concept and training leaders a mixed bag of programs and institutes. Those academics who do research on the subject tend to do so from the perspective of their own disciplines, and those practitioners who dare to put their reflections in print tend to do so almost exclusively from their own experience.

My personal experience of leadership began at a time when the emphasis in the United States was on the alpha male approach of command, control, and coercion, what has come to be known as hard power. Many of my male peers in college were fascinated with the model of the military leader who was assertive, authoritarian, and focused on commanding the behavior of others. Even in my studies of Western literature, the idea of a leader grew largely out of Homer's *Iliad* and *Odyssey*, an ideal of the brave warrior leading by example in the Trojan War.

It was some years later that I became more open to collaboration and more sensitive to soft power, although the world around me was still dominated by hard power. The leaders I admired were those who called us to a higher purpose, inspired us, elevated us, and appealed to our better nature. But that period was followed by an era in which many people seemed to be looking for the ordinary; someone in whose image they saw themselves, someone who looked like them, acted like them, and thought like them, if they thought at all. With the election of Barack Obama in 2008 as the president of the United States, this romanticizing of ordinariness seemed to have lost some of its hold on the American mind; but we have since learned that there are still relatively large numbers of people looking for leaders who fit their comfort zone.

## A Mandela Moment in the United States

On the day after the election of Barack Obama, some of my friends in South Africa compared this historic event to the election of Nelson Mandela in

1994. They called it "a Mandela moment in the United States." The euphoria was once again global, but while I was initially dubious about this comparison, I soon came to realize that my South African friends were offering both important insights and very useful cautions. They were commenting on the qualities we were now highlighting, and to some degree validating, as critical to leadership at a time of great challenge and change. But it was not just the long lines and the long wait at so many voting places that reminded them of South Africa's first fully democratic and inclusive election. It was not just the magnitude of the moment that spoke so loudly about the progress Americans had made in their efforts to form a more perfect union. It was not just the rebirth of hope and a momentary optimism in the face of alarming adversity.

To call the Obama election a Nelson Mandela moment in the United States was also to call forth an important caution. On Inauguration Day, the whole world seemed to stand in awe, with some calling it the intersection of hope and history. Yet while many understandably watched in amazement, we were in danger of seeing this change in American politics and history not as a new beginning, but as fulfillment and finality. Remembering the South African experience in 1994 when there was talk of a miracle, a new generation still struggling to fulfill the hopes of that moment was reminding us that while the election of Barack Obama was indeed an extraordinary leap forward, it was actually a turning point in a process that will continue long into the future.

It was my good fortune to work closely with Nelson Mandela for three years. As the U.S. ambassador to South Africa, I had a front-row seat as he orchestrated the transition from apartheid to a nonracial democracy and became one of the most respected and revered leaders of the modern era. Heads of state and royalty from around the world beat a path to his door for advice and counsel on the great issues of the day.

The irony is that after twenty-seven years of incarceration Mandela went from political prisoner to president. He was in prison while the world economy was becoming interdependent. He was in prison while we were developing the Internet. He was in prison when the cell phone was introduced in South Africa. He was in prison while we were being seduced by the notion that experience trumps wisdom and judgment. But he came out of prison, took over the leadership of his party and his country, and never missed a beat, because for him leadership was a way of being grounded in something deeper than simply the mastery of a set of specialized functions, management competencies, or public experiences.

Mandela's attractiveness and influence came from the power of his personality, the elegance of his humanity, the wisdom of his judgment, the loftiness of his ideals, the calmness of his temperament, and the depth of his commitment to forgiveness and reconciliation. He emerged from prison at a time when effective leadership was portrayed by many as the ability to bluff, buy, or bully one's way into influence. Even the projection of state power beyond national borders had come to be seen largely as the domain of what Arthur Schlesinger called the "warrior caste." Conversely, Mandela's influence at home and his standing abroad went far beyond what might be suggested by the size of the military or the gross domestic product of South Africa.

Mamphela Ramphele, who went from being a black consciousness advocate to heading South Africa's premier university and later serving as an executive director at the World Bank, likes to say that what stands out in looking back at Mandela's leadership style was his ability to make people feel that with him around, almost anything was possible. She likened his leadership to great inspirational conducting. The members of the orchestra are the specialists on their instruments, but they need a conductor to make their performance more than the sum of their individual endeavors.[2]

Mary and I made the pilgrimage to Robben Island more than a dozen times—including trips with Bill Clinton, Al Gore, and Mandela himself—but each time I was struck by how Mandela turned imprisonment into a time of reflection and personal renewal, not just for himself but for every political prisoner who served with him. Despite the harsh conditions of prison life, he exercised regularly, read widely, and urged others to do the same. He gave so much attention to personal growth, the continued development of the body, the mind, and the spirit, that the prison came to be described by the prisoners as Robben Island University. The spirit of Robben Island, with its slogan "each one teach one," helped prisoners to retain both their inner discipline and their inner dignity.

Mandela had another quality that enabled him to be more effective than others—his capacity to seduce when coercion was neither desirable nor possible. Much of the respect for him came from his ability to listen, to learn from others, and to show respect for their traditions while maintaining equal respect for his own. He was known as a skilled negotiator who won many concessions during the development of the new democracy because of his knowledge of Afrikaner history and culture. Mamphela called it a classic case of knowing your enemies well enough to charm them into respecting you. He could draw on lessons from key historical moments to illustrate why his proposals made sense in light of the Afrikaners' own history, especially their struggle to escape British domination.[3] Similarly, the Senegalese leader and great poet Léopold Senghor had first to demonstrate that he knew French literature, culture, and traditions as well as any Frenchman before he won respect for what he had to say about negritude and African culture.

The commitment to the public values that build community—forgiveness, reconciliation, justice, and so on—which so aptly described the uniqueness of Nelson Mandela, became the organizing principle of the unique experience provided for midcareer leaders in southern Africa and communities of color in the United States. After Hurricane Katrina devastated the Gulf Coast, we established a second program specifically for midcareer leaders in Louisiana. While the program served primarily leaders from minority communities, it also included others working to improve the quality of life of those communities. A new partnership was established with the College of Business at Southern University in Baton Rouge, and Professor Rich McCline, an academic who had also been a businessman, was added to our staff team.

Whether in southern Africa or Louisiana, no one more clearly demonstrated Daniel Goleman's contention that leadership is more art than science than Mandela. In his work on emotional intelligence, Goleman wrote about the importance of self-awareness, self-regulation, empathy, and social skill. To help cultivate these qualities in the midcareer and emerging leaders with whom we worked, we provided an executive coach for a year. Leslie Williams, whom I had not met but who had been a student at Pomona College when I served as chaplain, was an executive coach who shared both our view of the values essential for leadership in a badly divided world and our vision of how best to cultivate those values. She was recruited to put together an executive coaching team whose work quickly became a critical component of the program.

To Goleman's conceptual framework of emotional intelligence, we added three other dimensions of value-driven leadership as a way of being: moral, social, and spiritual intelligence. Cultivating these qualities was not only our objective; these qualities were already evident in some way in those chosen for the program.

### Moral Intelligence

Tony Ehrenreich was a fellow in the class of 2003. He was the director of the Congress of South African Trade Unions for the Western Cape. Tony was skeptical about the program because he was a union leader who had been nominated by a prominent businessman. I met him at the initial gathering of his class for the opening retreat in Cape Town and was very impressed with both his values and his understanding of how they should be integrated into his work. He was a self-made man whose academic education had been limited by apartheid. Yet some years later when I presented him for a conversation with some of my faculty colleagues at Duke, many assumed he was an economist. Not only was Tony heavily engaged in thinking about how comparative economies work around the world, he was also a man of considerable moral intelligence. Even now, more than a decade later, while he is a militant activist consistently engaged in calling attention to inequities in the Western Cape, whenever I see him he reminds me of his struggle with my suggestion of the need to respect the humanity of the adversary. As the leader of the opposition in the Cape Town city government, he is constantly engaged in confrontation, but he understands how challenging the policies and seeking to change the practices of his opponents differ from denying their dignity or disrespecting their humanity.

What we called moral intelligence in the leadership program focused on the role of ethics in our aggregate existence. It is not that we were unconcerned with private virtue. It is that organized religion does a good job in proclaiming moral absolutes, while there is not much guidance for public leaders who must often cope with moral ambiguities. Many question whether it is possible to identify moral prescriptions or standards for our public life that would be acceptable to all of humanity. They ask whether it is possible to identify a set of common values, a set of precepts so fundamental that they dissolve borders, transcend races, and outlast cultural traditions. My friend Rush Kidder, who wrote the book *Shared Values for a Troubled World*, traveled around the world in search of an answer to that question and concluded that it is indeed possible, that there are some values so universal to the human mind that they transcend theological and cultural boundaries.[4]

This is certainly true of the so-called Golden Rule that Christians claim as their own, but which cuts across all sorts of boundaries and can be found in many variations in faith communities around the world. The examples were numerous:

Christianity: Whatever you want done to you, do also to others.
Islam: No one of you is a believer until he loves for his neighbor what he loves for himself.
Judaism: What is hateful to you, do not do to your fellow man. This is the entire law; all the rest is commentary.
Buddhism: Hurt not others with that which pains yourself.
Hinduism: This is the sum of duty; do not unto others what you would not have them do unto you.
Confucianism: What you do not want done to yourself, do not do to others.

Bahaism: And if thine eyes be turned toward justice, choose thou for thy neighbor that which thou chooses for thyself.

Yoruba proverb (Nigeria): One going to take a pointed stick to pinch a baby should first try it on himself to see how it hurts.

It is clear from these quotes that the Golden Rule constitutes a precept that transcends national, cultural, and religious borders. So we are left with the question of explaining to young leaders why moral intelligence matters. The first answer is that most of the great issues of the day are moral issues. How we form a more perfect union is a moral issue. How we establish justice is a moral issue. How we promote the general welfare is a moral issue. How we provide for the common defense is a moral issue. How we ensure domestic tranquility is a moral issue. These are the public values that are prescribed in the preamble to the American Constitution, but they are rarely a part of the discussion about ethics in public life.

A second reason why ethics matter is pragmatic. More and more leaders are finding that it is in their self-interest to be ethical. At least half of the organizational leaders studied for the book *Value Shift* characterized ethics as risk management.[5] They tended to see values not just as a tool for ensuring fairness and preventing misconduct, but as a way of avoiding the high-profile missteps of government leaders and the great financial losses experienced by some business and nonprofit corporations because of unethical behavior.

A third reason why ethics matter is that while ethics has been used to domesticate and humanize power, we live increasingly in a world where ethics is power. It is power in business, as many executives are finding that in a market where so many products and services are of equal quality, many consumers are now making choices on the basis of what they consider to be responsible behavior: how the company treats its workforce; what are its policies regarding gender and race; as well as its impact on the environment. Some executive recruiters are now reporting that boards of directors and CEOs are giving them a new mandate. While they still want key executives who can make the company money, are willing to make tough decisions, and fit the management team, there is an even stronger interest in ethics, values, and goals. A friend of mine who is an ethics consultant was asked by a group of companies to assist in the development of a list of interview questions to help corporate recruiters learn more about the ethics and values of those they interview.

Ethics is also power in the nonprofit sector, where so many of the organizations that populate the space between the market and the state are now being forced to reexamine what it means to be accountable to a public. People now see nonprofit leaders as custodians of values as well as resources. Ethics is even power in international relations, where world leaders are discovering that while military power and economic muscle can prevent or inflict pain, it is diplomacy—acts of generosity, moral messages, and respect for local cultures—that can best develop the kind of influence that is most likely to endure.

Regardless of the reason for the renewed emphasis on values, it is increasingly obvious that the need for a moral thermostat is not confined to any one group or locale. Moral intelligence encompasses both what people should demand of their leaders and what their leaders should demand of them.

### Social Intelligence

Nceba Faku, a member of the class of 2002, was at that time the mayor of Port Elizabeth, one of the largest cities in South Africa and one of its largest seaports. Located in the Eastern Cape Province, Port Elizabeth, now called the Nelson Mandela Metropole, is a cosmopolitan city with continuing contact with the pluralism of the area and the diversity of the outside world, with which there is regular interaction. Mayor Faku reflected the sophistication of this coastal city, to which I had previously traveled while serving as an ambassador. He was a stalwart of the ANC and there were high expectations for his future. Because of this, I had asked Eli Segal, a veteran of political campaigns in the United States and a confidant of Bill Clinton, to serve as his mentor. When Eli and Faku met on Robben Island at the opening retreat in 2002, the tall, imposing mayor was wearing a Palestine Liberation Organization scarf around his shoulders. Eli was a close personal friend and I had not paid any attention to the fact that he was Jewish. On the last day of the retreat Faku showed up wearing a yarmulke. As I drew near to him, he remarked, "See what this program has done for me already."

Social intelligence helps leaders to embrace diversity. Their effectiveness comes from an ability to respect and value differences. Some leaders look at difference and want to homogenize it to fit their comfort zone. They fail to understand that the more diverse we are, the richer our culture becomes, and the more expansive our horizon of possibilities. Jonathan Sacks, the British rabbi who wrote the book *The Home We Build Together*, argues that if we were all the same we would have nothing unique to contribute, nor anything to learn from each other. Yet if we were completely different we could not communicate, and if we were exactly alike we would have nothing to say. So the rabbi concludes that we need to see our differences as gifts to the common good, for without a compelling sense of the common good, difference spells discord and creates not music, but noise.

Social intelligence also requires that effective leaders understand the relationship between leadership and context. My experience of authoritarian leadership in the military (see chapter 3) was followed by a period of organizing the civil rights movement in Tuscaloosa, Alabama, at that time the national headquarters of the much-feared Ku Klux Klan. The approach required was much more collegial. If the first leadership role was based on the power of position, this one was based more on the power of persuasion. I also spent ten years as a senior officer in business where I learned the power of principles, that being ethical can actually contribute to the bottom line. I spent another four years leading a bureaucracy that was best described as "authoritarian light," where an order can get lost or ignored as it moves farther from its origin. Some years later, as the head of a membership organization located in Washington, DC, but serving members in all fifty states and five continents, I learned the power of a platform. More recently, as an American ambassador, I learned the importance of soft power in a world long led by the ability to use hard power.

The relationship between leadership and culture is another central component of our curriculum. Culture influences many aspects of a leader's values, style, and strategy. In both the Louisiana program and the one based primarily in Cape Town, we found that local culture played a critical role in determining both those people selected to lead and who people chose to follow. In addition to providing a shared sense of identity and belonging, culture has traditionally provided a perspective on social organization and the authority to lead. It has also helped solve three types of problems: physical (how we feed, clothe, and shelter ourselves); philosophical (the meaning and purpose of life, and understandings about right and wrong); and relational (how we behave toward other members of our group and other groups).[6]

While globalization has changed many of the old patterns and expectations, there is, nevertheless, an increasing demand for leaders who can cope with the challenges of cultural diversity within their own communities as well as working across the geographical and cultural boundaries of others. A leader operating outside of his or her home culture will need to know what point host cultures have reached in the globalization process in order to determine what styles and strategies are likely to provide appeal or advantage.

Social intelligence also includes an understanding of the importance of various forms of networks. Christopher Howard is one of the youngest presidents of an American university. He was inaugurated in 2010 as the head of Hampden-Sydney College, a place where five U.S. presidents studied. After graduating from the leadership program in 2004, he was invited back to speak to a new class of fellows about networking for personal growth, to advance a cause, or mobilize a constituency. He shared with the new class his approach to networking, which included the selection of what he called his personal board of directors; not mentors in the traditional sense, but people who could help him network as his professional life unfolded. Esther Benjamin, a Rhodes Scholar and former White House fellow and member of the same class in our leadership program as Christopher Howard, emphasized the importance of finding the right institutions in which one can both contribute and grow.

## Spiritual Intelligence

The evening of February 28, 2012, was a glorious moment in the history of the University of the Western Cape in Bellville, South Africa. Established as a "bush college for coloreds" by the old apartheid government, this now internationally renowned institution was showcasing its status as a world-class university. Proud of its experience in the liberation struggle, the university is now taking equal pride in its role in nurturing the cultural diversity of South Africa and its commitment to excellence in teaching, learning, and research.

The occasion for the large audience and accompanying pageantry was the inauguration of Archbishop Thabo Makgoba as the new chancellor. He was succeeding former archbishop Desmond Tutu in this highly revered but voluntary position in the same way he had become one of Tutu's successors as archbishop of Cape Town. Tutu was among the assembled VIPs, but now older and both of us with much less hair than when we first met on my visit in 1974.

The focus on this night, however, was on the new chancellor. Mary and I were sitting up front as special guests, as we had done when Thabo Makgoba was installed as the new archbishop in similar pageantry at St. George's Cathedral in Cape Town. As we met his family and mingled with his friends, we reminisced about first meeting Thabo as a fellow in the leadership program. Since spiritual intelligence was a component of the program, each of the southern Africa classes included at least one religious leader. They were selected, however, not simply because they were engaged in a priestly ministry, but because they understood their calling as including a prophetic ministry as well. Each was a community leader with enormous potential for greater leadership in the larger society.

Our emphasis on spiritual intelligence went beyond what is normally thought of as parochial belief. Most leadership programs are grounded in the intellect. They use the word "spirit" with regularity, but they rarely deal with the soul of leadership. In this program, we look at leadership as a product of what is happening at the core of the true self, not just where you locate insight and imagination but in the ability to find meaning in mystery and to see the sacred in everyday life.

A friend of mine describes spirituality as a sort of privileged access to one's own soul. It provides not only the highest form of personal introspection but the highest form of personal renewal. Nelson Mandela, in a letter from Robben Island to his wife Winnie, emphasized the importance of finding a few minutes each day for spiritual renewal. He wrote that he had found it useful to set aside fifteen minutes each day to step back and look both inside and outside himself. This helped to center his life in something beyond his cell and the prison environment designed to break his spirit. He demonstrated a keen sense of spiritual intelligence when he advised Winnie not to forget that a saint is a sinner who keeps on trying.

Desmond Tutu, who was Nelson Mandela's ally and soul mate in promoting reconciliation, often pointed to the importance of his annual retreat as moments of renewal when he stepped back and disengaged in order to serve others more effectively. The inability of many younger leaders to understand the importance of renewal is best illustrated by the story of a man walking in the woods who came upon a logger cutting down trees. He greeted him and asked, "How are you doing?" The logger replied, "Not so well. I was doing so much better this morning, but this afternoon, I simply cannot cut as many trees." The passerby said, "Why don't you stop and sharpen the saw?" To which the logger replied, "Oh, I can't do that. I have too many trees to cut." In my work with younger leaders, I find many of them guilty of feeling that it would be selfish to stop and spend time on personal renewal, when instead it is often the most other-serving thing they can do because it enables them to serve others better. Over the years, from my days of organizing in the civil rights movement to my experience of the intensity of the engagement of many leaders in the aftermath of hurricanes, floods, and other disasters, I have found that some very good people burn out and lose their effectiveness because they have been on the front lines too long. They tend to think of personal renewal as selfish, when they really need to step back and sharpen the saw in order to serve others better.

We emphasize spiritual intelligence and the need for leaders in touch with their spiritual nature for a second reason. The effective leader must be both an agent of reconciliation and a purveyor of hope, and we use the word "hope" to convey something very different from optimism. Hope theology and hope psychology both argue that optimism adopts the role of the spectator who surveys the evidence in order to infer that things are going to get better. Hope, on the other hand, enacts the stance of the participant who actively struggles against the evidence in order to make things better.[7]

For a long time, hope has been considered an emotion and, therefore, ignored, discounted, or simply dismissed as an essential element of leadership. But psychology is now being joined by other disciplines in seeking to develop a cognitively based theory of hope and leadership. The basic premise of those scholars and researchers is that hope comprises not only emotion but thinking as well. They are now trying to understand the role of hope in sustaining innovation; the relationship of hope levels to stress, commitment, and performance; even the impact of hope in business organizations on profits, job satisfaction, and retention rates.

The capacity to cultivate hope may be the ultimate requirement of effective leadership, especially in a world in which anxiety is so pervasive that many people are even anxious about the fact they are anxious. Václav Havel, the poet and former president of the Czech Republic, wrote, "I can't imagine I could strive for anything if I did not carry hope in me. The gift of hope is as big a gift as life itself."[8] Cultivating hope was from the outset a central tenet of the leadership program.

# CHAPTER 16

# A Lexicon of Public Values

*What the Virtuecrats Did Not Tell Us*

Shortly after the publication of William Bennett's signature volume on virtue, I was invited to Indiana to present a lecture at Culver Military Academy as part of a convocation dedicating a new building. I was surprised to find that Bennett was one of the respondents. Our very polite and altogether civil exchange led me to think about the limits of private virtue and what a lexicon of public values might look like. Whenever I saw Bennett again, I called him Mr. Virtue, but I was always reminded of our first encounter, when it became clear that his emphasis on individual behavior did not sufficiently embrace my concern with ethics in our aggregate existence. It was not until I began writing this book that I realized the time for preparing my own list was at hand.

It is for this reason that my search for public values to guide our life in communities, institutions, and even bureaucracies—a moral journey that began at an early age—is the subject of this final chapter. Unlike Bennett in his *Book of Virtues*, I have identified a lexicon of social values that I found useful in trying to integrate values into my work in government, business, and civil society. Bennett's focus was on private virtues for individual behavior, and I am grateful for his contribution to the way we think about the microethics that build character.[1] But the experiences chronicled in this book have taught me that a different emphasis, and even additional values, are often required for a complex, interdependent world.

The publication of Bennett's book in the 1990s launched a new virtue industry, with a flood of writings on character and a renewed emphasis on individual behavior. The new industry now includes in its ranks economists and political scientists, conservatives and liberals, as well as futurists and historians. Some, like Bennett, have found that writing about virtue can also be lucrative.

People around the world are developing an increased appetite for literature that provides insight into moral reasoning, ethical decision making, and the cultural habits that constitute virtue. But social ethicists like Reinhold Niebuhr, who was the preeminent moral voice of the twentieth century, have fallen out of fashion with the "virtuecrats" of the twenty-first century who now dominate moral discourse. They reject notions of a moral dualism that draws distinctions between the moral sentiments of individuals and the moral imperatives of groups. They also reject the notion of moral ambiguities, especially Niebuhr's emphasis on the mixed and ambivalent character of human nature itself—regard for others overruled by self-regard, the impulse to build matched by the impulse to destroy, and so on. When they do turn to group morality, they offer their own dualism, dividing the world almost completely between good and evil and using moral absolutes as a way to condemn the actions of others rather than guide their own.

My concern is not only that individuals are tempted to play God to groups. It is also that public values often compete with each other. It is thus in the determining of which is to have primacy, and what is to be regarded as permanent, that I have been forced to probe more deeply than the preoccupation with private virtue would suggest. Francis Fukuyama, a political scientist who decided to travel the road once left primarily to moral philosophers and men and women of religion, argues for the primacy of trust. In his book *Trust: The Social Virtues and the Creation of Prosperity*, the former RAND Corporation scholar contends that there is a relationship between old-fashioned virtues like trust, honesty, and dependability, and the prosperity of nations.[2] The greatness of the United States, he maintains, was built not on the imagined ethos of individualism but on the cohesiveness of its civil associations, the strength of its communities, and the moral bonds of social trust. He warns that a radical departure from our past communitarian tradition holds more peril for the future of American prosperity than any competition from abroad.

Amitai Etzioni, the communitarian thinker and writer with whom I hosted a seminar for community foundation members of the Council on Foundations, writes about the myth of individualism and the powerful communitarian tradition. He contends that shared values are essential for social solidarity and community; there is no reason to pressure people to give up their heritage, their hyphen, when pluralism operates within a strong framework of shared values.

From my birthplace in Plaisance to the embassy in Pretoria, and many places in between, I have met people along the way who agree on the essential habits that should be considered social virtues. Like my high school teacher Mr. Douglas, who first interested me in philosophy although he was really my math instructor, many spoke of the contradiction between the widely accepted notion that all men and women are created equal, with the inalienable right to life, liberty, and the pursuit of happiness, and the fact that these rights have not always applied to everyone. And even today, there are men and women who would still restrict them to their own group.

These are wonderful slogans, but we continue to struggle with their meaning in the everyday reality of communities. What should the next generation of moral habits encompass? William Bennett assembled a collection of stories, poems, essays, and speeches to which he provided commentary to illustrate ten virtues he considered essential to good character: self-discipline, compassion, responsibility, friendship, work, courage, perseverance, honesty, loyalty, and faith. No one can really quarrel with this list, but we need to be equally concerned with the macroethics of communities and societies—whether they provide equal opportunity and protect human rights—as well as social institutions, including government, business, and voluntary organizations. Much has been made of the breakdown of families, but except for the writings of the largely academic communitarian thinkers, too little attention has been given to the breakdown of communities and how social virtues often serve as a prerequisite to the development of individual virtues.

Cummins Engine Company had provided a plane for my travel to and from Culver Academy where I first met Bennett, so I was not surprised when he asked if he could hitch a ride with me back to Washington, DC. I agreed, and we continued our conversation for a couple of hours. Although he had often been a lightning rod for political storms, Bennett agreed that we should not permit our disputes about thorny political questions to obscure our obligation to offer instruction to all our young people in the area in which we, as a society, have reached consensus: namely, on the importance of values and some of their particulars.

I have found it useful in the leadership roles highlighted in earlier chapters to think in terms of a complementary set of public values essential for the functioning of the many institutions, movements, and public and private organizations with which I have been associated. These social values require no special moral training or theological literacy to be understood, for they are part of the basic values necessary for the orderly functioning of plural societies.

While I agree with those who argue that it is difficult to separate public values from private virtues, when Martin Luther King Jr. spoke to our new movement in Tuscaloosa, Alabama, in 1963, he spoke of the need to link the duty of the individual to embrace the responsibilities of citizenship with the obligation to act in concert with others to ensure citizenship rights. He called on us to help transform both individuals and society.

Bennett's private virtues constitute a good starting point for identifying rudimentary forms of private morality. But while they are indispensable for individuals, my own experience has led me to conclude that far more is needed for a complex community or an interdependent society to thrive. The issues and problems of our aggregate existence are greatly aggravated by the fact that we are constantly dealing with people and systems with which we have no direct personal relationship. Personal responsibility is in many ways diluted. The directors of a business are individual persons, for example, but they are being asked to think as directors and shareholders. The private virtues to which they are committed may help them assess and monitor the private behavior of the chief executive officer, but where are they to find moral guidance in deciding on dividends, the welfare of the workers, or the obligation to the community in which the company operates?

The decision about dividends, like decisions about profits, where to locate a new plant, and how best to downsize, is likely to be regarded as morally neutral. But is it? If a decision affects the well-being of people, it is likely to require moral judgment and cannot be separated neatly from moral choices.

### Critical Public Values

The social virtues that have helped guide me in my relationships with others have encompassed a wide spectrum of moral imperatives, but at least ten stand out in very special ways as fundamental for our aggregate existence.

#### EMPATHY

A lexicon of public values should begin with empathy. It is the capacity to recognize and, to some extent, share feelings experienced by others that has led me to a lifetime of social activism. When Adam Smith, who wrote *The Wealth of Nations*, set out to develop a basic theory about how human beings could transact business with each other in an orderly and predictable fashion, he set forth the principle of empathy, the ability to feel what another person is feeling.[3] Knowing what gives others joy and pain because we know what gives ourselves joy and pain became the unstated basis for his economic theory in *The Wealth of Nations*.

Adam Smith is remembered best for what he had to say about economics, but he was a moral philosopher, not an economist. He wrote *A Theory of Moral Sentiments* before he wrote *The Wealth of Nations*. His economic theories were based on his idea about moral community, especially the notion that the individual has the moral duty to have regard for fellow human beings. This capacity for empathy is universal, but it needs to be nurtured. This ability to feel what another person is feeling can be thought of as a fundamental plank in the blueprint for building community.

The idea of empathy as an essential public value can also be understood as the blurring of the line between self and others, as in the Xhosa proverb "People are people through other people." It was for the South African tribes a form of transcendence over cultures and social conditioning in which one enters either momentarily or for longer periods of time into the mind and even the humanity of the other. It is those rudiments of empathy that enabled the high-profile acts of forgiveness that galvanized the attention of people in very different and distant places.

## COMPASSION

I was pleased that Bennett included compassion in his list of virtues. But it is easier to feel compassion for one's nearer neighbor than it is to generate the same emotion toward one's distant neighbor. Yet both forms of compassion are considered in all of the major religions as among the greatest of social virtues.

Compassion is certainly a virtue associated with empathy, but like empathy it is in danger of becoming a slogan with little or no substantive content. Like many others, the example I heard repeated most often as a child in the little church in rural southwestern Louisiana was the story of the Good Samaritan. A traveler comes upon a man on the side of the road who had been badly beaten. He stops and provides aid and comfort. But suppose the same man traveled the same road for a week and each day he discovered in the same spot someone badly beaten. Wouldn't he be compelled to ask who has responsibility for policing the road? His initial act of private compassion must inevitably lead him to public compassion, to matters of public policy. It is this progression from private compassion to public action that is often missing in our discussion of private virtue. Genuine compassion requires that we not only ameliorate consequences through the actions of individuals but also seek to eliminate causes through the action of groups.

It may be useful to remember that in Plato's inquiry into virtue he came to associate it with goodness. In one of his dialogues, Socrates meets the eminent Sophist Protagoras, who explains that his profession is the teaching of goodness. In the subsequent exchange, the emphasis is not simply on knowing the good, but on doing what is good.

## ALTRUISM

Our ability to provide healing and wholeness to badly fractured communities may depend to a large degree on our ability to develop altruism, the virtue most associated with empathy and compassion. The altruistic impulse is also universal. But it too may remain passive until activated. The cultivation of an environment where members of one community can see others as human beings like themselves and can care about those of another group and want good things for them is a necessary prerequisite for building and sustaining community.

Altruism, however, is not simply a matter of developing or practicing other-serving values. It has an element of enlightened self-interest as well. When the framers of the American Constitution sought to identify the values important to forming a more perfect union, they committed the new nation to establishing justice, ensuring domestic tranquility, and promoting the general welfare. Business corporations known for their charitable largesse are also aware that it is in their self-interest to improve the quality of life of their workers in order to enhance productivity.

## JUSTICE

It is not surprising that in the *Republic* the concern with virtue comes to focus on justice and kindness. Without a commitment to the promise of justice and the practice of kindness, virtue remains a concept with little content. We tend to think of justice in two primary ways: retributive justice, whose chief goal is to be punitive, and distributive justice, whose chief goal is to expand the distribution of wealth. When the Mandela government in South Africa thought about justice, it was pressured by some of its supporters to give primacy to either one or both of these two traditions.

But there were others, including Mandela himself, who called attention to another kind of justice, restorative justice, which, it was argued, was more characteristic of traditional African jurisprudence. Here the central concern was not simply distribution or retribution, but the restoration of broken relationships, a seeking to rehabilitate both the victim and the perpetrator in ways that reintegrate both back into the community. South Africa was, and still is, as our discussion of reconciliation demonstrated earlier, a very special place with very special circumstances, but the idea of restorative justice has wider implications.

## TRUST

A fifth public value essential to the orderly and effective functioning of community is trust. Like Adam Smith, Francis Fukuyama was pointing to a key element of the social glue that binds people together in community when he tied old-fashioned virtues like trust to the prosperity of nations. If we can accept that it is social trust that leads to the formation of both financial and social capital, we may be able to finally extricate ourselves from the paralyzing debate about the differing roles of the state and the market. Robert Putnam and Robert Bellah have both sought to remind us of the need to move a little more in the direction of community in the balance between community and the individual.

E. J. Dionne, in a more recent book, writes about our divided political heart, the tension between the role of individualism in the American narrative and the realities of the communitarian tradition in shaping our national union.[4] Some of our citizens give primacy to our love of individualism, while others emphasize our reverence for community. But while these two traits in the American character are sometimes in tension, they more often reinforce each other. While some Americans continue to celebrate the individual as the primary source of American greatness, others remind us that the ability to live and work together in community may have had something to do with it.

## TOLERANCE

To empathy, compassion, altruism, justice, and trust, I would add tolerance. While there are clearly behaviors and attitudes that cannot be tolerated, the primary moral question for me has been not so much "when is tolerance required?" as "when is intolerance justified?" Tolerance in public life has to do most often with group differences. People identify themselves in many ways, and they are in turn identified by others in many ways. But while they would prefer to be identified by who or what they are, they are often identified by what they are not. People who would find it strange to be identified as nonblack, for example, are quite comfortable in identifying others as nonwhite.

Race, however, is only one of the many factors that create both positive and negative bonding, others being family, community, nationality, class, gender, age, and other group characteristics considered important. The most devastating forms of conflict and intolerance usually arise when race, gender, or sexual orientation displace other loyalties and obligations to become the primary or sole basis of identity.

The form of tolerance offered by many people is to ignore differences and focus on similarities. The answer, they say, is assimilation. Yet, paradoxically, it is often preservation rather than assimilation that is most desired. This is particularly true when ethnic or racial identity is threatened. When people no longer feel free to express their identity through speaking their own language, practicing their own cultural traditions, or transmitting them to their progeny, they are less likely to feel common ground or affinity with the larger society.

Tolerance does not ignore differences. It recognizes and respects them. A sense of belonging to a larger community cannot be forced on people. They must adopt it voluntarily, and this will happen only when they feel that society respects them and their primary community of identity.

## RESPECT

Closely related to tolerance is respect. I have concluded that the most important challenge for a society that values pluralism may lie in finding the balance between respect for differences and respect for contributions to the common culture. It is right and good that we in the United States affirm the value and advance the vision of pluralism, but social inclusion requires that we do so in a way that does not diminish the role of any one group in fashioning what we call American culture. Nowhere is the need for inclusion more important, more challenging, and more provocative than in the canons that shape our intellectual ideas and moral ideals.

We must acknowledge that while the great books, ideas, and personalities that have been the interpreters and conveyors of much of our history and values—from Plato and Ptolemy to Hegel and Hemingway—are irreplaceable, we need now to make room for others who help many in our midst to understand the human condition as well as the struggle between good and evil. Kafka and Kierkegaard will not disappear simply because others join them in the canon of Great Books.

The last three social virtues that I have found to be particularly useful in thinking about how to build or sustain community are not new, but they may need a new emphasis and even new priorities. There are many reasons to believe that freedom, equality, and reconciliation will be increasingly at the center of our search for the social glue for communities that are integrating and fragmenting at the same time.

## FREEDOM

Freedom may be the most cherished value in Western civilization. Orlando Patterson, a distinguished sociologist who teaches at Harvard, has gone as far as anyone in examining why the concept came to achieve preeminence as the supreme Western value. In *Freedom in the Making of Western Culture*, Patterson traces the evolution of three distinct forms of freedom—personal freedom, civic freedom (the right to participate in public life), and sovereign or organic freedom (the freedom to exercise power over others)—from the earliest stirrings in Greece, Rome, and Christendom to the permutations of our modern world.[5]

Yet while those of us in the West, including both nation-states and freedom movements, speak of freedom as the one value for which we are prepared to die, it has only recently appeared on the radar screen of many non-Western peoples. Even in the West, many self-styled defenders of freedom have been more interested in defending freedom's privileges than in extending freedom's rights and opportunities. But as the concept develops expanded ownership— in eastern Europe, Asia, Africa, and throughout the developing world—it plays an expanded role as a public value.

It is precisely those people who have known the limits of freedom who are most committed to freedom as an essential value. They remind those who pay lip service to the concept, but easily deny it to those outside their group, that there can be no genuine community without provision for the protection of certain basic freedoms. Freedom of worship, speech, and assembly are usually singled out as preeminent and absolute, but there is no such thing as unbridled freedoms. They often compete with each other and must be related to a process for determining the public good.

Some political scientists, like the British intellectual and Oxford don Isaiah Berlin, have reduced this competition among the virtues of freedom to what they call positive and negative freedoms. They describe the individual freedom from government interference as negative freedom and the freedom to participate in the affairs of government as positive freedom. The focus of the first is on the well-being of the individual, while the second emphasizes the well-being of the community.

The staunchest defenders of negative freedom are often those whose primary preoccupation is with free markets and minimal government interference in their lives. They are happiest when left alone. The advocates of positive freedom, on the other hand, want public authority to be used to enable members of the community to pursue not just liberty but happiness. They are happiest when acknowledged and accepted as part of the community. In many democracies, these two forms of freedom are reflected in the values enunciated by the right and left of the political spectrum.

But to suggest that freedom is one of the most fundamental values of humankind is to suggest the need for a balance between what are often made out to be two profoundly divergent attitudes toward the public good. The most successful democracies are likely to be those that provide room for their citizens to strike a compromise between positive and negative freedoms.

## EQUALITY

Another constitutional or quasi-constitutional value likely to be found in the public documents of national communities is the idea of equality. The concept enjoys wide consensus as a public value essential to the orderly functioning of communities. But when I have tried to move an organization or a community from a celebration of the ideal to its actual implementation, I have found that it is here that the consensus begins to break down. Equality is a social virtue or public value easier to affirm than to practice. This is especially true of efforts to guarantee equality of opportunity where one group has been socialized into thinking that another group's difference in status is the result of a difference in kind. Stereotypical thinking is exacerbated by racial polemicists who surface from time to time to argue that cognitive abilities are genetically determined.

While we now know that an early move from a deprived home to an advantaged one can significantly boost a child's intelligence quotient, superficial characteristics like skin color are still used to postulate racial differences and foster racial intolerance. Biologically speaking, a person's color reveals very little about what is under the skin. Molecular biologists who examine genes have found that the overwhelming majority of the variations observed are among individuals within the same race. Moreover, so much racial mixing has occurred that the boundary lines between races are quite fuzzy. In many societies, race is largely a socially constructed category with limited biological significance.

A major barrier to community continues to be the legacy of racial discrimination that formally denies equality of opportunity to selected population groups because of their racial identification. While there is increasing agreement around the world that these barriers should be removed, there is very little consensus about how. The United States is not the only society that has tried to implement measures that consider race, national origin, sex, or disability in order to provide opportunities for groups that have been historically denied them. But this concept, often referred to as affirmative action, has caused so much controversy that it is now being rejected in other parts of the world as well. There are reasons to believe that it is the present language often used to describe affirmative action that is rejected rather than its original intent.

From the very beginning, affirmative action ran up against a problem of semantics, with many people repeatedly and inaccurately referring to the concept as racial quotas, preferential treatment, or the hiring of the unqualified. It is patently unfair and dishonest to use the terms interchangeably. There is no reference to preference or quotas in the original act that set up the U.S. Equal Employment Opportunity Commission, and there is certainly nothing to suggest an intention to require employers to hire unqualified members of an affected group.

The original intent of affirmative action was to provide affirmative opportunity to redress the imbalances of the past through recruitment, training, and other means. It is a mistake, however, to assume that barriers placed before individuals because of their membership in a group can be removed without taking group identity into consideration. It is also a mistake to assume that hiring those who are differently qualified is the same as hiring the unqualified. Business corporations regularly hire chief executive officers from industries very different from their own because they assume that their experiences are transferable. But when a black person with transferable experience is hired at a lower level, it is likely to be portrayed as hiring the unqualified.

## RECONCILIATION

To live together in community is to be constantly engaged in connecting or reconnecting with those who differ not simply in race or religion, but tradition and theology as well as politics and philosophy. Where there is diversity, there is likely to be alienation and separation. Conflicts are inevitable, and social relationships are constantly threatened and broken. Reconciliation thus becomes as highly prized a value in the age of interdependence as freedom was in the scramble for independence. Reconciliation has to do with reestablishing or sustaining a connection to a wider community. There is an implicit notion of brokenness, a relationship that needs to be built or rebuilt. But the estrangement individuals and communities face can be moral as well as social and political. As we have seen in chapter 11, the leading proponents and exemplars of reconciliation as a public value were the South Africans in the Mandela era who demonstrated that it can also be a public process for overcoming years of racial and ethnic division.

The need and process for reconciliation in the future will continue to be influenced by context and culture, but many of the conflicts will go beyond race to include a wide variety of additional forms of alienation. Moreover, the focus on nonstate actors will increase as nation-states lose their monopoly on the potential for superviolence. It is already true that substate, nonstate, or even individual actors can destabilize targeted states and societies. With the declining influence of the nation-state, intrastate conflicts will increasingly spill over national boundaries with one group's terrorists another group's freedom fighters.

Conflicts will also be economic as the influence of states as economic engines significantly declines. Of the largest economic entities in the world, many are now companies, not countries. One area in which conflicts between states will not only continue, but significantly increase, is in the competition for the earth's resources. While the present focus is on oil, the competition for water will create new tensions that present treaties and legal instruments will be hard pressed to contain. The rapid increase in population, accompanied by urbanization, poor land use, and drought have all led to a water-scarce environment. Disputes have emerged and will increase in a number of areas. In Africa, for example, all of the sub-Saharan countries share at least one river basin or lake, with more than eighty rivers or lakes shared by two or more countries. Although boundaries as a general rule are demarcated by treaties, the coming competition for water resources will raise many issues that present agreements and informal understandings may not be sufficient to reconcile.

Another way that present conflicts are likely to intensify is in the role of religious zealots who claim to have a special pipeline to ultimate truths. While I do not subscribe to the predictions of the doomsayers who see a clash of civilizations ahead, it requires no great leap to say that religion is becoming as divisive as race has been. But instead of a clash between Christianity and the 1.2 billion Muslims who now populate all regions of the world, I suggest the clash will be increasingly across religious lines, between believers who accept and adapt to change and traditionalists who share a common desire to return to some form of golden age they see as ordained by their sacred scriptures.

The South African model of reconciliation is certainly not a blueprint for the myriad forms of conflict on the horizon, but it should at least remind us of the potential of the human spirit, that no alienation is absolute, and as Nelson Mandela argued, if we do not resolve conflicts with our brains, we may be driven to seek resolution with our blood.

It is difficult to commit oneself to others and seek to build or sustain community without these ten public values. They are as essential to building community as Bennett's ten virtues are to building character. The virtuecrats of the 1990s had a special appeal to those who were searching for something more meaningful and fulfilling than the selfishness and greed of the 1980s. But far too much of what passed for virtue was simply prescriptions for individual behavior by groups that used the language of religion and morality to disguise partisan political agendas and hide their true colors. Hopefully, we can now ignite and ennoble a new conversation fit for the realities of the new world of the twenty-first century.

## Building Community by Design

The signs and symbols of a united America that emerged after the terrorist attacks of September 11, 2001, led many at the time to conclude that the divisions in American society exposed by the 2000 census had now been bridged. Americans of all races, religions, and regions were united in their pain and grief, but throughout the many months of flag waving that followed, I remained skeptical about the lasting power of the apparent unity.

This tragic and trying episode in American history brought back memories of another time when large numbers of Americans had come to believe that we were close to forming a "more perfect union." At no time in my own life had this seemed more likely than in 1963, when more than a quarter of a million Americans came together at the Lincoln Memorial in Washington, DC, to bear witness to Martin Luther King's dream, the American dream.

This was also the year that I left Yale to join the civil rights movement in Alabama. Like so many other Americans at the time, I felt confident that the March on Washington marked a great turning point in the long struggle for full citizenship by several generations of African Americans who had known either slavery or the intentional underdevelopment that followed. But a few years later when Dr. King was assassinated, we learned that nothing is more volatile than the frustration that comes from high expectations followed by dashed hopes. The whole nation watched as American cities went up in flames.

In the immediate aftermath of the tragedies of September 11, 2001, there was once again a feeling that Americans had reached a new level of community. Surrounded by so many examples of how we are both healed and bound together by our response to those in need, it appeared that we had finally answered Rodney King's troubling question, "Can't we all get along?" One heard regularly that we were no longer a divided people; that we were united as never before. Americans everywhere waved the red, white, and blue flag and sang patriotic songs. Journalists wrote about the new patriotism and politicians praised the new nationalism. There was even talk of a new civility.

My own experience was not quite that reassuring. I began to notice the decline of the new civility within weeks of 9/11. The people in the long lines at the airport were rude and nasty again. The New York cab drivers still passed me by in favor of white passengers. White women in elevators still stepped as far back as possible when I entered.

Despite signs of the reemergence of the stereotypes and prejudices I had encountered before, I remained optimistic that the potential for remaking America I wrote about in an earlier book was still alive. As the new national chair of the board of directors of the National Conference for Community and Justice, I traveled the country urging our regional organizations to accelerate their efforts to combat bias, bigotry, and racism.

It was in this capacity that two months after the terrorist attacks I was invited to speak in Las Vegas for a prayer breakfast hosted by the mayors of the nearby region. As Mary and I left the auditorium filled with many of the region's mayors, top business executives, and nonprofit leaders, we came upon two men engaged in a rather heated conversation. One looked like the all-American tourist and the other appeared to be an Arab vendor. As the prosperous-looking tourist walked toward us, we heard him describe the other man to his wife as a "sand nigger." We had not heard that particular expression before, but we knew what "nigger" meant and felt, for a moment, a special connection with the man described in this way.

He was a stranger, but we felt an affinity that had not been there before. It was not the first time I realized the many ways in which even negative forces can trigger the sense of solidarity that leads to community. The communal embrace was fleeting and in need of a more enduring connection, but the memory of the debasement of another human being because of his group identity lingered on.

At the same time, I continued to worry about the other side of the new nationalism, the many people ruled out of its embrace. It was not simply that so many Americans were seeking and reaffirming national community in an increasingly postnational world. There was also growing evidence of a new internationalism. But it soon became clear that the sudden embrace of globalization by once-ardent isolationists was a pragmatic response to the need to build coalitions against international terrorism rather than a fundamental acceptance of our interdependence.

It was not the antiglobalists in the streets that concerned me, but the neosovereigntists in national capitals. The first group was concerned with the fact that globalization creates winners and losers, yet few nations are dealing seriously with the plight of the losers. These voices of dissent were primarily from representatives of civil society. The second group was concerned, they asserted, with the impact of multilateral institutions and protocols on national sovereignty. The voices we heard came primarily from isolationists in the political sector and those academics and analysts who helped shape their thinking.

There was, indeed, an extraordinary increase in the expression of patriotism and national unity across the United States after 9/11, but the new spirit of community was forged out of crisis. While many leaders were congratulating the nation on its new solidarity and apparent coherence, no one seemed to be addressing the question of how to sustain that sense of community when the intensity of the crisis was no longer felt so keenly. We were united in our pain and grief, but could we remain united in the realities of daily life? I could not help but recall the statement by the eminent psychiatrist and writer Scott Peck that we build community out of crisis and we build community by accident, but we do not know how to build community by design. The problem with building community out of crisis, he argued, is that once the crisis is over, so usually is the spirit of community.

Nowhere was this more evident than in my experience of the American response to Hurricane Katrina and the devastation of New Orleans. People were outraged not simply by the suffering and neglect brought home to them by the television coverage, they were equally upset by the preexisting conditions the hurricane exposed. The American people were united in both their moral outrage and their response to the victims in need. They responded with billions of dollars for charitable relief and urged a slow-moving government to provide quick assistance to rebuild the physical infrastructure of communities and restore the health and spirits of those whose lives were shattered. There was no doubt that the crisis created a new sense of community and an upsurge of compassion.

But could Americans find a way to sustain the common ground they now shared? Could they now move beyond the neglect of the poor and the racial divide that made Katrina far more devastating than it should have been? I served as chairman of the board of directors of the Louisiana Disaster Recovery Foundation established by Governor Kathleen Blanco, and I found that there are usually three elements or stages in the response to a disaster—relief, recovery, and reform. In the first stage the disaster is most dramatic, the public attention most pervasive, and the public response most immediate. Survival is at stake, and there is an outpouring of public support to provide relief from suffering and to maintain order. In the case of Katrina, the public contributed billions of dollars at this stage.

The next stage in the disaster response continuum is recovery, taking stock of what has happened, working together to return both private and public life to normalcy, and reinforcing the need for prevention and mitigation of future disasters. The focus of the first stage is almost exclusively on people, on lives to be saved. The second stage leads to a concern with infrastructure and policy, why the disaster occurred in the first place and what policies are needed to ensure that it does not happen again or, if it does, that there is a well-coordinated plan and sufficient resources to deal with it. Most disasters arise from failed policies that either enabled the disaster or made it inevitable.

The third stage, reform, shifts the crisis response paradigm not just to risk reduction but to using the crisis as an opportunity to improve conditions and rebuild smarter than before. Following the 1927 floods in Mississippi, Herbert Hoover is reported to have described this third stage as the most difficult and discouraging of all periods, for there is no longer the excitement of catastrophe, the stimulation of heroism and laudable sacrifice. That has certainly been my experience in Louisiana. Private donors provided billions of dollars for relief, and the government provided billions of dollars for recovery, but neither group has been willing to provide much for reform. Scott Peck was right. Once the intensity of the crisis passed from daily drama to yesterday's emergency, so did the strong sense of community and caring. Within a few years, the sense of affinity and connection that saw New Orleans embraced as part of a larger community with civic obligations and national ties dissipated into simply a racially divided, vulnerable, and economically struggling region with its own unique problems.

So we are left again with the question that followed 9/11. How do we build community that is sustainable once the intensity of the crisis has dissipated? How do we build community by design rather than by crisis or accident? How do we transcend our natural tendency to think and act as us and them?

These questions in the aftermath of Katrina brought back memories of my first encounter with the inspirational thoughts of the African American mystic, poet, and theologian Howard Thurman, whose writings and meditations would shape my thinking about community for the rest of my life. As a young second lieutenant just out of college, I often put on my civilian clothes and braved the icy cold winds and snow-covered roads of Boston winters to slip into the back of the chapel at Boston University to hear the dean of the chapel, Howard Thurman. He had been an early mentor of Martin Luther King Jr. and was fond of saying, "I want to be me without making it difficult for you to be you."

When I first read Scott Peck's warning about the absence of a blueprint for building community by design, I thought of Howard Thurman. His notion of community and his writings about the search for common ground had led me to say often in my own public utterances, "I want to be an American without making it difficult for Africans to be Africans, Asians to be Asians, Arabs to be Arabs, and Australians to be Australians." I had long concluded that if I was to be involved in any way in helping to build community by design, I must be able to say also, "I want to be a Christian without making it difficult for Muslims to be Muslims, Jews to be Jews, Buddhists to be Buddhists, or Hindus to be Hindus."

One place Americans, in particular, have sought to find a blueprint for building community by design is in the founding documents of our nation. The framers of the Constitution did not believe that they had *formed* a more perfect union. They set out to lay the foundation for *forming* a more perfect union. The emphasis on justice, tranquility, security, and the general welfare has always seemed to me to be a good starting point for a blueprint for building community, not just in the United States but in an interdependent world.

A second place Americans are likely to search for the social glue that can sustain a sense of community is in what the Frenchman Alexis de Tocqueville described well over a century ago as the uniqueness of the American society. He thought he had stumbled onto the unifying element, civic participation. He mused about everyone "taking an active part in the affairs of society." But those who analyze civic engagement—voting, volunteering, and other forms of public action—tell us that America's social capital is on the decline.

Another foreigner and keen observer of American life was Gunnar Myrdal, the Swedish economist and sociologist who wrote *An American Dilemma*. He saw the unifying element as "the American creed," that cluster of ideas, institutions, and habits that affirm the ideals of the essential dignity and equality of all human beings, of inalienable rights to freedom, justice, and opportunity. But the affirmation of these highly cherished public values has been largely subsumed by our preoccupation with private virtues. It is too often the case that those who talk most about promoting good values want simply to argue that someone else has bad values.

Others have found the potential for common ground in what was once called America's civil religion. But many prominent and powerful voices are arguing that the ethic that once undergirded the civil religion is waning. We see instead an increasing conflict over fundamental conceptions of moral authority, exacerbated by the politics of virtue and the parochialism of dogma.

The idea of a unifying creed is obviously in trouble. The bonds of social cohesion and community are increasingly fragile. Moral theologians, political philosophers, opinion leaders, and pundits of all sorts are once again in search of common ground. Yet it may be that they have simply been looking in the wrong place, assuming that American society was somehow fixed and final rather than a community that is always in the making. What has sustained me in my efforts to help build a new and altogether just America has been the notion that our uniqueness as a people lies not in the occasional assumption that we have finally formed the ideal community, but in the fact that we are always seeking to form a more perfect union. I have no illusion that a perfect union is possible, but my own personal journey has found me, wherever I have been and whatever I have done, stretching the canvas to approximate the ideal as closely as possible.

As I travel around the country, indeed, around the world, I am persuaded that three ideas are converging to create a common ethic of community. The first is that of civil society, with its emphasis on sharing and caring, on using the space between the state and the market to serve a public good. This very popular movement that brought down the Berlin Wall and caused the collapse of communism and the dismantling of apartheid deserves to be celebrated for both its universality and the particular ends achieved.

Still, it is important to remember that civil society includes more than simply the citizen action and nongovernmental organizations that have achieved so many positive social changes in communities and cultures across the globe. As we are increasingly reminded by scholars who study the social sector, the elusive concept of civil society covers a bewildering array of the good, the bad, and the bizarre. The hate groups I have encountered over the years—growing up in Louisiana, working to eliminate segregation in Alabama, and mobilizing various publics in California against the Vietnam War—are only a few of the citizen activists who now use the Internet to serve less than noble purposes. There is no doubt that the almost universal embrace of civil society carries with it the potential to reshape and unite a divided world, but those of us who seek to build the ideal community must not oversell its strength or overidealize its intentions.

The second idea that is converging to create a common ethic of community is the idea of a good society—the notion that a truly benevolent community depends as much on the goodness of individuals as it does on the soundness of government and the fairness of laws. In the 1990s I traveled to eastern Europe, Central America, Asia, and southern Africa, and everywhere I went I found people taking matters into their own hands because they had come to believe that while some governments in some parts of the world were working reasonably well for some of their people, no governments anywhere in the world were working well for all of their people—especially those on the margins.

The third idea is that of a transforming society, the notion that when neighbors help neighbors, and even when strangers help strangers, both those who help and those who are helped are transformed. As I have suggested in previous chapters, my own experience has taught me that getting involved in the needs of the neighbor provides a new perspective, a new way of seeing ourselves, a new understanding of the purpose of the human journey. When that which was "their" problem becomes "our" problem, the transaction transforms a mere association into a relationship—one with the potential for new communities of meaning and belonging.

I have found along the meandering journey chronicled in these pages that doing something for someone else—what John Winthrop called making the condition of others our own—is a powerful force in building community. It was as I tried to deal with the problems of the poor and the marginalized on Native American reservations and on the isolated islands of Micronesia that I found common ground. It was as I helped people in Mississippi and Alabama to reclaim their rights as citizens by registering to vote and to restore their dignity as human beings by securing a decent job that I came to understand the genesis of community. It was as I helped develop or promote programs to enable South Africans to find housing or regain their health that I discovered how to build community by design.

One of the most powerful messages coming out of my own personal journey is that meeting the needs of others is a quiet form of soft power in a world where many people are still fascinated with hard power. People who come together out of a common commitment, a common vision, or a shared moral message are likely to develop a more fundamental connection than can be achieved through the coercion of military or economic power. Those who continue to depend on hard power to help shape the new world order will soon find they are out of step with the realities of the twenty-first century. The years ahead will see challenges to our ability to live together that military and economic power cannot resolve alone. These challenges to world peace and national stability will also be out of the control of any nation acting alone.

We cannot build community either at home or abroad unless we are willing to address both the predicament and the issues that breed frustration, hostility, and hatred, not only within marginalized groups in other countries but among those within our own borders who share their race, religion, culture, or ethnicity. The one message that 9/11, suicide bombing, and terrorists with tanks supporting oppressive regimes convey is that none of these emotions stop at national borders.

No one country can solve these problems alone. But each country can work with others to tackle the cause of the many problems that fragment our world into "us" and "them." Nations can also set important examples by the kind of society they build at home. If the United States can form a more perfect union out of its own diversity, for example, it not only will have mastered the first requirement of soft power—providing a moral message that captures the imagination of others—but will demonstrate to the world that diversity need not divide, that pluralism rightly understood and rightly practiced is a benefit, not a burden and, equally important, that the fear of difference is a fear of the future.

I share the optimism of those who argue that we human beings are better than we think we are, and that a caring community is as much within the reach of our daily lives as it is a part of our hopes for the future. Accordingly, our success in building community by design will depend on our basic goodness, the capacity to empathize with each other, the refusal to allow others to suffer, and the active engagement in efforts to promote human happiness, not just for ourselves but for an interdependent world.

Many of my years since graduating from Yale Divinity School in 1963 have found me trying to integrate values into my work in business, government, and civil society. While I never chose to serve a parish, I regard everything I have done in the intervening years as a form of ministry. My many speeches were actually sermons in secular places. My emphasis on the importance of spiritual intelligence has been directed to those—young and old—seeking to find meaning in mystery. Even in my worst criticisms of injustice and my many active challenges of the status quo, I have tried to be a purveyor of hope and an agent of reconciliation. While the journey from a rigidly segregated South to citadels of power across the United States and beyond has not been easy, I discovered along the way that the most effective critic is likely to be the one who is willing to be a servant and the most effective servant is likely to be the one who is willing to be a critic. I continue to be both.

# NOTES

## 1. Growing Up Black in Cajun Country

1. Colbert King, "Old Lessons for Obama," *Washington Post*, April 19, 2008, A15, A16.
2. William Chafe, *Civilities and Civil Rights: Greensboro, North Carolina, and the Black Struggle for Freedom* (New York: Oxford University Press, 1980), 6–10.

## 2. Sunday Mornings in Louisiana

1. Quoted in Liliane Crete, *Daily Life in Louisiana, 1815–1830*, trans. Patrick Gregory (Baton Rouge: Louisiana State University Press, 1981), 147; Robert C. Reindeers, "The Churches and the Negro in New Orleans, 1850–1860," *Phylon* 22, no. 3 (1961): 241–48.
2. Cornel West, *Restoring Hope: Conversations on the Future of Black America* (Boston: Beacon, 1997), 196.
3. David Chappell, *A Stone of Hope* (Chapel Hill: University of North Carolina Press, 2003), 5.
4. Jespar Svartvik, "In Memory of Krister Stendahl on His Idea of 'Holy Envy,'" Public Forum, Shalom Hartman Institute, Jerusalem, March 24, 2009, www .svenskakyrkan.se.

## 4. A Spiritual Journey at Yale

1. Harvey Cox, *The Future of Faith* (HarperCollins ebooks, 2009), 11.

## 5. Alabama

1. Allan Stanglin, "Sledge Hammers of Truth!," AllanStanglin.com, November 11, 2010, http://www.allanstanglin.com/sledge-hammers-of-truth/.
2. "MIA Mass Meeting at Holt Street Baptist Church" (Montgomery, Alabama, December 5, 1955), *The Papers of Martin Luther King, Jr.*, vol. 3: *Birth of a New Age, December 1955–December 1956* (Berkeley: University of California Press, 1997), 72.

3. Quoted in Joseph Fletcher, *Situation Ethics: The New Morality* (Louisville, KY: Westminster John Knox, 1966), 91.

4. John Danforth, *Faith and Politics* (New York: Viking, 2006), 215.

5. Danforth, *Faith and Politics*, 215.

6. Danforth, *Faith and Politics*, 215.

7. Niall Ferguson, "The Next War of the World," *Foreign Affairs*, September/October 2006, 61.

8. Ferguson, "The Next War of the World," 61.

## 6. California

1. United States v. Seeger, 380 U.S. 163, 1965.

2. Al Gini, "Moral Leadership and Business Ethics," in *Ethics and Leadership Working Papers* (Chicago: Academy of Leadership Press, 1996), 2.

3. Immanuel Wallerstein and Paul Starr, "The Columbia Statement," in *The University Crisis Reader*, ed. Immanuel Wallerstein and Paul Starr (New York: Random House, 1971), 23–47.

## 7. Cummins Engine Company

1. Clay Risen, *The Bill of the Century: The Epic Battle for the Civil Rights Act* (New York: Bloomsbury, 2014), Kindle Reader Summary, Loc 125.

2. Cummins Inc., "Cummins Mourns the Loss of Visionary Leader; Former Chairman, Chief Executive Officer J. Irwin Miller's Legacy Touched Thousands," *Business Wire*, August 16, 2004, http://www.businesswire.com/news/home/20040816006023/en/Cummins-Mourns-Loss-Visionary-Leader-Chairman-Chief.

3. "Dark Side of the American Dream," *International Herald Tribune*, February 3, 1999.

4. "Dark Side of the American Dream."

5. "Dark Side of the American Dream."

6. *Cape Times* (Cape Town, South Africa), February 23, 2009, 22.

7. Peter Gumbel, "Rethinking Marx," *Time* 173, no. 5 (February 2, 2009): 44.

8. Benjamin R. Barber, "A Failure of Democracy, Not Capitalism," *New York Times*, July 29, 2002, A19.

9. Barber, "A Failure of Democracy."

10. Michael J. Sandel, *What Money Can't Buy: The Moral Limits of Markets* (New York: Farrar, Straus and Giroux, 2013), 3.

11. Al Gini, "Moral Leadership and Business Ethics," in *Ethics and Leadership Working Papers* (Chicago: Academy of Leadership Press, 1996), 5.

12. General Robert Wood Johnson, quoted in Frederick Harmon and Gary Jacobs, "Company Personality: The Heart of the Matter," *Management Review*, October 1985, 10, 38, 74.

## 8. Debating Disinvestment

1. Gideon-Cyrus Makau Mutiso, ed., *Readings in African Political Thought* (London: Heinemann, 1975), 116.

2. "Divestment from South Africa," Outside Criticism, Wikipedia, last modified October 11, 2014, http://en.wikipedia.org/wiki/Disinvestment_from_South _Africa.

## 9. The Carter Administration

1. Jimmy Carter, "Crisis of Confidence," July 15, 1979, *American Experience*, http:// www.pbs.org/wgbh/americanexperience/features/primary-resources/carter -crisis/.
2. Peter Drucker, "The Effective Decision," *Harvard Business Review*, January 1967, 1–19.
3. William James, *Pragmatism* (Buffalo, NY: Prometheus, 1991), 9–10.
4. Alasdair MacIntyre, *After Virtue* (Notre Dame, IN: University of Notre Dame Press, 1984), 220.
5. Aldo Leopold, *A Sandy County Almanac* (New York: Oxford University Press, 1968).
6. Mary Anglemyer, Eleanor R. Seagraves, and Catherine C. LeMaistre, *A Search for Environmental Ethics: An Initial Bibliography* (Washington, DC: Smithsonian Institution, 1980), 7.
7. Editorial, "Trust and the Interior Department," *New York Times*, September 18, 2009, A26.
8. Neil A. Lewis, "Justice Dept. Investigates Ex-Official's Ties to Shell," *New York Times*, September 18, 2009, A12.

## 10. Civil Society

1. CIVICUS, *Citizens Strengthening Global Civil Society* (Washington, DC: CIVICUS, 1993), 3.
2. "Spotlight Falls on Aid Brigade," *Business Day*, August 24, 1999, 15.
3. U.S. Senate Committee on Finance, *Treasury Department Report on Private Foundations*, 89th Cong., 1st sess. (Washington, DC, 1965), 5.
4. Michelle Goldberg, *Kingdom Coming* (New York: Norton, 2006), 112.
5. Goldberg, *Kingdom Coming*, 112.
6. Lester M. Salamon, "Of Market Failure, Voluntary Failure, and Third-Party Government: Toward a Theory of Government-Nonprofit Relations in the Modern Welfare State," *Journal of Voluntary Action Research* 16, no. 1/2 (1987): 29–49.
7. Robert Reich, *Tales of a New America* (New York: Times Books, 1987), 170.

## 11. From Activist to Diplomat

1. The Nelson Mandela Centre of Memory, Nelson Mandela Foundation, Houghton, Johannesburg, South Africa.
2. Jordana Lewis and Jerry Adler, "Forgive and Let Live," *Newsweek*, September 27, 2004, 52.
3. William Henry Chafe, *Private Lives / Public Consequences: Personality and Politics in Modern America* (Cambridge, MA: Harvard University Press, 2005), 5.

4. Heather Boushey and Christian E. Weller, "What the Numbers Tell Us," in *Inequality Matters*, ed. James Lardner and David Smith (New York: New Press, 2005), 27.

5. Boushey and Weller, "What the Numbers Tell Us," 27.

## 12. Dismantling Apartheid

1. Uri Ra'anan, "The Nation-State Fallacy," in *Conflict and Peacemaking in Multiethnic Societies*, ed. Joseph Montville (Boston: Lexington, 1990).

2. Jonathan Sacks, *The Home We Build Together* (New York: Continuum, 2007), 10.

3. "Transcript of Jacob Zuma's CNN Interview in Davos," The Presidency, February 1, 2010, http://www.politicsweb.co.za/politicsweb/view/politicsweb/en/page71651?oid=158352&sn=Detail.

4. Briefing, "South Africa over the Rainbow," *Economist*, October 20, 2012.

5. Kader Asmal, "Sense of Loss behind Anti-Mbeki Tirade," *Sunday Independent*, April 8, 2001, 9.

6. David Smith, "Mamphela Ramphele Defends Decision to Quit Election Pact," Guardian News and Media Limited, February 3, 2014.

7. David Smith, "Mamphela Ramphele Announces She Is Quitting Party Politics," Guardian News and Media Limited, July 9, 2014.

8. Bekezela Phakathi, "Ramphele to Take a Break from Politics," *Business Day* (Johannesburg), May 16, 2014.

## 13. Ethics and Statecraft

1. Theodore Roosevelt, "The Man in the Arena," Speech at the Sorbonne, Paris, France, April 23, 1910, theodore-roosevelt.com.

2. Office of the President Nelson Mandela, "Address by President Mandela at the 53rd United Nations General Assembly," African National Congress, 1998 [cited 2006], http://www.anc.org.za/show.php?id=3052.

3. "Speeches and Messages by Nelson Rolihlahla Mandela," June 13, 1994, http://www.mandela.gov.za/mandela_speeches/index.html.

4. Jeffrey Sachs, *The End of Poverty* (New York: Penguin, 2005), 189.

5. Sachs, *The End of Poverty*, 189.

6. Sachs, *The End of Poverty*, 190.

7. Sachs, *The End of Poverty*, 191.

8. Desmond Mpilo Tutu, *No Future without Forgiveness* (New York: Doubleday, 1999).

9. Amitai Etzioni, *From Empire to Community* (New York: Palgrave Macmillan, 2004), 6.

10. Secretary-General Kofi Annan, "In Address to World Economic Forum, Secretary-General Says Globalization Must Work for All," United Nations, 2001 [cited 2006], http://www.un.org/News/dh/latest/address_2001.htm.

## 14. Presidential Diplomacy

1. *Lions on the Move: The Progress and Potential of African Economies*, McKinsey and Company, June 2010.

### 15. Leaders Learning from Leaders

1. Daniel Goleman, *Emotional Intelligence* (New York: Bantam Books, 2005).
2. Mamphela Ramphele, *Laying Ghosts to Rest: Dilemmas of the Transformation in South Africa* (Cape Town: Tafelberg, 2008), 35.
3. Ramphele, *Laying Ghosts to Rest*, 34.
4. Rushworth Kidder, *Shared Values for a Troubled World* (San Francisco: Jossey-Bass, 1994).
5. Lynn Paine, *Value Shift* (New York: McGraw Hill, 2002).
6. Terence Brake, *Managing Globally* (London: Dorling Kindersley, 2002), 28.
7. See, for example, Cornel West, *Restoring Hope* (Boston: Beacon, 1999).
8. Quoted on "Inspirational Quotations," Appreciative Inquiry Commons, appreciative inquiry.case.edu.

### 16. A Lexicon of Public Values

1. William J. Bennett, *The Book of Virtues* (New York: Simon and Shuster, 1996).
2. Francis Fukuyama, *Trust: The Social Virtues and the Creation of Prosperity* (New York: Free Press, 1996).
3. Adam Smith, *The Wealth of Nations* (London: W. Strahan and T. Cadell, 1776).
4. E. J. Dionne, *Our Divided Political Heart* (New York: Bloomsbury, 2012).
5. Orlando Patterson, *Freedom in the Making of Western Culture* (New York: Basic Books, 1992).

# INDEX

Roosevelt, Eleanor, 37
Roosevelt, Theodore, 217
Rosenwald, Julius, 15–17
Rouillard, Larry, 90
Rousseau, Jean-Jacques, 159
Rubin, Robert, 228
Russell, Richard, 95
Rwanda, 197

Saarinen, Eero, 97
Sachs, Jeffrey, 222–23
Sacks, Jonathan, 199, 259
Sagebrush Rebellion, 134
Salamon, Lester, 160–61
Salazar, Ken, 148
Salole, Gerry, 251
Sampson, Anthony, 231
Sandel, Michael J., 112
Sarkozy, Nicolas, 110, 111
Savimbi, Jonas, 223
Schacht, Henry, 103–4, 107, 116
Schlesinger, Arthur, 255
Segal, Eli, 171, 249, 259
segregation, 19–20, 60, 65, 185; in armed
    forces, 38–39, 46; of churches, 24–25;
    of higher education, 34–36, 55, 86–87,
    198; of primary schools, 15–17, 41, 198;
    of public facilities, 57–58, 68, 72. *See also*
    discrimination
Selma march, 72
Senegal, 223, 250, 255–56
Senghor, Léopold, 255–56
September 11 attacks (2001), 277, 278, 280, 284
sexual orientation, 50, 65, 271
Shack, Ruth, 164
Shakespeare, William, 15
Sharpeville massacre (1960), 194–95
Sheen, Fulton J., 15
Shelton, Robert, 55, 60
Sierra Club, 146
Sisulu, Sheila, 251
Sisulu, Walter, 195
Small, Robert, 119
Smith, Adam, 267–68
Smuts, Dene, 237–38
social intelligence, 252, 256–59, 259–61

Socrates, 15, 27, 269
Solidarity movement (Poland), 150
Solomon, Theresa, 234
Somalia, 223
Sonn, Franklin, 234, 238
Sorensen, Phillip, 96, 102
Soros, George, 109, 110
Sotheby's, 109
South Africa, 132; ambassadorship to, 41,
    120, 127, 179–81, 195, 214–33, 249; black
    homelands in, 116, 121–22, 125; censor-
    ship in, 118; Clinton's visit to, 219, 220,
    232–46; Council on Foundations in, 157;
    documentary on, 126; educational policies
    in, 121, 123; housing policies in, 121; job
    discrimination in, 122–23; racial identity
    in, 118, 197–99
Southern African Development Community,
    219–21
Southern Christian Leadership Conference
    (SCLC), 59
Southern University (Baton Rouge), 27,
    34–39, 41–42, 86–87
Soweto, 120–21, 132, 186, 243
Sparks, Allister, 187
Spinoza, Benedict de, 52
spiritual intelligence, 52, 252, 256, 261–62, 284
Star Light Baptist Church, 24, 29–30
Stendahl, Krister, 33
Stevens, N. W., 57
Stillman College, 54–58, 61–62, 72, 81
Stone, Christopher, 145–46
Student Christian Movement, 71
Student Nonviolent Coordinating Commit-
    tee, 101
Sudan, 183, 197, 223
Sullivan, Leon, 116
Sunshine in Government provisions, 131–32
Suzman, Helen, 116, 194
Swaziland, 191

Tambo, Oliver, 207, 222
Tangeman, Clementine, 126
Tanzania, 227
Tax Reform Act (1969), 166
teleological theory, 138